PRAISE FOR
OUT OF THE SHADOWS

In 2019, to mark the 75th anniversary of the liberation of Paris from Nazi occupation... Michel Jeruchim, a French child hidden during the war, published a deeply moving biography of his life, there and then, and later in America. Drawing on multiple layers of memories...meticulously retrieving rich and varied details...he draws out of the shadows a past buried for many decades. The fascinating chronicle structured in an original cinematic reverse motion explores...an early youth in Normandy with a family that sheltered him and reminiscences, happy, humorous and painful, that emerge through the prisms of his innocence and his losses. The voice of a boy paired with the deeply humanistic perspective of an adult... sifting through conflicting emotions, Michel remains...attached to the country where he was born, the language he spoke first, and to the early events imprinted in his very soul.

—*Danièle Thomas-Easton,*
Former Counsul of France in Philadelphia

Out of the Shadows is a remarkable memoir ... of a resilient life, fashioned out of turbulent beginnings. Michel Jeruchim, is one of many Jewish children....who survived the Holocaust in War II ... due to the heroism of families and organizations that hid them at great personal risk. Although Jeruchim avoided the Nazis in occupied France he tragically lost his parents... who perished in Auschwitz. Jeruchim eventually made his way to the United States, where he persevered and became a prominent and successful electrical engineer. Written for his family, *Out of the Shadows* sends a wider message about resilience in the face of tragedy...the importance of education and the promise of America to immigrants. Out of the Shadows makes this reviewer recall other notable writings, e.g. *The Diary of Anne Frank*, *The Portrait of the Artist as a Young Man*, and *Suite Française*.

— Martin Garrell, Professor of Physics, Adelphi University

With few exceptions, those among us who...were victimized by the Nazi-driven disaster were silent—for decades. But, as Michel Jeruchim writes, the experience never left us. Even suppressed into our unconscious minds, it was with us, within us. But in time, encouraged to bear witness, some among us have spoken out.... It took nearly 50 years for those who suffered the same fate to be able to speak out about their early-life pain-laden experiences. ... Remarkable how ... Michel built a life that is productive and gratifying, driven by superb strength of character, a man of vigor, optimism and resilience. ... This telling is not just writing, it is reliving. And doing this, he bears witness..

— Henri Parens, MD; Professor of Psychiatry, Thomas Jefferson University, Sidney Kimmel Medical College

OUT OF THE
SHADOWS

Tree of Life Books
Stockton, NJ 08559
www.outoftheshadowsmemoir.com

Publication Design: Tim Ogline / Ogline Design
Cover images: Private collection of the author

ISBN: 979-8-9866188-6-9

Publisher's Cataloging-In-Publication Data

Jeruchim, Michel
    Out of the Shadows: A Memoir, Survival in Nazi-Occupied France
    and Making a Life in America
    Second Edition

1. World War (1939-1945)—Paris, France (Montreuil)—Memoir 2. World War
(1939-1945)—Normandy, France—Memoir 3. Holocaust (1939-1945)—Memoir
4. Hidden Child, Normandy, France 5. United States—Brooklyn, New York—
Memoir 6. United State—Philadelphia, Pennsylvania—Memoir

OUT OF THE
SHADOWS

SURVIVAL IN NAZI-OCCUPIED FRANCE
AND MAKING A LIFE IN AMERICA

—— A MEMOIR ——

MICHEL JERUCHIM

Tree
of Life
Books

CONTENTS

This memoir is dedicated to the memory of my parents,
Sonia and Wolf Samuel, remembered with sadness and love;

To my sister, Alice, and my brother, Simon,
who were always there for me;

To my wife, Joan, our children, Claude & Kenny,
and our grandchildren:
Serah, Gloria, Hope, Joseph, Eric, Alan, and Alina

May they know only peace.

ה הההה הההה ה ההה ה ה ה

THE PAST IS NEVER DEAD.

IT'S NOT EVEN PAST.

WILLIAM FAULKNER

YOUR PAST IS ALWAYS YOUR PAST.

EVEN IF YOU FORGET IT,

IT REMEMBERS YOU.

SARAH DESSEN

SONIA SZPIRO m.
SAMUEL JERUCHIM

ALICE n
SIDNEY GOLDMA

SIMON m
CÉCILE (née ROJE

MICHEL m
JOAN (née WOLFGANC

STEPHANIE m.
STEVE KAUFMAN

SONYA

BENJAMIN

ELI

AVIVA m.
PAUL DAVENPORT
(second marriage)

WILLIAM

TALIA m.
ALAN HIRSCH

NORA

AVIVA m.
MICHAEL ABRAHAMS
(divorced)

DANIEL m.
KYLA
(née GUIDOBONI)

ADAM

LINDA m.
JONATHAN SAWYER

SAM

BRYCE

SERAH

GLORIA

KENNETH m.
KAYLA
(née DROGOSZ)

HOPE

JOSEPH

ERIC

CLAUDE m.
OLGA (née STAVISKIY)

ALAN

ALINA

PREFACE

The first edition of this memoir took somewhat less than twelve years to complete. Why so long? Writing, as you may know, is a demanding enterprise, but a memoir has a special challenge: in a word, it's memory. We all know how elusive, misleading, and self-serving memory can be. I think it's incumbent to be as true to the past as possible, and this requires research: digging up old letters, photographs, documents, interviewing relatives or other contemporaries, and searching public records. All of this is doubly challenging when most of the individuals who could have given a glimpse into the past were victims of the Shoah. Plumbing the past is thus a very slow process. But, to a degree, that is actually beneficial, because time gives one perspective and unhurried reflection; it also allows one to gradually come to terms with one's past, to the extent that it is ever possible.

Thus, I was satisfied that I had done all I could to render an objective description of events and circumstances, except for this: The "situation" in St. Aubin, the small town where I was hidden during the war. By "situation," I mean the occupation by the Nazis and the liberation by the Allies. No amount of searching, in English or French language sources, brought more than a smidgen of information, even on the website of St. Aubin, itself. Resigned to this state of affairs, I let the publication go forward as it was.

But the ghosts of World War II would not stay quiet. A tap-tap inside my head would randomly remind me that I forgot something. And I agreed. So, I called my friend, Danièle Thomas-Easton, the former French consul in Philadelphia, to help write a letter to the mayor of St. Aubin, and ask them to search their archives. However, Danièle thought searching academic sources would be much more fruitful. And indeed it was. Shortly after, she found a PowerPoint presentation entitled *Actions de la Résistance en Seine-Inférieure*, authored by a Professor Michel Baldenweck at the University of Rouen, the main academic center in the region of St. Aubin. This discovery opened up a world of information, likely unavailable otherwise.

I contacted Professor Baldenweck, and he most graciously agreed to help me. We now have been in frequent email correspondence since the beginning of July 2021, and the ghosts are happy. In the frequent references to Professor Baldenweck's contributions, for economy of words, I will refer to him as Professor B. I am also grateful to Dr. Jean-Marc Dreyfus for many clarifications of the war conditions. I have also greatly benefited from two seminal books about the occupation, one by Michael Marrus and Robert Paxton, *Vichy France and the Jews*, and the other by Jacques Sémelin, *The Survival of the Jews in France, 1940–1944*. I will have occasion to quote from these books in what follows. I now have a reasonably full understanding of the occupation and the liberation of "my" town, and my sense of amnesia about that time has been relieved. I hope to make this dramatic time clear to you, as well.

PROLOGUE

In 2008, my wife, Joan, and I received the gift of our first grandchild. Motivated by her arrival, I embarked upon the pages that follow. I hesitate to call this narrative a memoir, at least for the first dozen years or so years of my life, and especially the first five. The word comes from the French mémoire, which means memory. Memory is a central tenet of Jewish culture and practice. Yet, I have essentially no recollection of the most traumatic and dramatic events of those first five years, and for some period of time immediately following. So, how could I write a memoir without memory? Fortunately, my brother, Simon, seven years older, and my sister, Alice, nine years older, have a sharp recollection of many of the events in that period. *They* are my memory about the early years. I prefer to think of this writing as a conversation with you, the reader, and like all good conversations, the topics meander, triggered by a word, an unspoken or hypothetical question, or a random thought.

In the summer of 1989, Joan and I took a trip to France to try to find the French Catholic family that had sheltered me during World War II (WWII). Joan, a psychologist, was insistent that we take this trip. She understood the necessity. The result of that trip was to open a crack in the wall of self-protection that I had built around myself for decades. I was five years old when I saw my parents for the last time, separated from my older siblings, dislocated from everything that was familiar to me, and thrust into the hands of strangers.

Two years after our visit to France, in the spring of 1991, I attended a conference for children who were hidden during WWII. During and immediately after that conference, the crack grew into a major fissure, which allowed me to confront my early experience and begin to talk about it. Since that time, I have tried, little by little, to grasp a tangible sense of my lost childhood. This goal took a positive step forward when my brother published a memoir in 2001, *Hidden in France: A Boy's Journey Under the Nazi Occupation*. But slowly, the need to tell my own story could not be denied. Strange as it may seem, prior to the 1991 conference, we had not talked much among one another, if at all, about many of the details of our family life, or of the circumstances surrounding our dispersal in 1942. It would have been too painful.

I now have lived much longer than those early tumultuous years, but their effect has never escaped me. Those years loom large in my rational and irrational thoughts, my interpretation of events, and my view of the world. Yet, they have not subdued me, nor controlled every aspect of my life. After immigrating to the USA, I adapted, because I *had* to adapt. I slowly became an American. I became a Brooklyn Dodgers fan. I went to public school, high school, college, graduate school, and built a career. I married and had children and grandchildren. I lead a good life, but it's colored by a past that's been my constant companion.

How often have we heard people say how much they regret not having interviewed their parents or grandparents while they were alive about their families' histories? Here, I'm anticipating that interview one day, but the real incentive has been for me to try to emerge from the shadow of WWII and reconstruct a lost childhood, one that was shattered by the Nazis, and which I've had a yearning to touch ever since. This reconstruction is not only to find myself as a child, but to "find" my parents, about whom I think almost on a daily basis. Not compulsively, not in a maudlin way, but about what we both missed. It's not my aim to write history, but only to make a small and incomplete documentary on myself.

THE UNLOCKING

My awakening arrived on May 20, 1991. The occasion was the First International Gathering of Children Hidden During World War II. It took place at the Marriott Marquis in Times Square. There had been other gatherings of survivors in other places, but this was the very first specifically aimed at hidden children. Why the first time, after so many years? Not long after the war, survivors began to organize and form support groups. At that time, "survivor" implied only someone who had lived through the death camps. Hidden children were not generally considered to have experienced significant trauma, certainly not in comparison to camp survivors. However, hidden children had trauma of their own: separated from parents and family and bewildered by circumstances they could not understand nor articulate, resulting in lifelong psychological repercussions.

In the immediate postwar years, we hidden children were not telling our stories. What could we say? We were children! We felt the effect of our trauma in our core, but we didn't have the adult language to express our hurt or the maturity to put it in a context that would have made sense to us even though it may not have made sense to others. And for many, the sequence of events that landed us in hiding places would simply have been unknown. But if a child had actually ached to tell his or her story, would they have trusted the adults to hear it? How do children talk about their parents who have disappeared?

Hidden children were "invisible," and no one asked for our stories anyway, so we kept these stories locked inside. It took some years before we "children" became adults and were able to speak for ourselves. Mental health professionals, many who had been hidden children themselves, understood that we had endured significant trauma. We could now be identified as a distinct category of survivors. Thus, the conference that took place in New York almost half a century after the end of the war was born.[1] The stories that wanted to be told could now be safely tiptoed out of the locked drawer.

The gathering was buzzing with sixteen hundred no-longer-so-young people like me, and most of them older. People crowded around a large bulletin board, on which hundreds of index cards were pinned with messages seeking persons from their original neighborhoods, or asking if anyone knew the whereabouts of their brother or sister or other relatives. The air was crackling with energy, as if the pent-up repression of grief for nearly half a century was about to erupt. And it seemed to for most participants.

We were like children impatiently waiting to unwrap a gift, in this case an encounter with our own lost childhoods. The presence of so many who shared a similar history, to whom nothing needed to be explained, with whom this mutuality was understood, produced such a high of well-being that it shattered the natural reticence of hidden children who had now come out of hiding so many years later. I was fifty-four years old and taking baby steps to recover from a trauma inflicted nearly half a century earlier. Even as I write this remembrance many years later, my eyes water involuntarily.

My brother, Simon, and my sister, Alice, attended as well. They were initially resistant, as was I, a typical symptom of our experience.

At the time we ourselves did not identify as survivors of the Holocaust. We still reserved that term for people who survived the death camps. It was also probably true that we did not want to open ourselves up to the inexpressible pain of the loss of our parents whose fate we actually did not know at that time. Since then, I have changed my mind about the definition of a survivor. I now think that any Jewish person living in parts of Europe controlled by the Nazis who lived through the war to be a survivor, because it was the Nazis' goal to kill *every* Jew in Europe. Jews were hunted animals, and once caught were slaughtered. Males were especially vulnerable; a suspicious Nazi could force him to strip, and circumcision was a death card.

Surviving took place in various forms: hiding, false papers, fleeing if possible, and luck. For children, "hiding" took place in different ways. The word often conjures up a literal interpretation: secreted in a cellar, under a trapdoor; in a room sealed off from the outside, in the hayloft of a barn. Many children were hidden in convents, and many, like me, were hidden in plain sight under a false identity. This is not to suggest that every means of survival was an equivalent experience. Nothing can compare with surviving a death camp. Nevertheless, all Jews were at risk, at any moment.

It may seem that "hiding" in plain sight would be foolish, and even possibly dangerous, but it turns out, according to Professor Sémelin, that this was not unusual at all in France. In supporting his thesis, Professor Sémelin makes the observation (among many others) that the situation in France was very different from that in other countries, even those in relative proximity and similar populations like Belgium and the Netherlands. Here, I would like to quote some phrases from his book that reinforce this notion:

One of the most tenacious clichés about the anti-Semitic persecution during this period holds that Jews had to hide in basements or attics to escape arrest.

It is often believed that Jews were forced to live hidden in attics with secret rooms or annexes like Anne Frank's family in Amsterdam. This cliché is not true in France. While a minority of Jews did go into hiding, most did not. But they could have been denounced.

The first plenary session, organized by the Anti-Defamation League (ADL) was set in a large ballroom. Abraham Foxman, the president of the organization, and himself a survivor from Poland, addressed us. When he spoke of the Polish woman who had sheltered him, his voice quavered with emotion. I found myself sobbing uncontrollably, but quietly. I think this was the first time I had allowed myself to cry for my parents.

After Foxman's speech and those of other speakers, we sat down to lunch with Joan and Cécile, my brother's wife. Cécile had been hidden in a convent in Belgium. At that meal, for the first time in fifty years, Alice, Simon, and I spoke about our parents with love, with wistfulness, with humor, and with regret, and we reminisced about our childhood. It was as if a weight had been lifted, and we could speak about our parents as people with foibles and celebrate their lives, rather than mourn them as numbered victims. All this, of course, was unsaid: I don't know if Alice and Simon registered the moment in that fashion, but I did. At the time of this conference, we still had not known our parents' fate in detail. For some years after our arrival in the States, I had fantasized that they would turn up; perhaps they had escaped to Russia, as had happened to some, or perhaps they didn't know where we were. These thoughts were unrealistic, of course, and little by little, I discarded this hope. The facts of my parents' deaths were not to be revealed until about ten years later, through Simon's tireless research.

I know now that my emotional preparation for this conference took place two years earlier, when Joan and I planned a trip to France. For some time, Joan had been quietly lobbying for that trip. She was somewhat insistent that we take it, even if I wasn't sure that I was emotionally prepared. We would return to the town where I was hidden, St. Aubin-lès-Elbeuf in Normandy, about seventy-five miles northwest of Paris, to find the family who had sheltered me. We engaged the services of Jacques de Larsay, a travel specialist for France, to map out an itinerary that would have been (and was) lovely in itself, with lodgings at picturesque farmhouses or small châteaux. One such place was relatively near St. Aubin.[2] My ambivalence was such, however, that prior to landing in Paris, I had actually not yet decided whether or not I would go. Many years after the fact, I am sure that my hesitation to contact them so long after the fact had a component of embarrassment if not shame for not having done so long before.

My brother and sister had also spent the war in Normandy. After Normandy had been liberated, we started to write letters to one another. My brother had known from the start where I had been hidden. We kept most of those letters and they are now preserved in the Holocaust Museum in Washington, DC, to which they were donated. From one of the immediate postwar letters, I discovered that the Lecleres were on my mind at least as late as 1948. One such letter from my brother provided me with their address, which I had requested. Did I write to them? I don't remember.

You might ask, why did it take forty-four years to find the Lecleres and thank them for protecting me? I was twelve when I left France, and I was too young to realize what a debt I owed them. At that age I was only looking forward. I was excited to be in America and I wanted to fit in. France was in the rearview mirror. Then there was school, and work, and life. Returning to see the Lecleres would have taken too much emotional energy. As time passed, it eventually became very clear that I did owe them a great deal, if not my life, but by then I had such a sense of awkwardness—how could I explain this long absence to them? But then, with Joan's help, I took the plunge.

We rented a car and planned to pass not too far from St. Aubin, since our first destination was to be the landing beaches in Normandy. The cemetery and memorial there was deeply moving for me. I had not expected it, but gazing at the field of markers, the simple crosses and a few scattered Jewish stars, brought such a sense of loss and sadness. I cried there, not only for my parents but for all those young men.

After the beaches, we were to head further west to Mont St. Michel, turn south and repair towards Paris along the Loire valley, where we would stop at many of the beautiful castles along La Vallée des Rois (the Valley of the Kings). Our first stop after leaving the Paris airport was in the town of Saint-Pierre-du-Vauvray. There, in St. Pierre, we checked into L'hôtellerie St. Pierre, a very charming inn selected by Jacques, on the banks of the river Seine, where from our window we could see barges lazily drifting past. Somehow, just seeing the countryside, the river, the fields, triggered a sense of joy, a primitive reconnection to the land I remembered from my childhood. It's possible I'm over-romanticizing this memory, but I don't think so. It just felt so satisfying.

We had dinner at the hotel and then collapsed from the long trip. Refreshed in the morning, I decided that it would be impossible not to take this opportunity to visit the Leclere family. I was also tempted to visit Cailly-sur-Eure, the site of the first orphanage where my siblings and I found ourselves after the war (about which, more later), which was less than thirty minutes away. But it was in the direction opposite St. Aubin. Going there would simply have been a delaying tactic, and

I was afraid of losing my "courage" if I delayed my visit. It happens that St. Pierre is across the river from a town called Louviers. The sign to it immediately brought to mind a song I used to sing as a boy, "Sur la route de Louviers." As we set out for St. Aubin, I couldn't help mumbling and humming the song to myself:

♪*Sur la route de Louviers (bis), Y avait un cantonnier (bis), Et qui cassait des tas d'cailloux, Pour mettre sur le passage des roues.....*♪

It so brightened my spirits that my anxiety almost melted away.

After the fact, I realized how unrealistic it was to assume I would know exactly where to find the Lecleres' house, as if time had stood still since the day in 1945 when I was "reclaimed" by my uncle. It would not have been realistic to expect an eight-year-old to have such pinpoint recall. Yet, I had a strong mental image that I thought would guide me to the right place. St. Aubin had grown quite a bit from the little village I thought I remembered. Even more, I had not only forgotten the address but the correct spelling of the Lecleres' name! After innumerable twists and turns and retraces in our rented car, I was ready to give up. I just couldn't accost someone on the street and ask, "Do you know the Leclere family?" But then, while going around a square, out of the corner of my eye, I spotted a sizable building on one side: It was the Mairie, the town hall. I decided it was worth a try to go in and see what the civil servants could do for us.

We entered the reception area and addressed a young lady behind a counter. "Bonjour, Mademoiselle. J'ai vécu ici pendant la guerre, et je me demande si vous pouvez me donner l'adresse d'une famille que je connaissais alors, la famille Leclere," I said to her.

I explained somewhat vaguely that I had lived in this town during the war and was trying to find the family with whom I had stayed, without giving further detail than their name, which of course sounds the same, whether spelled Leclere or perhaps the more common Leclerc, which I had always thought it was. She furrowed her eyebrows for a moment, said that she could not be of help, but there was a certain Madame de Latour in the back office, who had been around a long time and might be of assistance. She went and fetched Madame de Latour, to whom I gave the same information, namely, that I had lived during the war with Marcel and Suzanne Leclere, and was trying to find them.

Of course she knew the Leclere family, she said, and in fact lived near them. I further learned that the first name of the man of the family was Léon, although everyone referred to him as Marcel, his second middle name. She apparently knew the family well, for she knew that Gaston, their son, had recently had heart surgery and was in *retraite* (retirement).

At that moment, I imagined hugging Suzanne and clasping Marcel in a tearful and happy reunion. But before the thought had fully crystallized, Madame de Latour explained that Suzanne and Marcel had passed away some years prior. That reunion was not going to happen. I had half-expected that they might not be alive, but still, I felt really sad.

My mood turned around again when, to my surprise and delight, Mme de Latour said that she was about to take her lunch break and would be happy to guide us to Gaston's house. We accepted and the three of us took off in our rented car. Very soon after, we arrived in front of a small brick house with a white picket fence. At the gate, Madame de Latour said *Attendez ici*, while I go in and tell the occupants of the house that we are here. The protocol in France for "dropping in" is not the same as in the States. The French are much more formal. In this case, however, it was more than formality. She said she did not want to shock Gaston, especially since he had had recent heart surgery. Although I had been circumspect about the exact nature of my connection with the Lecleres, I suspect she knew more than I had said and wanted to prevent a double shock.

I watched Mme de Latour emerge from the house along with a portly ruddy-cheeked woman: Micheline, Gaston's wife. She was clearly protective and wanted to make sure I was not an impostor. I told her who I was, and why I was there, and I suppose I gave her enough detail no one else would know, satisfying her that I was the genuine article. She then returned to the house and re-emerged with Gaston.

He shuffled up to the gate and looking me straight in the eye, said "Alors, c'est vraiment toi?" So, is it really you?

I never thought about what kind of reception I would receive. Perhaps there was a hint of reproach, as if he meant "where have you been all this time." I had only thought of my separation from the Lecleres as a loss for me, but I had never thought about the possibility that my departure would have been a loss for them. As I learned later, the Lecleres had wanted to adopt me after the war. Had they fallen in love with a little orphan boy? So it would seem.

My unease was quickly put to rest. Gaston smiled and forty-four years melted away. I felt so good, and yet so bad at that moment because I still ached with the realization that I would not ever see Suzanne and Marcel. It may be that, to some extent, I have conflated the Lecleres with my parents. I do not remember the immediately ensuing moments, but soon after Joan and I were ensconced in their house and Micheline couldn't stop fussing. We spent the day with them, eating and bringing one another up-to-date, if one could only remember forty-four years of happenings. Their current house, while similar was not the one that I had been sheltered in, but we took a walk to where that was, a small pilgrimage that I should have taken years before. The address of that house had been 88 rue de Tourville (the street was renamed after the war), and I have wondered if it's pure coincidence that the house in Paoli, Pennsylvania, where I lived for nearly forty-two years, before moving to Philadelphia, is numbered 88.

During that walk, Gaston took us next door to his parents' neighbor, a sprightly eighty-two-year-old Mme Louise Brida. When Gaston told her who I was, she broke out in smiles, hugged and kissed me. Although I had completely forgotten about her, I had apparently spent a lot of time with her and her family—she had seven children. Because the Lecleres worked, she took care of me when I returned from school at which time no one was yet home. She used to give me a tartine (a snack) till it was time to go. She invited the three of us in the house and gave us un *petit coup*, a "drop" to drink. The French use any excuse to open a bottle! It was such a happy reunion. I can't say that memories came flooding back, but her joy was so infectious that I almost felt like that schoolboy again.

During one of our conversations, I learned that Marcel had been in the Résistance, the source of a connection that landed me in the Lecleres' home.[3] One thing that astounded Joan was the stack of letters sent to me by my brother and kept for forty-four years by the Lecleres. One might think that they had simply burrowed them somewhere in the house and forgotten about them until we showed up. But that's not the case. First of all, these letters were delivered to the Lecleres' original house, and something meaningless would not have been transported to their new one. Gaston knew exactly where they were and proudly showed them to us. I can only conclude that these letters were somehow a link to me that they didn't want to lose.

I have difficulty smiling for cameras. But here is a photograph taken by Joan of Gaston, Micheline, their grandchildren who were there that day (Cécile and Étienne) and me, sitting around the dining room table, with the quintessential companion—a French poodle. My smile is as wide and genuine as has ever been taken of me, for on that day I recovered a part of my childhood.

From left to right: Micheline, Étienne, me, Cécile, and Gaston

They didn't want us to leave, and wanted us to stay overnight. I was torn. Our original plans had not accounted for a possible stay with them. We had an itinerary and reservations elsewhere. In retrospect, I should have said "the hell with those reservations," but I didn't. So, at the end of the day, we bid them goodbye, promising to return toward the end of our trip. At the gate, we hugged and kissed (in the French way) and Gaston said "à la bonne retrouvaille." That trip was magical in many ways, though this feeling was no doubt generated to a large extent by the glow of this *retrouvaille* (finding again). After saying au revoir to Gaston and Micheline we headed north. The following day we went to the landing beaches.

Years later, I mused about how the gods of chance had dealt me several aces on that day: First, that moments before I was about to give up the search, I happened to spy a large building. Then, for an unknown reason, that I approached it and discovered it was the town hall. That, against my initial impulse, I went in to see what might happen. That, against all odds, there was a civil servant working that day who knew the Lecleres and took us to their house. If every single step of that lucky sequence hadn't happened, I wouldn't have discovered Gaston, and the lasting psychological lift from that encounter and all that ensued from it would not have come into being, including this memoir. This visit may have been the trigger for my view that life hangs on a razor's edge and that we can fall on one side or the other due to circumstances not under our control. Several other chance events took place to reinforce that view, as I will recount later.

That evening, after departing from the Lecleres, we stayed at a farmhouse and fell asleep to the bleating of sheep and were awakened in the morning by the crowing of roosters.

Looking out the window, we could see a fine mist hovering over the field, the animals peacefully grazing, a scene which would have looked the same centuries earlier. There was something so reassuring and satisfying about that timeless scene, a sense of peace and stability that said: This is France, the way it was and the way it will be. It was a taste of France that I hadn't known, and I liked it. I think that every time I visit France, I'm trying to recreate a feeling that I may never really have had about belonging. After petit déjeuner we headed to Brittany where we intended to visit the famous Mont St. Michel. However, before we got there, we made a stop.

Prior to our departure, my sister had suggested we might want to stop and visit the Ledauphin family who had sheltered her during the war and she gave us their phone number and address. They lived in a little Norman town called Saint-Hilaire-du-Harcouët. I was somewhat ambivalent about doing so because I had never met them. However, since I had now embarked on a career of impromptu drop-ins, we drove to the little town where they lived, and found on a square the little photography shop owned by Willy, the son of Madeleine, the head of the family[4] who worked the tenant farm in the commune of Savigny-le-Vieux, where Alice had stayed during the war. After the war, the Ledauphin family had moved to St. Hilaire, just a few miles from Savigny-le-Vieux (see the map on page 63).

Entering the shop, we introduced ourselves to Willy who seemed genuinely delighted that we came and, despite our protests, immediately closed the shop and took us to his home. His wife, Danny, his mother, and his son were there, also. The mother, Madeleine, was the woman in charge when Alice lived there during the war, and was by now elderly. Their hospitality could not have been more *chaleureux* (warmth to the highest degree). We had a wonderful dinner and talked about all sorts of things: family, work, that strange culture called America. I brought them up-to-date about Alice, for whom their affection was visible. I translated for Joan, also with the help of their son, Fabrice, a student who was decently familiar with English. At the end of the evening, we intended to move on to our next destination, but they so strenuously insisted we stay, that we did. No first-class hotel would have had a lovelier room or a more welcoming environment. We slept well and were treated to a beautiful petit dejeuner, which wasn't so petit. The feeling of unpretentious hospitality and openness warmed my heart. Were my feelings amplified by the fact that my sister survived the war at Madeleine's farm? No doubt. After making our goodbyes with many thanks, we resumed our itinerary.

En bref, as the French say, we then headed to Mont St. Michel, climbed an impossible number of steps to the actual monastery which is on top of a steep promontory. It always amazes me what humans could do centuries ago without the help of modern machinery. Tour buses lined the roadway, crowds of tourists and perhaps pilgrims mingled along the cheap commercial stalls at the base, hawking all kinds of made-elsewhere replicas of saints and other so-called souvenirs. It reminded Joan of the pilgrims in Chaucer's *The Canterbury Tales*, whose feigned piety is subtly exposed. Nevertheless, the place itself was impressive. The less-than-savory impression that we were left with from the hawkers was totally redeemed some time later when we stopped spontaneously at a restaurant off the roadside. We had one of our best lunches ever, in a courtyard surrounded by flowers. It was one of those settings that belonged in a movie. And the dollar was still king! I told myself, this is the real France.

Not long after, we again stopped spontaneously, lured by a sign that announced local pottery. There, craftsmen were at the pottery wheel making all kinds of objects, probably with the same techniques and styles as was the case for their forbears. We bought several plates and mugs, in a shimmering deep blue glaze, which we still have today as a reminder of that trip. And every time thereafter when I sip my coffee from one of those mugs, I breathe in that sense of rural France. Afterwards we set our course for the Loire Valley, starting at its gateway, Angers. Along the course of several days, we visited small and large castles, varying from enormous fortresses to elegant petits châteaux, almost all of which, unfortunately, had little of their interiors intact, as most of them had been looted during the French revolution in 1789. We typically saw one in the morning and one in the afternoon, roughly in this order: Château de Chambord, Château de Blois, Château d'Amboise, Château de Chenonceau, Château de Langeais, Château d'Azay-le- Rideau, and Château de Chinon. As I said earlier, I have always held in wonderment many of the towering structures built centuries ago without the help of computer-aided design or heavy machinery, and many of these castles reinforced this feeling. Of course, these medieval and Renaissance châteaux have nothing to do, per se, with my personal history, but they took me back to French history lessons in l'école primaire that I had attended where we were taught about the kings who had built these castles. I liked school; there was a sense of order, and in those classes I could feel like everyone else.

We were deep in the wine country of the Loire Valley, vineyards stretching on both sides of the road, to the horizon, and we started to get hungry. There were no signs to restaurants, nothing in sight. At last, we spotted a sizable structure in the distance, which we hoped was a restaurant or an inn. We took a dirt road that led to it, and as we approached, we could hear laughter and conversation. That settled it for us: This must be a hotel of some sort. We parked and approached the entrance, climbed some steps, and asked the first person we saw if this was a restaurant. Soon after, someone appeared and informed us that this was their home; they owned the surrounding vineyards, and the substantial crowd present were celebrating the birthday of the wine master, the person speaking to us. I explained, in French, that we were Americans touring the Loire Valley. He remarked as to my almost flawless French, to which I replied that I had studied some French in my youth.

I don't know whether his subsequent invitation to join the party was due to the goodwill engendered by a French-speaking American, or whether he was naturally hospitable. But we spent a good part of the day enjoying the food and wine at what turned out to be a sprawling villa with a large pool in which people cavorted with wine glasses in hand. The wine master took us down to his cellar to show off his produce. It was more than a "cellar." It was a huge cave carved out of the local stone, deep underneath, with racks of barrels and bottles lining the walls. He offered us sample after sample of his wines, of which we took only modest sips since we had to drive. Why did I enjoy this accidental afternoon so much? It wasn't the food or wine; it was in some way feeling accepted in the land I had to leave. Late in the afternoon we gave our thanks and made our goodbyes.

Eventually we found our way back to Paris, but it was a little adventure, or perhaps misadventure, to find our hotel, Relais Christine, on the banks of the Seine. I had a huge map of Paris, but its streets are not laid out in a New York grid, and soon I was lost. At one point, I pulled behind a cab and proposed to pay him if he could lead us to our destination. He declined, but gave us very clear directions, and without further misadventure we found our place. We did the usual in Paris, the Louvre, the Musée d'Orsay, and others I don't remember. We had great meals and finally on the day before last, we returned to St. Aubin to have lunch with Gaston and Micheline. We promised to stay in touch and we did. The year following, Gaston, Micheline, petite Cécile, and Micheline's sister-in-law, all came to the States, their first visit ever. They toured Washington for a couple of days and then took the train to Philadelphia. We picked them up, and they stayed with us for about a week. Subsequently we drove them all to Simon's house, where he hosted them also for about a week. The summer following, Gaston's granddaughter Cécile came by herself, and again stayed with us for a week and then the same amount of time with Simon. Unfortunately, Gaston died the following year and I felt a loss. The connection to this part of my past was now gone. I kept in touch with Micheline, with an occasional letter, postcard, or phone call, and gift parcels at Christmas, but of course, it was not the same without Gaston. Sadly, after this was written, Micheline also passed away.

The trip to find the Lecleres was magical. Everything seemed to work out better than I expected, the sun shined brighter, there was no rain. Joan and I have returned to France many times, to different parts, and my perspective and reason for going is not simply to see something new. There's a feeling of going home, as much as I have other negative feelings stemming from the war. It's a primitive reaction.

Hearing French spoken around me in France is almost like hearing music. It brings me back to my childhood, not to any particular place, or particular experience, just a generally warm feeling, like putting on a coat when it's cold. I was twelve years old when we immigrated to the States, and under the circumstances of my life till then I hardly knew much of France other than where I had lived. Discovering France is always a delight, apart from emotional and tragic connections, but perhaps I can't separate the two.

OPENING UP

Over time, fragments of my story would leak out during conversations, and some people would urge me to write it. Although I was tempted at different junctures to begin writing this story, I resisted for many reasons. When people suggested that I write my story, what they were really referring to, primarily, was the Holocaust experience. Part of my reluctance to write was no doubt the desire not to bring up those painful feelings, but also, I considered that part of my story to pale in the spectrum of painfulness relative to others who had suffered so much more brutally. And I despaired of being able to put into words the depth and complexity of my feelings about the Holocaust. In this, of course, I am not alone.

In 1991, soon after the Hidden Children gathering, I was contacted by one of the organizers, Stefanie Seltzer, who happened to live not too far from us. Stefanie, who was herself a hidden child in Poland, is a dynamo and has dedicated herself to helping survivors psychologically and materially. She started a group called Child Survivors of the Holocaust – Philadelphia Chapter, and our first meeting was at her house. There, about two dozen or so of us gathered and started sharing our stories. It was painful but cathartic, and it felt safe to do so.

Stefanie was also on the organizing committee for the Yom

Hashoah (Holocaust Remembrance Day; האושה םוי) observance which takes place every year all over the world in the spring. In Philadelphia, Yom Hashoah is observed at the Holocaust Memorial Plaza, a triangular space at the intersection of Arch Street, the Benjamin Franklin Parkway, and 17ᵗʰ Street in Philadelphia. There, a bronze sculpture by the Polish sculptor Nathan Rapoport dedicated to the six million martyrs depicts two women, two children, hands holding daggers, a rabbi, and a Torah, all surrounded by the flames of a menorah. I was no doubt aware of Yom Hashoah before 1991, but I don't think I had made a special effort to observe it one way or another, and I'm sure that I was unaware of the Philadelphia event. I didn't want to think about such things.

After Stefanie informed me of it, at the first opportunity to attend, Joan and I went. I must admit that I was not eager to go, but the rabbi of the congregation we then belonged to, Ron Kaplan, convinced me that it would be a good thing to do, and actually offered to take us there. When I looked at the program, I expected it to be boring; but I was transfixed. The program began with the Israeli consul reading a long list of victims, but not simply a random list. He chose to read the names of the members of specific families that had been wiped out, and the drone of one name after another, all with the same last name made the air feel heavy and sad. During his speech, a violinist from the Philadelphia Orchestra played in the background, a plaintive Jewish melody that accented the tragedy. That set me up for what came later. Towards the end of the program, a cantor sang El Maleh Rachamim, a prayer from traditional Jewish liturgy. The words mean "God full of compassion." It is the prayer said on the anniversary of a person's death. But it is also usually chanted during Yom Hashoah observance because for the victims of the Holocaust, who knows the actual date of their murder? The cantor's chanting was the closest to crying that singing could ever come to, and it triggered just that in me.

The Child Survivors group met about every other month, and in those meetings people started to tell their stories in turn. Every story was different and every story was similar: hiding unseen or in the open, in one country or another, with adequate food or bare pantries, with protectors they didn't want to leave after the war, and it goes on. It was painful to tell and painful to hear. After a time, silence would fall upon the group, as if, by unspoken consent, we needed to exhale and return to the mundane. Social hour had arrived. The host would have coffee brewing, and all of us had brought our contribution to the potluck. Schmoozing ensued about family, children, and random topics. I had many conversations with one person in particular about religion and God. In spite of his experience, he had remained observant and a believer. This was not so unusual among survivors, but a state of mind I could not fathom. Our "argument" had probably been duplicated many times and in many places.

"How could there be a just God," I would argue, that would allow such carnage to occur.

"Man was given free will to do good or evil," he would reply.

I would counter something along these lines: If "man" was created in His/Her image, as some believe, what does that say of the original?

The explanation given by some, for the unexplainable, is that humans are too limited to understand God's plan. To me this makes no sense. We were given reasoning ability—what plan could include such cruelty? This debate could have gone on indefinitely, but we knew that neither of us would convince the other. We called a truce and went on to other things, with coffee and cake from the buffet table.

After a year or two, and after we had all told our stories, the tone of the meetings began to change. The reason for the formation of the group, namely support, had now been largely fulfilled, and the cohesiveness of the group, which had been based on the commonality of the Holocaust experience, now started to give way to individual characteristics. Some wanted the group to support older survivors, some wanted to be politically active, and others wanted no part of either. We now began to see a set of individuals rather than a set of survivors. I used to say to Joan that someone who was obnoxious before the Holocaust did not alter their personality because of it and would likely still be obnoxious afterward. Indeed, if anything, some became even more bitter. So, after having served a very valuable function, the group dissolved.

Sometime after 1991 and probably after the formation of the Child Survivor group, during a conversation with a friend, Joan had mentioned my story, more or less in passing, and this person tendered an invitation through Joan that I address her Hadassah chapter. I accepted with butterflies, for this was to be my first "outing." I was accustomed to addressing large audiences on technical subjects, but this was different. In my mind, I was still "hidden" in terms of the general public, but now I was exposing myself. My rational side told me, don't worry, this is America, but my other side stayed wary.

I was fine once I started speaking, although I choked up a couple of times, an unstoppable eruption welling up in my body that required a small time-out to regain my composure. This wasn't caused by anything I said in particular. I was simply telling my story. But emotion has its own will.

These presentations (of my story) are time-limited, so I basically related that I landed in a Catholic family in Normandy, following a Nazi raid in Paris. I couldn't say much more because I wasn't aware of all of it at the time. It may be that, by voicing my story in public, the reality of it could no longer be suppressed, and that's what triggered the emotional reaction. The end result, however, was again cathartic. Subsequently, I have spoken on a number of occasions to one group or another. But until more recent years, I still had discomfort about these speeches. Not because of speaking in public, but revealing myself in public. When I say "revealing," I mean simply telling what happened, but that telling in itself meant I could no longer suppress the emotional reaction. Subsequent to the publication of this memoir, I presented my story a number of times, in person or on Zoom, and I "learned" to present my story without a pause for composing myself. But after all these years, instead of an initial reluctance, I view my talks as an obligation to remind the world.

In 2001, I had another breakthrough which allowed me to open up a little more. Joan was a member of the American Jewish Committee (AJC), an organization dedicated to human rights in general and for Jews in particular. We joined a trip to Poland that was organized by the AJC. The occasion was to be the dedication of a memorial in the Polish town of Jedwabne, about one hundred miles northwest of Warsaw. In Jedwabne, on July 10, 1941, the Jewish population was rounded up and herded into a barn which was then set on fire. This massacre had always been blamed on the Nazis, but in a book called *Neighbors*[5] by the Polish historian, Jan Gross, it was concluded that the massacre had actually been perpetrated by the townsfolk themselves. This caused a furor in Poland.

The Poles, rightly so, considered themselves victimized by the Nazis and could not acknowledge that their compatriots would behave just like their invaders. Of course, Poland does have a reputation for being anti-Semitic, but in some sense, I feel uneasy in painting an entire country with the same brush. We met wonderful Polish people on this trip, who sincerely wanted rapprochement between Poles and Jews, and it is also true that there are more Poles honored in Israel for saving Jews in WWII.[6] This anti-Semitic label also ignores the fact that Jews had lived in Poland for a thousand years before the onset of WWII. While it wasn't always brotherly, for many centuries during that millennium Poland had been the most hospitable country to Jews in Europe, in spite of repeated efforts by the Polish Catholic hierarchy to denigrate and marginalize them. Nevertheless, the sense of horror and shame that this act, the Jedwabne massacre, evoked made the population refuse to believe it. That is, until additional respected Polish historians added support to the truth of the accusation. The Polish government eventually acknowledged the Jedwabne massacre and decided to publicly admit the fact, as well as sponsor a weekend of ceremonies, which included the dedication of a gravestone for the martyrs in a field in Jedwabne.

As with the trip to France in 1989, Joan was the initiator because she thought it important to be a witness. Initially, I could not bring myself to go because one of the stops on this trip was to be Auschwitz. But, at the last minute, I changed my mind and I'm glad I did. The first stop took us to Warsaw. I'm not sure whether I had a moment of reflection upon touching Polish soil knowing that I could be walking on a street where my parents might have walked as young adults and in love. But events were moving too fast for much reflection.[7] We stayed at a French hotel (yes!), a Sofitel in Warsaw. The morning after we landed, we were picked up by a bus: "We" were the US delegation, which consisted of members of AJC, Polish Catholics, and émigrés. About half of the delegation were Holocaust survivors. Police on motorcycles escorted our bus to Jedwabne, which is a couple of hours from Warsaw. We attended the dedication ceremony, along with Polish government representatives: a few priests, but none from the Catholic hierarchy; and a number of Orthodox Jews, at least one of whom was a rabbi, dressed in their typical black suits and hats. One of them recited prayers for the dead. A stone had been erected, memorializing the event that had taken place there. Perhaps the ceremony had been intended to be healing, but for me it wasn't. I couldn't forget that the souls for whom these prayers were said had been burned to death. After a few minutes the assembly dispersed, we climbed back on the bus and we returned to Warsaw with the same escort. I felt depressed and resigned—what was different in Jedwabne than had happened elsewhere in Nazi-occupied Europe?

Back in Warsaw, we went straight to our hotel to retrieve our invitations to the prime minister's concert and the president's reception. These events were attended by only a few hundred people and we were fortunate to be among them.

The evening concert was hosted by Prime Minister Jerzy Buzek, a Lutheran, unlike most Poles. It took place in the Augsburski Evangelical Church. Prime Minister Buzek welcomed us in Polish and English. The concert had three selections: first, a piece by a medieval composer, Gomółka, related to Old Testament psalms; next was a composition by Gustav Mahler, on the death of his child, "Kindertotenlieder;" and the last piece was by a contemporary Polish composer, Krzysztof Knittel, entitled "A Cantata on El Maleh Rachamim," the blessing for the dead I mentioned earlier. Thus, we expected it to be traditional sounding, but it was far from it. It began with almost deafening dissonance, implying the destruction wreaked by man's inhumanity to man. Then the piece ended with a chant of El Maleh Rachamim by a choir, accompanying the orchestra. This part suggested sadness but was melodiously soothing, as if to caress the bereaved, making a startling contrast with its beginning. The whole effect was *foudroyant* (like a lightning bolt), and again, I couldn't help melting into tears. Later, we attended a reception at the presidential palace. I happened to bump into Mr. Knittel and told him that his music had brought tears to my eyes, to which Mr. Knittel replied, "That is the highest honor."

We stayed in Warsaw for a few more days. We met with a delegation from Parliament and also with the president of Poland at the time, Aleksander Kwaśniewski, and, since life goes on, we shopped.

After leaving Warsaw, the delegation traveled as a group, by train, to Auschwitz. I dreaded this part of the trip, but it really was the reason I had forced myself to go in the first place. Of course, the camp had been sanitized. So, the impact at first was not staggering until we approached a simple gravestone. On the stone was inscribed:

"In memory of the men, women and children who fell victim to the Nazi genocide.

Here lie their ashes. May their souls rest in peace."

In front of that gravestone, one of our delegation, Alvin Rosenfeld, recited the Kaddish (prayer) for the dead. This was as close as I would ever come to a funeral of my parents. Some joined in the prayer, but I did not. First of all, I do not know it by heart, but even if I did, I still would not have joined in. The prayer is not to honor the dead, but heaps praise on God.[8] Even though I found the cadence of the prayer somewhat comforting, I could not possibly join in that praise, standing in front of a memorial for an untold number of murdered people that God, if he exists, couldn't or wouldn't protect from that savagery. Here, even though this was the most wrenching part of the trip for me, I could not cry. Tears were insufficient for the magnitude of the evil that had taken place there. My emotions were a jumble, in part rage, but strangely I also felt a measure of peace, having finally "found" my parents, in the sense that, at last, they were "here." I can understand the extraordinary effort that people make to recover any part of a loved one's remains. Here this was not possible, but somewhere "here" their ashes were scattered. So, this brief ceremony would be the closest to a funeral that I could ever hope to have for them. And with this trip to Poland, I felt more urgency to explore and write about our family tragedy, although action did not follow for some years.

Aside from the birth of Serah, my first grandchild, I had an additional inspiration that set me down to write. Coincidentally, in January 2008, the month of Serah's birth, I read a book that Joan gave me. It was *My German Question: Growing Up in Nazi Berlin*, by Peter Gay, himself an escapee from Germany. Professor Gay is a distinguished historian, Jewish by birth, but like me not taken to religion. In his writing, I found an amazing confluence of thought and feeling, and at many junctures a rage that matches mine.

Ever since the birth of our first son, Claude, I have been very conscious of the fact that my existence and the continuation of my family name is not merely my best but my only revenge or response against the Nazi attempt to wipe us out. Given the uncertainties of life, this memoir may be the only way that any grandchild will get to really know me, although such a possibility is becoming more realistic for my older grandchildren. As I write this it strikes me that, perhaps unconsciously, I am following the path of my much-loved father-in-law Ernst, who took copious notes as life unfolded. I am also coming to the conclusion that I am writing this story for myself, to try to fill the void created by never really knowing my parents and never having had a sense of family history to ground myself in.

Unlike Ernst, I did not document events as they were happening. There were too many other things to attend to. And during those critical early years I was, of course, too young to either remember the events surrounding me or recognize their significance at a reasoning level. Even at later ages I was too focused on surviving the day to make a conscious effort to record the details. I mentioned earlier that I consider this story a conversation with you, but one might also call it impressionistic. Like the shimmering paintings of a previous era, the details may be somewhat fuzzy but the overall picture is quite clear. What I say or have said may not be exactly what a camera would have recorded, but a camera does not record thoughts, feelings and impressions.

III

ANTECEDENTS

A memoir often contains reminiscences about the writer's childhood: vacations, celebrating holidays, visits by, or to, grandparents, maybe even great-grandparents, uncles and aunts, friends of the family, and so on. In a conventional family, and in peacetime, there is a slow evolution through the stages of growing up. There is time for the brain to record people and events by repetition: birthday parties, secular and religious holidays, vacations. A person's formation often rests on these family experiences and models. A phrase from liturgy comes to mind: "from generation to generation," which implies a continuity fed by stories and myths recounted by parents and grandparents, feeling connected to long-ago forebears that one never knew. I believe there is a need for people to feel grounded in this continuity.

As I was growing up, from the time that I left the Lecleres to the time that I married, my sense of family consisted essentially only of my siblings. There were no repeated encounters with grandparents, great-grandparents, or tales from prior generations. I had only fleeting encounters with other relatives, like my uncle in Paris, or my grandmother, or even my uncle in Brooklyn, with whom I lived for a few years. But these connections were too shallow or infrequent to fill that emotional empty space.

For most survivors the connection to the past was severed because their immediately prior generations were murdered before questions could be asked. Simon's book provides a small bridge to the past, but his narrative intentionally starts only near the beginning of WWII. I must admit that for a large part of my life I did not consciously miss this connection to the past. In my earlier years, I was too focused on the future: schooling, dating, professional development, forming my own family, and so on. Now that those stages of life are in the past, I have increasingly looked backward, and since I began to write this story, I started to get a bit of a nagging curiosity about who these people were, whose genes I inherited.

A BIT OF HISTORY
ON MY MOTHER'S SIDE

In 2009 I asked my sister (nine years older) if she could shed some light on our past and she sent me a long letter. What she describes occurred before I was born. She was fortunate, as a child, to have traveled to Poland with our mother and to have heard our mother's stories as well as those from our grandmother. On that single trip she also met our grandparents on both sides. She relates that our mother took her and Simon to visit our father's family in Warsaw. What I find fascinating is Alice's statement that she recalls playing with our cousins and chatting with them in Yiddish, which she says was her first language! She remembers little else about that side, except that our grandfather had a beard. Serendipitously, in 2005 my son Kenny visited one of our cousins, Reuven, who was living in Israel, and who had a fairly detailed memory of some of the family on my father's side. I will relate more about that side later on.

Alice remembers much more about the Szpiros, my mother's side of the family. This is a transliteration of our mother's maiden name.

Szipiro was modified to Spiro by her brother Chil, who also renamed himself David when he settled in France. Her older brother Sam changed it to Shapiro when he settled in America long before the war. Our mother's mother was born Tessie Uchein (that last name means *student* in Polish). Her parents ran a tavern and she was familiar with the names of French liqueurs, such as *Courvoisier* and *Bénédictine*, which would have been Martian to the average Pole. Tessie's marriage was an arranged one, and she went to live with her in-laws in Garwolin, Poland. She mentioned that her promised dowry failed to materialize because her parents had some money problems. Because of that she felt less than welcome in her husband's family.

That family owned a large hardware store, a very early version of a Home Depot, selling building supplies, farm equipment, nails, and tools of all sorts. Eventually, our grandfather (her husband) ran the business, while his father retired to read the "Holy Book." He would come out sometimes, particularly at harvest time. The peasants trusted no one but our great-grandfather to go into the warehouse and pick out the long scythe they bought for harvesting the wheat. He would feel the blade and say this is a good one, and the peasants were satisfied with his judgment.

Tessie and Isaac had six children. The oldest was Simcha (or Sam) and the youngest our mother. Uncle David was the next youngest. Our mother's given name was Syma, and I was under the impression that she changed it to Sonia in France, but Alice says that she called herself Sonia to appear more Polish (than Jewish). When Sonia was just an infant, her father died. It appears that he was traveling by train, probably on business; the train crashed or derailed and he was killed. Alice was told that the railway company offered compensation, but Tessie was ill-advised to sue. After Isaac's death, Tessie moved to Warsaw to look for her own lawyer: She had never been happy in her in-laws' house, anyway. The older children came to live with her, but she left the young ones, David and Sonia, in the care of her sister-in-law and their grandparents. While well taken care of, the young ones missed the affection of their mother. Meanwhile the lawsuit dragged on, and it appears that the lawyer was crooked so the suit came to naught.

Our grandmother had to survive on her own and she opened a "restaurant," probably more accurately labeled an eatery. I assume that this idea came to her because she was familiar with "catering," from her experience with her own parents' tavern. Alice describes her imaginings of this eatery and its environment:

> *"I picture the Warsaw scene where they lived as a warren of workshops of all kinds: cap makers, tailors, leather-goods workers, shoemakers, watch makers, etc. These workingmen had to have lunch somewhere and they went to our grandmother's place, which I imagine as a table d'hôte setup: no menu, just something simple, maybe kasha with a piece of meat and a hunk of rye bread, or borsht and a boiled potato..."*

Eventually the younger children rejoined their mother. This is how David's career was decided. For some reason, jobs such as a tailor or similar trades were deemed too *déclassé* (pedestrian) by the Szpiros, so Tessie inquired of one of her customers, a watchmaker, if her son could be taken in as an apprentice. And so it happened. In due time, he became a skilled watchmaker and went to work in an *atelier* (workshop) where, as luck would have it, a certain Wolf Jeruchim was also employed in the same profession. The photo below, probably taken in the early 1920s, shows our father in that workshop, second from the left, and our uncle David third from the right.[9]

In the watch-making workshop in Warsaw c. 1926

Our mother, who had now come to Warsaw, worked as a governess for a wealthy Jewish family. She also worked as a kindergarten teacher. By-and-by, we can infer that David introduced his sister to Wolf Jeruchim and, in 1926, Sonia and Wolf became engaged. The second photo following was probably taken around that time. That photo shows my mother on the far left, my father on the far right, and my uncle Chil (David) next to my mother (his sister). I don't know for sure who the other young woman in the photo is, but Alice thinks it's one of our mother's sisters.

Both our parents and their parents lived through the First World War (WWI), which brought much hardship to the Szpiros in Warsaw. There was little food, and consequently they were hungry and malnourished. Uncle David was a teenager at that time, and his small stature may well have been caused by this shortage. Our mother fell ill with typhus and used to tell the story of the night when the illness peaked, and in the morning they found that their little cat had died. So, the story went around that the angel of death had come by that night to pick up a soul and took the cat's, thereby saving our mother's life. In Poland, especially in the rural parts, people were still somewhat superstitious in those days, a fact that one can deduce from reading Isaac Bashevis Singer's stories. Singer, who became a Nobel laureate in his later years, wrote many short stories among other works. I loved these short stories. In a colorful and evocative style, Singer depicted the life of the Jews in the shtetls, a now-lost world where superstition and magical thinking held their own against logic and reason. I chuckle every time I think about drowning a fish in "The Fools and the Carp." My boys loved this story!

Our father was drafted near the end of WWI, around 1917, and worked in a telegraph unit. This is all Alice remembers our father saying about his war experience. Our uncle Simcha (Sam), my mother's eldest brother, took a more drastic approach to avoiding service: he maimed himself by somehow poking a hole in his ear. I remember that he was always hard of hearing when I knew him. Uncle David did not remember his father. There were no photographs, but he did know that his father had dark hair and a dark beard. Uncle Simcha, on the other hand, had his mother's coloring, fair and blue-eyed.

Uncle David and our mother were raised in a very pious home. Most Jews in the small town were Hasidim.[10] Yom Kippur was truly a Day of Awe, when the Day of Judgment did really feel "awesome" in their souls. After coming to France, our parents left behind their religious upbringing, casting off what they called "superstitions." At home, we sometimes had jambon (ham) for a sandwich, but our mother never partook, nor did she ever cook pork or shellfish: old habits are hard to break.

Sonia is on the left; next to her is Chil (David); on the far right is Wolf

Alice and Simon grew up knowing very little about our Jewish heritage, wanting to be French and were a little confused about our parents' background. Were they Polish, though they didn't speak much Polish at home? Of course, they were émigrés, Polish Jews who wanted to become French citizens, but whose origins made them much more vulnerable than Jews of French origin after the Nazi invasion.

Our parents could read and write both in Yiddish and Polish. They read Polish writers as well as French and Russian and English writers in translation. Warsaw in those days was a vibrant capital. People wore the latest French fashion and our parents (who were engaged then) went to concerts and to the cinema. In Poland they saw Charlie Chaplin, whom they loved in *City Lights*. When they moved to France and had children it was difficult for them to take in spectacles and Alice reflects that their years together in Warsaw were probably more exciting and carefree than their life in France. But France offered a better life overall than in Poland, especially for their children.

Alice and Simon had strict and excellent teachers in the elementary grades. There were free clinics for the children and free summer camps. The French government encouraged "large" families because of the staggering loss of lives, men in particular, caused by WWI. We were *une famille nombreuse* (a large family) at a time when most families had only one child and, as such, we received a special allocation each month. Alice still remembers the kind gentleman who delivered this money, which he carried in a grand leather pouch.

Our father read the French newspapers, one morning and one evening paper. He especially liked *Le Populaire*, but Alice does not remember our mother reading the papers. She does not know for sure whether our mother could read in French, or simply that she was too tired or busy from the day's chores. It was very hard to manage the shopping, the cooking, and especially the cleaning and washing in our small apartment, where a washing machine would have been such a life saver! Her hands and finger nails were raw from the harsh soaps that she used constantly for she was a fanatic about cleanliness. For larger items like sheets or heavy loads, we had a laundress, Madame Bronzini, who, it turns out, also sheltered Alice in the summer of 1942.

In 1954, after their wedding, when Alice and her new husband Sid went to Paris, they stayed with *Oncle* David and *Tante* Berthe. Alice used to wash her and Sid's underwear daily and hang it over the bathtub. Tante Berthe said to Alice on one occasion, "You're always washing, just like your mother!" Alice took this as a great compliment.

Our mother was generous and helped other people. Though we were not rich, our father always provided, and he always seemed to have work to do, even in the thirties when the Depression spread to Europe as well. But mother met people worse off than we. She heard about German refugees who could not afford to pay for the storage of the piano that they had brought from Germany, so she bought the piano: Its name might have been Hermann. It was a tall upright with three pedals, and it came with two candlesticks and a swivel stool (*tabouret*). Mother found a piano teacher for Alice. Her name was Eleanor: She was the daughter of Russian refugees who had aristocratic airs about them. Alice learned some pieces which she played for company, but it turned out that Eleanor was no teacher. When mother took Alice to a "real" piano teacher, the latter was horrified that she (Alice) had not been taught the rudiments of *doigté*, the correct positioning of fingers and hands.

Alice remembers vacations before I was born. Our municipality arranged for children's summer vacations, either in a *colonie* or with individual families. One summer, it must have been 1935, Alice was sent to the countryside (*colonie de vacances*), on the Ile de Ré, an island off the west coast of France, near *La Rochelle*, which has now become a more fashionable destination. But then, it housed a huge fortress which was a prison. She was haunted by fear because they passed by it every day, and her memory of that vacation is not so pleasant. That same summer, Simon was in the region of *Morvan* (east-central France, Burgundy region), with a family consisting of an old woman and her daughter. He came home happy and with wonderful stories, so the following summer, in 1936, our mother asked if both Simon and Alice could stay with that family. In the middle of the summer our mother came to the village, took a room in a hotel and visited with Alice and Simon. Shortly afterwards, however, she didn't seem to approve of their surroundings. She found lodging with a farm family and removed them, to Alice and Simon's disappointment.

Eleanor's father was a photographer of sorts. When Grandmother Tess was in France, the family *sans moi*, because I wasn't born, trooped to their apartment for a group picture.

From left to right: Simon, our father, Grandmother Tessie, Alice, our mother

But then our father came to visit. It was a happy time and our parents seemed in good humor. They hired a driver (what a luxury!) to take everyone to a nearby spa, *St. Honoré les-Bains*, for the day. Alice felt rich as the family strolled the manicured gardens and ate in a restaurant. Already, Alice could hear adults discussing the Spanish Civil War and worrisome news about a certain Hitler in Germany. I was born the following year

A BIT OF HISTORY
ON MY FATHER'S SIDE

Until relatively recently, much less was known about my father's side of the family. I asked my brother and my sister if they ever heard our father tell stories about his parents or grandparents, but they say they had not. "And, even if we were curious about it," my brother added, "it wouldn't have come to mind to ask such questions. It was adult talk."

At the beginning of his memoir, my brother assembled a sparse family tree. It said our father's parents, Abraham and Sarah, had six children: my father, Wolf Shmuel[11] (1898); his sister Fela (1900); and his brothers, Jacob Aron (1902); Simcha (1904); Moshe (1906); and Zvi (1910). The tree also showed that Jacob married Yeda, and Fela married Abraham Weinberg and had two children, Vladik and Renya.

It turns out that my grandfather's name was actually Shlomo (Solomon), and my father had been preceded by an older sister, Feiga (1896), which made it seven children. But all of this information tells us very little about their lives.[12] Once again, fate intervened with a small gift. Sometime in the late sixties, my brother received a letter from a man living in Israel named Reuven Jeruchim who turned out to be our first cousin whom we hadn't known existed. Reuven, who had changed his name in Israel to Yeruchin, had wondered if there were other survivors who had the same name. He did a search, and lo and behold discovered Simon's name in the USA. Reuven is the son of Jacob, one of my father's brothers. In 1970 Simon and his wife Cécile visited Reuven and his family in Israel and Reuven came to the States some time later. Thus was the personal connection made.

In 2005, our younger son, Kenny, went to Israel and visited Reuven. During his stay, Kenny interviewed Reuven and took notes, the essence of which I now relate. But only so much can be unearthed in a short time, and many details that I would have liked to know were not given, or perhaps not known. So, to fill in the blanks, I have constructed a narrative.

Here is Reuven's story: The Jeruchim side of the family was originally of Litvok background. "Litvok" was the name by which Lithuanian Jews were generally referred to. At some point in time, probably in the nineteenth century, the Jeruchim family immigrated to Poland where they had adopted one of the Chasidic rites. That is, one of the several strands of Judaism that flowered in the eighteenth, nineteenth, and the beginning of the twentieth century in eastern Europe. Lithuania and Poland shared a common border and both had large and vibrant Jewish communities.

My grandfather (my father's father), born in 1872, was originally from a town called Ostrów Mazowiecka, a town in northeastern Poland (this is the Polish name; it was called Ostrowa by the Jewish population). Ostrów Mazowiecka is about 60 miles northeast of Warsaw and about 120 miles southwest of the Lithuanian border. I give you this information because, without a mental image of the map, these place names might as well be on the moon. And with this map, it becomes clear how families migrated from one place to the other, how close Poland and Lithuania are to each other and to Germany; and thus how helpless they were to resist the Nazi war machine. The excerpt below sets the atmosphere of that town:[13]

> *Among the large and small communities of Jews in Poland, Ostrów Mazowiecka occupied a distinguished place with regard to its rabbis and righteous men, whose names were famous and whose deeds glorified their congregations. Their books were like teachers of Jewish law whose words were heard and accepted by many, even beyond the borders of the towns where they officiated.*

This was the environment that nourished my grandfather. He apparently had rabbinical ordination, and became known as "Reb (Rabbi) Shloime" Jeruchim. (Reb is an honorific and indicates respect; Shloime is an affectionate Yiddish rendition).

I'm conjecturing that Ostrów Mazowiecka was so full of righteous men that it was hard to break in, so to speak. In addition, Ostrów Mazowiecka was a small town and the opportunities were correspondingly limited. Around 1900, the Jewish population was only about six thousand, while Warsaw had a population of about three-quarters of a million. So, at some point my grandfather decided to move to Warsaw. There, employment would likely have been much more available and Warsaw was generally much more secular. In fact, my grandfather apparently found employment, not as a rabbi, but as the gabbai (generally, someone who helps a synagogue run smoothly) and *chazzan* (cantor). It is said that his singing was so beautiful that the women in the neighborhood would open their windows just to hear it waft from the nearby synagogue. A rabbi is generally supported by the congregation he serves, but gabbai/cantor is not a full-time occupation. So, Shloime needed another source of income and became a glazier (a trade in glass/window repairing).

My grandmother, Sarah, born in 1875, came from a very small town called Czyzew, approximately eighty-five miles northeast of Warsaw. Czyzew in the nineteenth century was predominantly Jewish. Reference is made on the Internet about a "brown" plague which devastated the town, but little appears to be available about how or when this occurred. Reuven also says that Czyzew was completely destroyed in 1939, presumably by the Nazis.

How Sarah met Shloime is open to speculation. Here is mine. Czyzew is only about twenty miles due east of Ostrów Mazowiecka. It would not be surprising that at some point Sarah, most likely with her parents, traveled there, perhaps to attend a service by one of the famous rabbis, and there she could have encountered Shloime. Marriages were arranged, or semi-arranged, in those days, and it may be that on one of those visits Sarah's parents and Shloime's parents made a deal.

In due course, Shloime and Sarah were married. Since my father, Shmuel (Samuel) Wolf, was born in 1898, Shloime was no older than about twenty-five when Shmuel arrived and Sarah three years younger. Early marriage was typical in those days. Following the biblical injunction to "be fruitful and multiply," which was generally followed by Orthodox Jews, Sarah and Shloime had seven children.

Even without war, lifespan was short, especially for women who had the burden of multiple births, cooking, cleaning, and every other chore while the men in the rabbinical profession spent their days studying the Torah and writing interpretations, although I suppose Shloime must have spent some time practicing his craft. I hope Sarah took her tasks in stride and found pride and satisfaction raising her children.

The stories of Shloime and Sarah's children up to the Nazi invasion are like those of most people: growing up, marrying, but not all, and having children. It does not appear that any of their children survived the war, as far as we know, but four of their grandchildren did: my brother, my sister, me, and Reuven, my Israeli cousin. The siblings had different occupations and foibles like everyone else. Fela's husband, Abraham Weinberg, worked in the printing industry, but was a gambler and had trouble keeping financially solvent. Jacob was a small business owner. Simcha took over the business of Shloime as glazier. Little else we know. They were all my uncles, aunts, and cousins, and I am very sad that I never got to know the colorful and large family on my father's side.

It's not clear if all of Shloime's and Sarah's children had been born by the time they moved to Warsaw, but my father was born in Ostrów Maziowecka. On his passport and documentation, my father listed Ostrow as his birthplace. There are many towns in Poland that have Ostrow as their name or part of their names. I'm conjecturing that he didn't say Ostrów Maziowecka because he would immediately have been identified as Jewish.

We have no record of the daily life of Shloime and his family. Probably, on the Sabbath, he would sing at Friday and Saturday services and otherwise did his gabbai duties as required, and worked as a glazier when needed. However, one episode related by Reuven is interesting.

A church in Warsaw was going back and forth between Polish and Russian authority, as was the area generally in those days. (It also seems from the context that this story must have taken place prior to 1917, the year of the Russian revolution.) The Russians wanted to remove and replace the stained glass in the church, which seemed to be specific to the Catholic Polish community. Reb Shloime was asked to create the glass pieces. However, because the glass was for a church, and because it may have had Christian religious imagery, Reb Shloime felt uncomfortable about going forward without first consulting one of the authoritative rabbis of the community. The rabbi at hand told Reb Shloime that not only *could* he do the job, but he *must* do it. The rabbi's response seemed to rest on the principle that not creating the glass pieces could create an anti-Jewish sentiment amongst the Russian authorities. And so, Reb Shloime completed the job and was rewarded with a fancy Russian knife. The knife remained in the family through WWII but was lost after that time.

Our family had many relatives elsewhere in Poland and as far as Prague. Several lived in Bialystok, the regional capital, which was perhaps 50 percent Jewish before the war. Reuven relates that he used to visit family in Bialystok and that he was amused by the differences in cuisine and speech. Reuven was accustomed to gefilte fish that was much simpler, and in Bialystok and Ukraine the gefilte fish was spicier and peppery. In addition, he remembers visiting a family in Bialystok where their pronunciation of Yiddish differed substantially from his. For example, where he said "Ziche" for sugar they said "Zucher."

There was a family member living in Prague, we are told. He had become a lawyer and judge or some kind of government bureaucrat. He sent a picture of himself to the family in Warsaw once he had achieved this position. The photo, taken in his office, prominently showed a cross which indicated that he might have converted to Christianity in order to be permitted to take the position. This was no doubt a requirement for any Jew in eastern Europe, probably western Europe as well, to join the civil service. The family members who received the photo decided that perhaps it would be best not to show the picture to other more religious members of the family.

It was not uncommon in the religiously traditional communities for a son, at least one son, of a rabbi to follow in his father's path. (In eastern Europe at least, "traditional" observance was universal; today we would call this Orthodox since several variations in practice have emerged.) This does not seem to have been the case for any of Shloime's sons. It is certain that my father did not. In fact, as my sister relates, and I mentioned earlier, he considered religion a "superstition." How this came about, having been raised in a very religious home, I can only speculate.

What is likely, however, is that my father was swept up in the new political and social currents sweeping through Europe in the early part of the twentieth century: socialism, communism, nationalism, Zionism, and other "isms" which rejected traditional norms. I have inherited my father's skepticism, as have my siblings. If I have any religious tendencies, it would not be in organized religion. My leanings could be described as humanism, a belief that people should act ethically and morally toward one another, independently of any deity.

Reuven was the only grandson who lived in Warsaw with Reb Shloime, and accordingly they had close rapport. While Shloime's and Sarah's children were not as religious as their parents, (indeed some espousing communist/atheistic views) there seemed to be no contradiction to Reuven that he participated in our grandfather's religious life, while at the same time living in a mostly secular environment.

In September 1939, their world collapsed. Germany had just invaded Poland and soldiers were shooting down civilians in the street (particularly in the Jewish towns). Reuven remembers praying with Reb Shloime during that Yom Kippur with a special fervency. "It was the last time I really prayed," he said.

What happened to this large family? None lived after WWII, save Reuven, though not all died at the hands of the Nazis. Simcha died of tuberculosis (TB) before the war, as did Zvi, who never married. Jacob also died of TB, probably in Treblinka. Fela and her husband were murdered by Ukrainians. Wolf Samuel and Moshe had moved to Paris before the war. About Wolf, my father, I'll say more later. Shlomo lived in Warsaw when the Nazis invaded Poland and he and Sarah were forced into the Warsaw ghetto. Reb Shloime died of sickness in the Warsaw ghetto. Sarah was taken from the ghetto to Treblinka concentration camp, where she undoubtedly perished.

Reuven was trapped in the Warsaw ghetto with his parents. His father, Jacob, died of TB, probably also in Treblinka. Miraculously, Reuven and his mother escaped the Warsaw ghetto and found their way to Siberia, where they lived out the war. In 1948, they were able to immigrate to Israel. And then, many years later, he found us.

IV

THE EARLY YEARS

DRAMA, TRAUMA AND SURVIVAL

April 4, 1937 was the day I made my entrance in Paris. My birth certificate says I was born at 74 *rue Denfert Rochereau*. I was initially puzzled: this looks like an ordinary street address. I looked it up and it turns out that this address is today *l'Hôpital Saint-Vincent-de-Paul* in the fourteenth *arrondissement*. It was founded in 1638 as *l'Hospice des Enfants-Trouvés* (basically a foundling home), but not at this address and underwent multiple incarnations. Its maternity ward was only created in 1934, and had a different name when I was born. At the time, my family lived at 95 rue Diderot in Vincennes, a neighborhood just east of the boundary of Paris. About a year later, we moved to 71 *rue Colmet Lépinay*, in Montreuil, a section just north of Vincennes. This is where we lived when the Germans marched in.

I am told that I was named after one of my father's brothers, Moshe, who drowned in the Seine. It was reported as a suicide by the police. My sister says that, one day, she happened to be rummaging in my father's rolltop desk and stumbled on a yellowed clipping from a newspaper about the discovery of my uncle in the river. Our father snatched the clipping from her, but did not discuss its content.

On the tattered copy of my birth certificate that came with me to the States, my parents' names are inscribed as Wolf Samuel and Syma. My parents spoke Yiddish to each other and my mother called my father *Shmiel*, a Yiddish version of Samuel, and my father called my mother *Soniou*, an affectionate version of Sonia. I am touched that my granddaughter, Serah, is named after her. Into this household I had been preceded by my sister Alice, born February 18, 1928, and my brother Simon, born December 25, 1929, whose first given name was actually Isaac, after my mother's father. Simon's nickname was *Zizi*, one of the variants of Isaac, but once in hiding he started to use the more French-sounding Simon; Isaac would have been a dead giveaway. My sister says that, when I was quite young, I used to call her *ta sœur* because people used to point to her and say to me "c'est ta sœur"—that's your sister! Many years later I sometimes joked, without intending disrespect, that Simon was at least the second Jewish boy to have been born on that date. I have always found it hard to fathom Christians' hate of Jews when the Christian God incarnate led his life as a Jew.

Sometimes I see a bumper sticker with words like "my boss is a Jewish carpenter." Would that every Christian be so inclined. It was probably in college, but possibly in high school, when I became interested in religion as a subject, not as a personal goal. Although I am not a student of history, I have read a fair amount of it, and I concluded long ago that religion was such a force for misery that I could not bring myself to be a follower of any.

I have no recollection of the first five years of my life. I know there are people who say they have very early memories. But, in my case, whether the lack of them is a result of the ensuing trauma is useless speculation. The only relatively sharp image that I have is being in a bathtub playing with rubber soldiers. My brother confirms that this was the case. Fortunately, my brother and sister, seven and nine years older, respectively, have a fairly sharp recollection of our family life up to the summer of 1942. Among other things they tell me that I was the treasured baby in those first few years and I believe that the infusion of love that I received from my family then was an important factor in surviving psychologically.

The fall of France to Germany in 1940 was as unexpected as it was swift. The French were defeated in a matter of six weeks in May/June 1940. This catastrophe doomed the world to years of carnage.[14] But prior to the French capitulation, as the reality became clearer, Parisians began to leave in droves. I was then three years old. Fear of bombardment or fear of the invading army soon resulted in a wave of refugees seeking safety to the south or the west of France. Two million people fled Paris proper and its *environs*. By the time the Germans entered Paris, two-thirds of its inhabitants had fled. But the stream of refugees had swelled to eight million, the Parisians having been joined by refugees from Belgium and northern and eastern France; the French referred to this episode as *l'exode*. This was no orderly evacuation. The quoted fragment of the article below gives a small sense of what it must have been like:

> *As the German invasion progressed unchecked, the Parisians began their exodus from the city ahead of the invading army. The foreign correspondent, Walter B. Kerr, described the atmosphere of the city in the last edition of the newspaper, the International Herald Tribune, distributed in Paris on June 11, 1940.*[15]
>
> *Paris, before dawn yesterday, was a city of men, women, and*

children fleeing to safety, of countless thousands of families joining the millions of refugees from the north who have fled before the German mechanized army in these last few weeks. All day long streams of cars and trucks, loaded down until the springs gave way, poured out of the city. It was heartbreaking to watch them for there once more was that sad old story that has been told so many times, of twisted lives, of poverty, of flight before an invader, of separation perhaps forever from mothers and fathers and children. They lined up at railroad stations, carrying overwhelming bundles. They piled into old cars that hammered and pounded their way along the roads.

I do not know exactly when they began to realize their city and perhaps their lives were in danger...

One of the many photos of people fleeing the German army in 1940.[16]

There is a 2003 French film *Les Egarés (Strayed)* that will give you a *real* feeling for the chaos. But it wasn't only chaos; German and Italian fighter planes randomly swooped and strafed the long line of weary refugees, causing people to dive into the ditches along the road. One hundred thousand people died on this journey. My family was part of this exodus. It felt prudent to separate, so my father and my two siblings went as one group and my mother and I as another. My brother recalls on this journey having dived into a ditch with my sister and father as a German plane started to strafe the column of refugees. I have no memory of this exodus, but the fear and anxiety that must have pervaded the atmosphere must surely have been transmitted to a little boy.

By the end of June 1940, the Nazis had vanquished France in record time. Toward the end of June an armistice was declared and overt hostilities ceased, in France at least. The refugees were permitted to return to their homes. Almost immediately, the Germans partitioned France into occupied and unoccupied zones, the latter usually referred to as Vichy France, where, for a time, less stringent conditions were imposed.[17] For a while, life seemed to be returning to "normal" if one can use that word under the circumstances. But for Jews, life never became "normal" again. Soon, life started to become perilous for Jews. Already in the fall of 1940, on September 27, the authorities declared that Jews were to report to their local police station to get identification cards. Of course, it was the Germans who mandated this requirement, but it was the French administration (i.e., the Vichy government), in particular the police, who carried out the task.[18] Initially, at least, it was the "foreign" Jews who were targeted, those like my parents who were legal residents but not citizens. This is another sad story—a devil's bargain between Vichy and the Nazis. My friend Jean-Marc Dreyfus, a historian, tells me that the Germans did not have sufficient personnel to carry out the roundups. So, the bargain was that if Vichy were to allow its police to do the roundups, the Germans would not pursue "real" French citizens. Of course, this was a false promise. If the war had continued, no Jew in France would have been spared, French born or otherwise.

My parents dutifully obeyed the order to report and register. At that time, most people would comply with orders from "authorities," although Susan Zuccotti in her book, *The Holocaust, the French, and the Jews*,[19] says that many Jews were suspicious enough not to comply. My sister points out that Jews from eastern Europe were "used to" oppression from the authorities in their country of origin and were naturally leery of official pronouncements. At that time, however, my parents had been in France for about fourteen years and perhaps by then their natural sense of suspicion had been eroded.

The word "*Juif*" was stamped across the identification card in red letters. This already made them a target. But on June 7, 1942 Jews now had a literal target on their chests. The German military commander in France ordered all Jews over six years old to wear a yellow star. I did not have to wear one because I was not yet six. However, long before this decree, life was already becoming fragile. In 1941, major arrests, or raids (*rafle* in French), started to take place. In Paris, raids took place beginning on May 14, August 20, and December 12, 1941, and were usually carried on over additional days.[20] Those arrested were held in French internment camps before eventually being sent to Drancy, outside of Paris. From there, they were transported by train to concentration camps and death. This trip was not what one might imagine by a "train trip." It was 1,500 kilometers of misery, typically lasting several days. Packed in cattle cars, just like cattle, standing all the way, without food or water, many died before reaching their destination. For them, I'm afraid to say, it was even possibly a blessing, compared to what would ensue. However, the fate of those arrested was not fully known at the time. Nazi propaganda circulated the fiction that they were going to work in camps or factories. These raids just mentioned were only the prelude in France. My parents and their neighbors were well aware of these random arrests, and my father no longer went outside our apartment to deliver his work. My mother took over this task.

Even though the real story was not known, the prospect of work camps in Germany was in itself to be avoided.

Early in 1942, the "Final Solution" was made official Nazi policy. The infamous Wannsee Conference, held on January 20, 1942 in a Berlin suburb, attended by senior Nazi officials, formulated the "Final Solution," namely, the elimination of the Jewish people from Europe. But even before this official policy, the Nazis had long begun implementing it—wanton and rampant killing was occurring in conquered countries. In Poland, Ukraine, and Russia, killing squads in the wake of the German army had already murdered two million people, not only but mostly Jews. In Paris and its surrounding communities where a majority of Jews lived, the Nazis and the collaborationist French police set this policy in motion. The largest roundup of Jews in the Paris area was now scheduled for July 16, 1942.

The deviousness of the registration edict, of course, is that when the Nazis wanted to "collect" Jews they would know exactly where to go, and they had already made use of that information in the previously mentioned raids. And so it happened. For some time, the Nazi overlords, with complicity from the French police, had been planning a major roundup of all Jews in the Paris region, which included Paris proper and its nearby environs.[21] This roundup (rafle in French) was scheduled for July 16, 1942. It started at four o'clock in the morning; 4,500 French policemen, with over twenty-seven thousand index cards, started knocking on doors. In the end, 13,152[22] Jews were arrested and nearly all were sent to Drancy, just outside Paris, or to the Vélodrome d'Hiver ("Vel d'Hiv") in Paris proper, and eventually transported to Auschwitz. Given the apparently detailed preparation by the police for this roundup, a surprisingly large number of people avoided arrest. They were either warned by the French resistance, civil servants with a kernel of decency, or uncomfirmed rumors; hidden by neighbors; or benefitted from a lack of motivation and purpose in some policemen. We were the beneficiary of one of those circumstances. The "number," 13,152, is just that, a number. It doesn't convey the misery that each person suffered. Susan Zuccotti imparts a sense of that misery with these chilling words:

> *This book is dedicated to the more than 3,500 Jewish children under the age of fourteen who were arrested in Paris on July 16, 1942, and forcibly separated from their mothers at the French camps[23] of Pithiviers and Beaune-la-Rolande two weeks later. Their mothers were deported. The children had to fend for themselves until they too were deported, bewildered, terrified, and alone, in sealed cattle cars without light or air, to be murdered upon arrival at Auschwitz.*

Ultimately, it was serendipity and my mother's presence of mind that saved her three children and eventually brought me to the Leclere family in the Norman town of St. Aubin-lès-Elbeuf.

It should be emphasized that this was the very first raid where children were "arrested." The age did not matter—from infants to teen-agers. The depredation of the Nazis knew no bounds.

The critical period was a bare two months, from July 15, 1942 to September 11, 1942. Events were happening in rapid fire, anxiety and fear reigned, and of course no one was stopping to take notes.

It happened that our mother had an appointment with a dentist on July 15, one day after *Le Quatorze Juillet*, the day France observes its liberation from the monarchy in 1789.[24] The dentist was Jewish, and one of his patients was a French policeman who told him about the impending roundup. That dentist, in turn, told my mother.

That warning in itself would have been no guarantee of safety. Not everyone would believe that this wasn't just a rumor. In fact, it appears, according to my brother, that my father thought it was just that, although I'm surprised that he may have been hesitant because of what my sister told me, which is this: The random arrests that had been taking place in various Parisian locations were conducted in public and broad daylight and were well-known. Furthermore, my father no longer left our apartment even to conduct his business. As mentioned earlier my mother now took over some of those activities, going to a district in Paris to purchase parts or other items that he needed for his watch-making, and delivering finished watches to clients. In any case, my mother, who was perhaps more *streetwise*, took the threat of the raid seriously and invited close friends to our apartment to discuss this possibility and they jointly decided that it might be best not to be home that evening.

We spent the night at the home of a Polish lady who did laundry for us. Daylight revealed that the policeman's warning was all too true. If it hadn't been for my mother's serendipitous appointment and her decision to believe a "rumor," my siblings and I would have suffered the exact same fate as the children who were arrested the night of the raid. This fits again in my theory about the fragility and randomness of life.

After the raid, it was clearly unsafe to return home. We did not know if the police would return to try to collect those they had missed. It turns out that they didn't, but how were we to know? So, from one day to the next we became essentially homeless. Earlier I noted that, before I was born, my parents and siblings had lived in Vincennes, a nearby suburb of Paris, adjacent to Montreuil, where we were now living. There, my mother, who was a very gregarious person, had become friendly with many people in the neighborhood, including local shopkeepers. Alice remembers coming home from school and smelling fresh brewed dark coffee, and our mother entertaining a newly found guest she had met somewhere. Many of the people our mother knew became our temporary protectors. Among the shopkeepers was a Monsieur Lefèvre, who owned a hardware store, and Mme Garnier, who owned a pharmacy, though it was perhaps closer to a homeopathic dispensary. Madame Garnier proved to be an indispensable connection to safety. Our mother was troubled by chronic indigestion; perhaps today we would call it acid reflux, and she regularly purchased bags of dry *tisanes* (herbs) from Mme Garnier. I find it ironic, or perhaps another instance of the unpredictability of life, that my mother's ailment led to this relationship, which led to our salvation.

Here I must interject another difference between my siblings' memories. It illustrates the well-known fallibility of eyewitnesses. Our family, like many Parisian families, took our vacations in the countryside in a village called Richebourg about forty miles west of Paris. There was no direct way to get there, but the town of Houdan, about three miles south of Richebourg had a train station. From there, we would go and walk (I assume I was carried some of the time) the rest of the way to Richebourg where we rented a large room with simple kitchen facilities. The house was owned by Madame Balossier.

Next to Madame Balossier's house there was a farm. When on vacation, my parents went there regularly to buy eggs, fruit, vegetables, chicken, and what have you. Over time, my parents and the farmer became friends. My sister and my brother romped in the farmer's fields, snatching fruit from orchards and building "secret" hideaways with branches. My parents' friendship with the farmer was providential. As fate would have it, I was sent there early in 1942.

At the end of the summer of 1941, we had returned home to a quasi-normal life. My siblings went to school and I attended a *crèche*, a sort of kindergarten attached to their school. By then, rationing had been in place for a year and the shelves in stores were nearly empty. In the beginning of 1942, my mother thought it best if I went to Richebourg—it was probably after the *vacances de Noël* (Christmas vacation). It would lighten her load if she had to queue up in Paris and she wouldn't have to worry about what to do with me if she had to go get parts for my father or do other errands. My mother arranged to have me stay with the aforementioned farmer *en pension* (i.e., as a boarder), and on that farm, where food was available, if not plentiful, I could be fed. This would relieve my mother of at least *that* worry. This is why, according to Alice, I was not at home on the day of the *rafle*.

Alice and my brother would take the train from *la Gare Montparnasse* and visit me and bring back the valuable vegetables, chicken, eggs, the farmer had available. Here is the divergence of recollections between Alice and our brother Simon. My brother is certain that I was at home with everyone else on the day of the rafle, but my sister says, "No! He was still in Richebourg and was brought back by Madeleine Bonneau."

I can't help thinking about what *could* have happened if my family *had* been arrested on the night of the rafle and I hadn't been there—or if I had been there. Either of these two possible *dénouements* could be alternate scenes in a play, or forks in a road, but as it turns out this point is a moot one.

Immediately following the *rafle* my siblings and parents separated. Apparently, my parents thought it best to scatter so that we would not all be arrested together, should such an event have materialized. Alice says that on a seemingly random basis, my siblings and parents stayed for perhaps a night or two in different households whose owners my mother had befriended. According to Alice, my parents also sometimes stayed in different hotels for a few days and spent time in the home of the Bronzinis where my father worked on his watches in the garden. Soon after, my mother persuaded the Bronzinis to take Alice with them, as they were about to go to the countryside on vacation—another instance, I think, of my mother's attempt to keep us separate and safe. Alice also said that she and my mother went back to our apartment (how often she doesn't know) to take clothing and other possessions, which could not have been taken in the haste we had to leave on the night of July 15. My father also went back, at least once, to retrieve a satchel that contained many watches under repair that had been accidentally left behind on the day of the rafle. His sense of rectitude would not let him rest till he had retrieved other people's objects left in his care. He was so conscientious that almost any risk was worth saving his reputation.

On the surface, this strikes me as foolhardy because I would have thought that the police could come back at any time to homes where the occupants had been absent during the roundup. Of course, we didn't live in Paris proper, and there weren't that many Jews in Montreuil relative to Paris. But we learned afterward that the police did not return. So possibly it seems the police thought they had done their "duty" and weren't going to bother further in that neighborhood.

Providence smiled on us, at least temporarily, in the person of Mme Garnier. She was a friend or acquaintance of Monsieur and Madame (Albert Charles and Irma) Bonneau and their daughter Madeleine. Mme Bonneau was also a client of the pharmacy and happened to come into the store where Madame Garnier told her about our plight. Mme Bonneau said she would be back in a few days with a solution, and so she was. She invited us (and another family, the friends of our parents who had been hiding with us, Monsieur and Mme Krum and their son Joseph) to come to her home, which was nearby. Because it would have been impractical and dangerous for all to remain there, the initial plan was to find safe haven for the children. On the day we entered the Bonneaus' house, a man by the name of Monsieur Ernst was waiting for us. At this time, my sister hadn't yet returned from her stay with the Bronzinis.

What ensued at the moment was unexpected by our parents. It appeared that Monsieur Bonneau wanted Monsieur Ernst to take me immediately to his house in the country outside a town in Normandy called Saint-Aubin-lès-Elbeuf. Why the hurry? No one articulated it, but as I said, the focus was on saving the children. The countryside was a clearly safer environment than the Parisian urban setting. And, I surmise, the fewer "guests" in the Bonneau house, the less likely to be discovered by nosy neighbors.

But, imagine this scene. My parents had not previously known the Bonneaus, nor Monsieur Ernst, and had no idea what would happen once we arrived at this home. So, it must have been quite a shock to my parents that I was to leave more or less immediately. My brother recalls an animated discussion between my mother and Monsieur Bonneau.[26] My mother was probably shocked and frightened to give her youngest child to a stranger. Monsieur Bonneau must have convinced her it was best for all present for me to depart first. One of the few things remaining in my brother's observation is my mother animatedly beseeching Monsieur Bonneau with these words, "Please make sure that my children get a good education."

How the Bonneaus made the connection with Monsieur Ernst, no one knows. Much later, on a trip to Paris in 2012, we went to the

Paris City Hall where there was an exhibition commemorating the seventieth anniversary of the July 1942 *rafle*. On the wall there were copies of letters from children who had been arrested along with their parents, but were later separated. They had written to their parents, full of hope to be reunited, which was not going to happen. I felt such sadness reading those letters. What subsequently happened to these children was chillingly captured by Susan Zuccotti in the dedication to her book that I quoted earlier. Also on a wall, there was a poster where I read about *Réseaux de Sauvetage* (rescue networks) that had been established by Protestant churches, and it may well be that the Bonneaus, who were Protestant, had been moved to join, perhaps by a sermon.[27]

My brother nominated the Bonneaus to be honored as "Righteous Among the Nations" in Yad Vashem, Israel's official memorial to the victims of the Holocaust. After much time and paperwork, they were granted that honor.[28] Those so honored, sometimes erroneously called righteous gentiles (because not all were), risked their own lives to save Jews.

Almost immediately after arriving at the Bonneaus' home, Monsieur Ernst took me on a train trip to his home, in Normandy, which would have been fraught with danger since police and gestapo watched all train stations and checked papers. But luck was with us. It was an uneventful trip, likely aided by the fact that it was summertime and, as was typical, many people left Paris for the countryside. A grown man with a small boy was probably not an unusual sight. Still, I am always struck at how many instances of disaster could have occurred that did not. What if an overly eager French policeman or gestapo or SS officer had stopped us and asked questions? It gives me the chills to contemplate that possibility. I must have been coached by my parents, or the Bonneaus, on how to behave. Did I even know what it meant to be

Jewish? Who knows how a five-year-old would react to an imposing person in uniform?

Monsieur Ernst traveled back to Paris a few days later to take Simon and Joseph as well. Luck was with them, too. I was by myself with a grumpy Madame Ernst for those few days, during which she apparently gave me no emotional support, for when Simon came back, I ran to him in tears of joy (so he told me) and I said I hated this *sorcière* (witch). But, Madame Ernst, who had raised three grown sons, declared that she was not up to taking care of a young child. After some weeks, Monsieur Ernst made arrangements to transfer me to a family they knew in the same town, St. Aubin-lès-Elbeuf. This was the Leclere family, Suzanne, Marcel, and their son Gaston.

It turns out, according to my brother, that the Ernst family sold meat on the black market and trafficked in stolen bicycles. For some time, long after the war, I had been wondering how the Lecleres and the Ernsts were connected because the latter were seemingly petty criminals and the Lecleres were solid citizens. This mystery was uncovered when Gaston visited us in 1990. During the week that he and his family stayed with my brother, Simon, the two had many conversations about what happened then. It transpired that Monsieur Ernst and Monsieur Leclere were *both* in the *Résistance*, and that must have been the connection.[29] I had also been puzzled about how the Bonneaus knew the Ernst family because, here again, the connection seemed unlikely. The Bonneaus were somewhat aristocratic and would not have been in the same social circle. Here, my sister gives the somewhat plausible speculation that the connection may have been linked to the black market, namely, that the Bonneau family purchased meat from the Ernsts. That may well be the case—in war (and in love), all kinds of unlikely connections take place, or, as the saying goes, make strange bedfellows.

The day that I was transferred to the Leclere family was a day of mixed blessings. On the one hand, I was suddenly separated from my parents and siblings. On the other hand, it was a very lucky day for me, given the circumstance I was in. For the next three years the Lecleres became a new family.

V

SURVIVAL PART 2

ST. AUBIN DURING THE OCCUPATION AND THE LIBERATION

I was now entering a new stage of my life, my hidden life, away from Montreuil, away from my parents, away from my siblings. I had survived the grande rafle, probably the greatest threat to my life. But who knew how long the occupation would last, if not indefinitely? France was occupied and danger could be lurking around the corner. Of course, such thoughts were not circulating in my brain. I was a five-year-old child, and children live in the present. All I could have been aware of at that moment is that I was living with a family called Leclere. Initially I probably did not understand that I was in a village called St. Aubin-lès-Elbeuf,[30] that I might have had difficulty pronouncing.

St. Aubin is in Upper Normandy, nestled on the east side of a bend of the Seine River.[31] I remarked in a footnote to the first chapter that "lès" in St. Aubin-lès-Elbeuf is an archaic term meaning "next to." In this case, Elbeuf could hardly have been closer. It is just on the other side of the Seine, a bit south and west, separated only by bridges. And in fact, the story of St. Aubin during the occupation and the liberation cannot be fully separated from what transpired in Elbeuf.

The map below shows an overview of part of northwest France and the towns where my siblings and I spent the war: St. Aubin, not far from Rouen, famous for its medieval cathedral; and Savigny-le-Vieux, the village I mentioned earlier, where my sister and brother had both been hidden, about two to three miles apart in the same commune. I cannot help contemplating how history follows us. Savigny is a very old town. It was founded by monks in the twelfth century, early 1100s, although the Vikings had made landfall there two centuries earlier. It's fascinating to think that only thirty-four years earlier, William the Conqueror had invaded the land across the straits, now the English Channel, and essentially founded what has become Great Britain, the foe that Hitler could not conquer. And here they were, my siblings, hidden in a town that had perhaps been imbued with the concept of sanctuary, launched into the future by those monks nine centuries earlier, and all the while the Nazi occupiers were close by. What was in the air in Savigny? At least thirty Jewish children were hidden within its boundary.[32] As a percentage of the population, perhaps a thousand or so, it was exceeded only by le Chambon-sur-Lignon.[33]

The map also shows Paris and the location of the infamous town of Drancy, around eight miles northeast of Paris, the point of departure of the trains to Hell, aka Auschwitz. Perhaps that association is unfair to the citizens of Drancy who may have not have had any notion of the true destination of those trains. And the same is true for the citizens of the town of Auschwitz, who may not have known the extent of the murders committed there, but must surely have known that something unholy was happening on those grounds.

Because of the nearness of our location to the landing beaches, around the time of the Allied invasion we saw or heard a lot of activity related to bombings, air-raid alerts, and armored convoys. But more about that later.

But this map does not show the true character of the Seine, which meanders through much of France like a snake that doesn't want to be tamed. The map on page 75 shows some of that character between the two towns of St. Aubin and Elbeuf. The strategic significance of the Seine will be revealed shortly when we speak about the liberation.

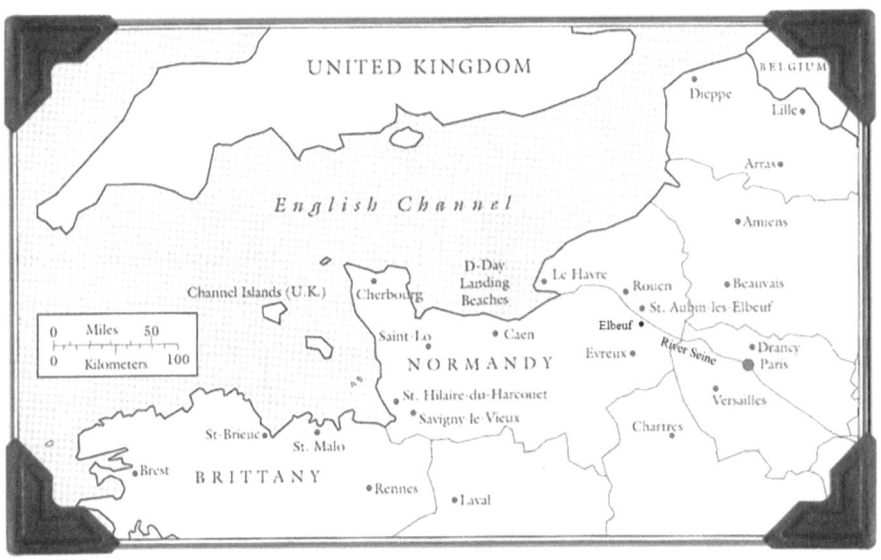

Map of part of northwest France showing the locations of St. Aubin and Savigny, and to the east and south, Paris and Drancy

Was I vulnerable to arrest in St. Aubin? It appears that there was not a Jewish community of any size in St. Aubin, or one so small it did not present an attractive target for the French police to raid the village looking for Jews on orders from the Nazis. I may have been a Jewish community of one, unless there were other hidden children. Even though no one knew my real identity, except two people named in Chapter 1, I could have been denounced by someone for a bounty. They didn't need to know I was Jewish. They could simply have been suspicious. Where did that little boy come from? Doesn't he look Jewish? This is not just an intellectual pursuit. Life for Jews at that time hung by a thread. My own survival to that point rested on the purely chance event that my mother had a dental appointment the day before the *grande rafle* in Paris.

The Nazis' obsession with eliminating all Jews from Europe could very well have been worth a short trip across the river to the police station in St. Aubin from Elbeuf, where indeed, in the latter town, there had been a small Jewish community who were all deported. So, it's not beyond imagination to think that catching one more Jew would have warranted the effort. In fact, the last train from Drancy left on 31 July 1944 with over three hundred children, less than a month before Paris was liberated.

Evidently, I was not denounced. I lived with the Lecleres for about three years, from July 1942 to the summer of 1945. The first two of those years were spent under the occupation and the third after the liberation of our part of France in the summer of 1944. I later learned that both Marcel and Gaston worked in a cookware factory where Marcel was a supervisor. Gaston was about sixteen, already of working age. In France, nothing stops la cuisine!

My brother was unhappy with the environment at the Ernst compound, and worried because trading in the black market for meat could lead to long prison sentences, if not execution by the Germans. So, he wrote to the Bonneaus, a risky thing to do, that he wanted out. Eventually, an elegant lady named Madame Mounier arrived and escorted my siblings to Normandy—to the village already mentioned, Savigny-le-Vieux. Mme Mounier was a guide for the OSE, a French-Jewish humanitarian organization (Œuvre de Secours aux Enfants) founded before the war, but developed a clandestine arm during the war to find safe havens for Jewish children.

In this family portrait, Suzanne is sitting, holding my hand.
Gaston is standing behind her, and Marcel has his hand on my shoulder

My memory of my time with the Lecleres consists of snapshots, rather than continuous film. I must have cried for my parents—it was so soon after our separation, but I have no recollection of being miserable for an extended period. Perhaps I was mollified by the fiction I was most likely told, that they would return soon. But I must credit the Lecleres with the sense of family, and the kindness and affection they provided, which somehow allowed me to sublimate my loss into an acceptance of my situation. The "family" portrait (taken toward the end of my stay there, with Marcel's hand protectively on my shoulder) speaks to an integrated family. I don't know how the Lecleres presented me to their friends or acquaintances. It would have been folly to tell the true story, at least before the liberation. They may have given me their last names, perhaps portraying me as a relative from another part of France. It's another missing piece that I would love to know.[34]

I picture myself in the street, whipping a *toupie* (top). I remember running and trying to keep a *cerceau* (hoop) upright. I remember going to church and Sunday catechism, though my skepticism about religion must already have been developed even at that early age.

Oddly enough I don't have an explicit sense of the daily activities that I must have participated in for the three years or so that I lived with the Lecleres, at that juncture nearly half of my life. For example, I can't place myself in the classroom of the school that I attended. But I have a strong sense of having played soccer in the schoolyard during recess. I was small, but quick! Furthermore, there is some evidence that my propensity for learning was already beginning to show. Simon writes that he received a letter from me in 1944 in which I mention receiving good grades and being rewarded by the Lecleres.

While I can't remember every detail, I have imagined daily life at the Lecleres. I would have had café au lait and perhaps a crusty piece of bread with butter before going to school, or church on Sundays; I must have sat at the dinner table. Even though food was rationed almost everywhere, I don't recall deprivation. I remember that Suzanne kept rabbits in the backyard, and I'm sure they were the source of a savory stew for the table. There was also a small garden in the front of the house, which supplied some of the vegetables. Madame Leclere grew beans and leafy legumes, perhaps cucumbers or tomatoes in the warm weather.

My introduction to French cooking, and acquiring a French palate, must have taken place during my stay with the Lecleres because my mother's cooking style was essentially eastern European, according to my sister. But if I try to picture sitting down at the Lecleres' dinner table, my mind draws a blank, similarly about bedtime. I can't conjure up a routine such as Joan and I typically did with our own children: perhaps a bath, maybe a snack (milk and cookies), brushing teeth, and a story. One thing I do remember clearly, however, is a hot brick. There was no central heating, and fuel was scarce. On really cold nights, Madame Leclere would place a hot brick, wrapped in a towel, in the bed. If my feet could sing, they would have said, "Merci."

And how did I address them? I'm frustrated by this lacuna, especially since I've always had a very good memory, but it's now more than seventy years ago. Equally frustrating is the same haziness about my emotional feelings towards the Lecleres. At first, I'm sure I was guarded. Did I simply tolerate them, or perhaps showed some level of affection as a survival response? Or did I slowly grow to be fond of them because that's what they showed toward me? It's quite possible that there is a psychological component to this haziness, in addition to time, but I attribute it to not having had a stable address until Joan and I were married. I have an analogy. When traveling by train and looking out of the window, we see a sight and for the moment it registers, only to be replaced a few minutes later by a different sight, and so on. At the end of the ride, little of all those sights remains etched in memory. Of course, my moves happened at a slower pace, but there were many of them, twenty in all till the present. However, it was not merely the change of address, per se, that caused a memory block. Each new address came with a change of residential and external environment, a change in persons in charge, a change in my companions, a change in expectations. Every move was like putting a new coat of paint on a wall, obscuring what was there previously.

About the Lecleres, I certainly would not have called them Maman and Papa—that would probably have stuck in my throat and the outside world would know that wasn't true. Monsieur and

Madame would have been too formal: Perhaps it was Oncle Marcel and Tante Suzanne? I wish I knew. One aspect of life that's typical for a young boy is having playmates. I don't recall having had any, except possibly in the schoolyard during recess, where I did play soccer with my schoolmates, but boys that age aren't interested in that sort of question. I'm not sure whether I longed for a friend, but I'm sure the reason I didn't have one was safety: If I had played consistently with a boy from another family, there might have been too many questions, probably not from the friend but from his parents.

I also have a copy of a letter, dated February 5, 1945, which I sent to my brother and sister. In this letter I say that "depuis la rentrée j'ai été 8 fois premier et une fois deuxième..." which means since returning to school I was first in my class eight times and second once. It does not seem to be the fashion to keep letters today, much less write them, but at the time it was the main mode of communication. In this case, however, I'm sure we kept the letters because in the aftermath of the trauma we three endured, they were the closest thing to family, next to physical proximity. Simon, Alice, and I had kept letters from one or the other of us as far back as 1945.

Some years ago, those letters were donated to the United States Holocaust Memorial Museum in Washington, DC. Simon also donated his watercolors from the war years to the museum, and I donated the tiny suitcase I carried on our immigration voyage. It contained all my worldly possessions: my passport, letters to or from Simon and Alice, and a precious gift from my brother, a comic book that he had written and illustrated for me following the Scout Jamboree in 1947, entitled *Les Aventures de Jambo*, detailing the exploits of a scout named "Jambo."

In many of these letters, I report to Simon or Alice my grades in various subjects. Looking at those grades today, they do not seem so superb, especially *calcul*, which is perhaps ironic given my eventual profession, but perhaps they were better than most of my schoolmates'. Schools in France, at least then, were run fastidiously, and the French were fond of ranking. There is, in fact, a hierarchy in the French school system, where the more promising students are identified through testing and prepared for the next level, the highest of which are the prestigious écoles supérieures.

For about two years after I arrived in St. Aubin, life seemed to proceed on an even keel, at least from my perception of the world, that is until the war reached us. The Allies (Americans, British, and Canadians, along with some soldiers from the occupied countries, e.g., Poland) began air raids around strategic locations in Normandy. It was not generally known at the beginning of 1944 that the invasion of France would take place where it did, on the D-Day landing beaches in Normandy. More important, the Germans did not know. The Allies had conducted an elaborate deception campaign that convinced Hitler the landing would take place at the Pas de Calais, the shortest distance between England and France across the English Channel.[35] The Pas de Calais is over two hundred miles north from the landing beaches, and this brilliant deception delayed German reinforcements past the point of effectiveness, at least in the sense of repulsing the landings. It may be that some of the bombardments were meant to deceive as well, but they had a real effect on the ordinary people on the ground.

Here is a liberal translation of an introduction to the table on page 70.[36]

From January to mid-September 1944, the bombings in Haute-Normandie became a daily reality. From the beginning of the year until the landing, the Anglo-American air force targeted the main communication axes, destroying bridges and marshalling yards. These were part of the Operation Overlord plan, whose aim, among others, was to hinder or even prohibit the crossing of the Seine to German troops. On August 19, the encirclement of the German rear guard marks the end of the Battle of Normandy. After four years of occupation, Haute-Normandie is at the heart of the war. Indeed, the Allies are rushing toward the Seine. The battles of liberation take place from August 19 to mid-September. The surrender of the German garrison at Le Havre on September 12 marked the end of the occupation in the region. I have highlighted St. Aubin, of course, but also towns very near it. Given the imperfect accuracy of targeting at that time, bombs intended for one place could very well land elsewhere. But the entire list shows the price of war is not borne only by the enemy. Note the title of this table (not my words) and the word murderous. Today we would call the deaths of innocent civilians as collateral damage. But to those whose houses were destroyed and family members killed, the joy of routing the Germans would certainly have been superseded by despair and grief, and even anger.

CHRONOLOGY OF THE MOST MURDEROUS BOMBARDMENTS IN UPPER NORMANDY FROM PLANES OR ARTILLERY IN 1944

5 January	Saint-Léger-aux-Bois
7 January	Rouen
21 January	Belleville-en-Caux
10 April	Le Havre and its surroundings
19 April	Rouen, Amfreville-la-Mivoie, Blosseville-Bonsecours, Bois-Guillaume, Saint-Étienne-du- Rouvray, Sotteville-lès-Rouen
7 May	**Elbeuf**, Orival
7–8 May	Saint-Valéry-en-Caux
19–20 May	Dieppe, Neuville-lès-Dieppe
22 May	Les Ventes
26 May	Vernon
27 May	Rouen

30 May	Elbeuf, St. Aubin-lès-Elbeuf
30 May – 4 June	Rouen (Red week it was called)
2 June	Les Andelys
10 June	Aubevoie
12 June	Évreux, Conches
14–15 June	Le Havre and its surroundings
16 June	Auppegard
19 April	Rouen, Grand-Quevilly, Petit-Queville
24 June	Rouen, Déville-lès-Rouen
12 July	Damville
15 July	Rouen, Bois-Guillaume, Mont-Saint-Aignan
17 July	Eu
24 July	Elbeuf
26 July	Bernay
31 July	Le Havre
2 August	Le Havre
3 August	Ézy-sur-Eure
13 August	La Haye-du-Theil, Louviers, Le Neubourg
16 August	Brionne, Nassandres, Pont-Audemer
17 August	Appeville-Annebault, La Ferrières-sur-Risle, Pont-Audemer
26–27 August	Rouen, Grand-Quevilly, Petit-Quevilly
24–28 August	Elbeuf, Caudebec-lès-Elbeuf, Saint-Pierre-lès-Elbeuf
5–12 September	Le Havre and its surroundings

Finally, the day of reckoning arrived, June 6, 1944, aka D-Day. Fortunately, the Allies' deception campaign bore fruit because the deadly German Panzer divisions were held back near the expected landing at the Pas de Calais. Even prior to D-Day, the Allies had started almost continual air-raids to "soften" the enemy's positions, but the air raids continued well past D-Day because the German army fiercely resisted the Allies.

D-Day was an operation of seismic scale: Thousands of ships, landing craft, many thousands of men and equipment, aircraft, para-troopers.... Actually, D-Day also had a last name, Operation Over-lord. But I like D-Day because, for me, D stands for Deliverance. It was the beginning of the end of Nazi occupation on the western front.

My brother, who had been helping a farmer on D-Day, was an eyewitness to one such bombing air raid and captured it in a watercolor; he was fourteen years old.[38] During these air raids, I remember going into an underground shelter, which I later found out from Gaston was the cave of a small nearby château.

During the years of the occupation, I was in St. Aubin, 1942–1944, I don't recall seeing German troops. In fact, I was barely aware of the Boches as the German occupiers were derisively called (Boche implies something like "the Hun" or "Kraut"). My seven-year-old self's memory sees an isolated soldier or two patrolling the streets every now and then, rifle on shoulder. This relatively tranquil recollection was lodged in my brain and led me to believe, even long after the war, that St. Aubin must not have been a strategic location. The reality is quite the opposite. As I mentioned earlier, St. Aubin is bordered by the Seine River, which represented a strategic physical barrier to the Allied armies' eastward push toward Germany and an obstacle to the retreating German troops following D-Day. However, it appears that during the years of occupation, perhaps up to the Allied invasion, there were very few German troops in St. Aubin proper.[39] And this is consistent with my memory.

D-Day, however, (from my point of view) was a prelude to the liberation of St. Aubin which, of course, was the key event for me personally because it eliminated for good the possibility of being dragged by the Germans or the French police into a train heading to Auschwitz. This is not an idle statement. The Germans continued their relentless murder campaign even after their defeat became obvious.

How did the liberation take place? I have a visceral need to describe it and to relive it as if I had been there. The liberation has multiple psychological overlays. For one, there was a raw feeling of revenge in defeating and killing German soldiers. As of D-Day, there were about 371,000 German troops in Normandy. By August about two hundred thousand of them had been captured or killed.

And a reason to recount some of the details of liberation is a sense of having recovered part of my childhood. It's as if I've come out of amnesia. I was there, or nearby, and these events happened to me (and others) in the sense that I was physically present but I didn't understand them at the time. In my mind's eye, I see a split screen. One side is le petit Michel, seven years and five months old. Perhaps he's frightened by the chaos and explosions, but maybe he's at ease, reassured by Madame Leclere. Either way, he doesn't really understand what's going on.

On the other side, I see myself as I am now, on a rooftop like the fiddler, perhaps even higher, floating in space over the scenes below as they're happening, scenes that le petit Michel lived through without knowing their significance. Now his grown-up self relishes the Germans' defeat. He nods his head and says to himself, "So that's the way it was!"

And here is how it was, shortened in the sense that it will be a summary, and obviously I will be describing what was happening only in the region of St. Aubin. The "liberation" did not happen simultaneously in all of occupied France.

Once the landing beaches had been secured, at the loss of an estimated nine thousand lives in the first twenty-four hours, the Allies were able to proceed inland and disembark heavy equipment, tanks, trucks, and other supplies, as well as many more soldiers. German resistance yielded ground very grudgingly, almost inch-by-inch. But the Allies persisted and kept pushing the German forces back and back eastward. By mid-August the battle in the region of Elbeuf/St. Aubin was nearing the Seine River.

The Germans were desperate to cross the river and head east to defend their homeland or rejoin other depleted German units to form a more redoubtable counterforce. But they were trapped by the river, and the Allies wanted to prevent them from crossing it. There was a period of alternating bridge and ferry destruction and reconstruction. The Allies blew up bridges to prevent the Germans from retreating on the east side of the river. Once on the other side, the Germans did the same, i.e. blew up their own bridges to prevent pursuit from the Allies.

As early as the beginning of June, and perhaps earlier, the Germans understood that the Allies would eventually defeat them. They began to prepare for "rear guard" action, meaning that certain troops would not retreat. Their job was to slow the Allied advance enough to allow the bulk of their troops to regroup east of the river into a strong force which would produce a military stalemate. This, they hoped, would allow negotiated terms of surrender.

In the region of Elbeuf, the only crossing of the Seine was from Elbeuf to St. Aubin. Thus, the Germans began to reenforce their positions with artillery, machine guns, and other armament on both sides of the Seine. Elbeuf was on the west side and St. Aubin on the east. The idea would be to repulse, or at least slow down, the Allies at the point of crossing.

For a sense of the fierce and murderous battles between the Allies and the Germans, I must quote an abridged, translated, and liberally edited version of an account written by a French observer of and participant in the combat between the Allies and the Germans, as well as the Résistance. The author is Charles Brisson and his piece appears in the commemorative issue of the Bulletin of the Historical Society of Elbeuf, published in 1994, the fiftieth anniversary of the liberation. It is also supplemented by information supplied by Professor Baldenweck.

Beginning of June—we see works by the Germans on both banks of the Seine to allow the crossing by ferry for heavy vehicles: tanks and trucks. From June 6, these works allow traffic north–south of motorized or horse-drawn convoys of tanks, guns, trucks, and cars, toward Lower Normandy; also, installation of numerous anti-aircraft batteries, cannons, and machine guns on the wooded ridges around Elbeuf and elsewhere in the peninsula.

In the first days of August the Allied air harassment accelerates and intensifies still more. The entire valley trembles under the repeated shock of bombs and torpedoes: Elbeuf, whose quayside district takes on a chaotic aspect; Saint-Aubin where the train station is not forgotten; Cléon and Bédanne where military barges are stationed; Tourville[41] where a strategic connection has been established between the Paris and Serquigny lines which will never be used; Oissel where replacement of one of the viaducts by an embankment across a branch of the Seine was attempted; Orival whose fortifications remain formidable; and Freneuse and the locks district, where the most important ferry in the region operates, is a major objective. Not a day without the Allied squadrons roaring, stinging, and bombarding mercilessly!

From August 6, the press releases and radio broadcasts announce the progression of the war. On the sixteenth, they speak of a "push toward the middle Seine," on the twenty-first of a "withdrawal toward the lower Seine." No doubt we are witnessing with undisguised joy the feverish preparations of the occupier who, always methodical, is busy with a hundred preparations! No doubt we see with satisfaction that, not only have (German) convoys and reinforcements now completely ceased to go toward the front for several days, but that on the contrary, lines of trucks, guns, and even tanks descend from the plateaus and recross the Seine in the direction of Rouen. Unsurprisingly, we note the sudden disappearance of certain French "collaborators." But also, the noise, until then muted and distant, the cannonade becomes hour by hour more distinct and more intense: The battle is approaching, the front descends from the plateaus toward the valley. The press releases already speak of Mantes and Vernon (on the twenty-first), of Pacy-sur-Eure (on the twenty-third); the next day they will mention Louviers; and the day after, Elbeuf.

From August 21, the German reflux takes on the aspect of an extraordinary stampede. No longer are troops retreating in good order, homogeneous columns, and aligned convoys, but an indescribable procession, a rout, tumbling down from the heights of the plateaus, coming from different towns: Bernay, Evreux, and Louviers; piled up in a vast pocket which the Allied pressure quickly squeezes; the Germans do not have salvation except beyond the Seine…on condition, of course, to be able to cross it!

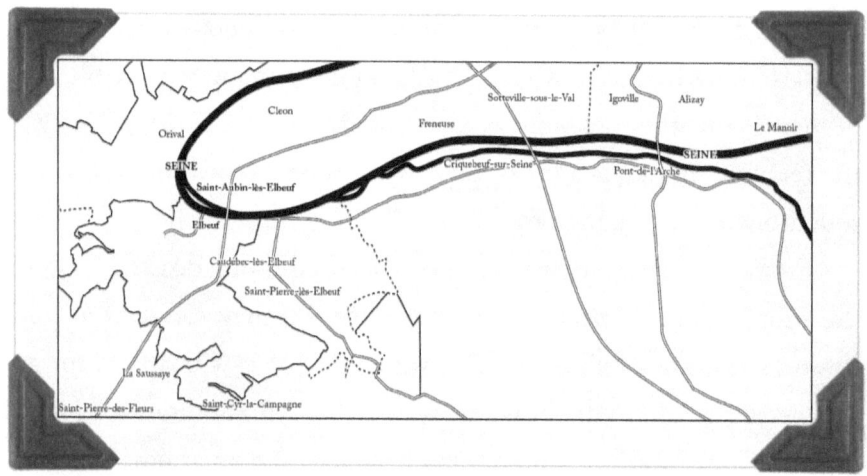

Illustrating the serpentine path of the Seine, which impeded the German retreat

Now the Allied aviation pounds roads and crossroads; it is an unprecedented debacle, a staggering amalgamation of vehicles and infantry, horses and engines. The flood flows interminably, day and night, on the roads, on the sidewalks, stopping, hesitating, starting again. The gray-green of the Wehrmacht juxtaposed with the gray-blue of the Luftwaffe, to which the black SS and even sailors mingle; few or no officers; here and there wounded. All these men are exhausted; many go into civilian dwellings, asking for food or some place to sleep. The tanks smash the sidewalks, dent the masonry; the vehicles advance in two or three abreast; and at each crossroads, there is a traffic jam. For this magma of men, horses, carts, cannons, and bicycles rush toward the river.

But now, the Seine can no longer be crossed! The understructure of the suspension bridge has had a "misfortune" as well as that of the Fairgrounds; the gates of Rouvalets Bridge have gone adrift. As for the locks of the river, the large ferry which, on its twin-decked barges, transfers seventy tons every half-hour has experienced an "unfortunate" event: A Saint-Aubinois patriot, the heroic Arsène Guerbette, employed in the service crew, scuttles and sinks it under the very nose of the Germans. On the twenty-fourth he was arrested and shot in Cléon.

Now, the human tide divides: Some continue toward Rouen, obsessed with the idea of bridges, moreover destroyed; by the thousands the vehicles will pile up on the left bank, from Saint-Sever to Quevilly, and be crushed there, set on fire by the RAF. The others stop at Elbeuf: in the streets, in the courtyards, and in the squares, they abandon their cars and their contents, they throw away equipment and ammunition. They "forget" trucks and caissons by the hundreds. The Fairgrounds, the banks of the Seine, and the quays are covered with them. Horses roam the city. The men cross the river themselves; they requisition rowboats, pay the "smugglers" without counting, cross at any cost, and throw themselves into the river to swim across. On the opposite bank, the exodus continues through St. Aubin—but this time, there are only foot soldiers. Not a single vehicle crosses the river.

A prodigious rout which we witness with hearts swelling with joy, eyes wide and shining, but lips mute: These thousands of men are armed, and the slightest imprudence could unleash harsh reprisals.

And this lasts until the twenty-third, while the cannonade becomes hour by hour more distinct and closer, sometimes interspersed with violent explosions.

The main body of the escapees has now gone; only isolated or very small groups of troops, latecomers, wounded, and stragglers, devoid of equipment, even helmets, still pass across. On the other hand, on the dawn of the twenty-fourth, organized formations appear which still seem to have a certain bite, but with low effectiveness; SS and tanks which protect the retreat by delaying skirmishes then "drop out" hastily.

The rumor has already spread that American soldiers and tanks coming from the Louviers region have reached Saint-Pierre. In Caudebec-lès-Elbeuf, German tanks have taken up positions at the main crossroads, while others are operating in the plain. The hour has arrived when the ultimate "game" for the fate of the city will be played out.

It is then that a new force will enter into play: Long isolated from one another, groups of Résistance organized themselves into a coherent and homogeneous formation, connecting with other such groups similarly organized in neighboring areas. The Force Française de l'Interiuer, FFI[42] are now coming out of hiding and will be able to work efficiently and valiantly. Until then, the almost complete lack of weapons has paralyzed them from any possibility of offensive action. Their hope of receiving arms by parachute had been disappointed; they would therefore have to use daring assaults to acquire rifles, submachine guns, grenades, and ammunition. But for weeks, their activity has been to focus on collecting and transmitting intelligence to the Allies on the enemy, its locations and movements.

Now, they can act in broad daylight, armbands proudly in full view. In Caudebec, where the Germans blew up one of their tanks in the city center, a stone's throw from the town hall, the Résistance groups explore the streets, search courtyards and houses, carry out a roundup of prisoners, and stock their armaments. Better still, a link can now be established with the Americans who occupy most of Saint-Pierre where, in the late afternoon, more than a hundred captured Boches can be dispatched.

Certain clues give rise to fears of an enemy counteroffensive; however, the American command, which does not yet have infantry support, does not want to engage its unaccompanied tanks. In Elbeuf itself, two groups of FFI move toward the bridge road which crosses the railway line and controls access to the city from the south. In spite of the close presence of a German tank, they fulfill their mission: The wire which was set (by the Germans) to initiate the destruction of the structure is cut. The bridge will not explode and the road will not be cut off; on the other hand, it will not be possible to save the neighboring bridge.

Patrols ceaselessly circulate in town, bringing back weapons and prisoners. In the evening, battles are organized in the woods south of Elbeuf, where enemy elements have been reported. In the town itself, various important points (the post office, the water factory, etc.) are reoccupied by the FFI.

Caudebec (just to the east and south of Elbeuf) is more or less empty of Germans, but they still hold the western part of Elbeuf and the neighboring heights, as well as the whole of the right bank of the Seine. The German batteries, installed in Orival, Cléon, and Freneuse, begin a heavy and murderous fire on the eastern part of the city. Incendiary and percussion shells of medium caliber rain down at random; in the evening, they set fire to an entire neighborhood bordering Elbeuf and Caudebec, where the fire raged for about forty-eight hours.

During the night of the twenty-fourth to the twenty-fifth, the Germans were able to prepare an offensive by regrouping and concentrating the tanks and men at their disposal, the aim of which was the recovery of lost ground. That is to say, to reoccupy Elbeuf and Caudebec and to stop the progress of the Allies stationed at Saint-Pierre. The situation appears to be critical, but the American command persists in not wanting to launch its tanks alone (i.e., without infantry). For the American command to make a decision, it would take the return of the enemy whose tanks are massing without having encountered serious obstacles. About ten tanks and around three hundred accompanying men—infantry and SS—take part in this desperate attempt.

However, the Americans finally begin to move in several columns. American infantrymen advanced along the national road, delayed by an ambush by a group of SS snipers hidden in a property which they defend inch by inch perched in trees. Other fights ensue in the fields and the very streets of Caudebec, where the tanks clash. The Allies still advance, gradually causing the Germans to bend and retreat, while the FFI courageously harass them. Soon, Caudebec is completely retaken, while only a few SS fanatics will resist, without hope, until the next day in the steeple of the church!

While the Americans continue their convergent and victorious advance toward Elbeuf, other elements—especially Canadians—

descend from the plateau where a tough encounter ensues: Bloody skirmishes, violent bombardments, and acts of terrorism take place in nearby towns heavily sprayed with shells.

From a different direction, American and Canadian infantry and tanks are approaching Elbeuf, meeting from street to street a desperate as well as useless resistance from the last enemy elements. Armored fighting begins in the main street, at the Carrefour du Coq, in the Saint-Louis district, and at the Bout-du-Couvent, while the shells launched by the German batteries from Orival and the right bank continued to rain down. On all sides wounded civilians and soldiers increase: In four days of fighting 250 casualties are sheltered in the underground hospital installed by the Passive Defense and the Red Cross, in the cellars of Hospice. The "Tigers" and other German armored vehicles are, for the most part, put out of order, destroyed, or captured.

Everywhere, there are only abandoned vehicles, equipment discarded at random, and weapons which the FFI will make use of to, along with the Allies, complete the cleansing of Elbeuf. Already flags are flying on all sides. We risk clamoring in the streets, we proclaim our joy, we run for the latest news, we breathe; we are free, free, free!

On the twenty-fifth of August, around nine o'clock at night, the Americans succeeded in reaching the destroyed town hall; later in the night, Canadians relieved them. But the Germans still resisted. Progress was slow because of the disproportional number of the forces present; against a single Canadian division there were still the remains of five German divisions, clinging to the Rouvray massif. The many civilians taking refuge in the nearby caves are protected from the Allied bombardments.

Now, while these events were taking place, near the western

extremity of St. Aubin, tragic events were developing—a perfect example of "the fog of war." Masters of the left bank, the Americans and Canadians had reason to suppose that the opposite bank still remained in the hands of the enemy, whereas in reality it was only anti-aircraft batteries exhausting their ammunition, and shells from just a few stray tanks. Admittedly, the firing of these German guns and armored vehicles from Freneuse and Cléon, firing which would continue for several days, could lead one to believe in a complete control of this natural redoubt by the Germans. However, as just mentioned, it was only anti-aircraft guns intentionally depleting their ammunition.

Having abandoned St. Aubin, the Germans set fire to one of their supply depots and a number of dwellings; their total withdrawal left the town in the hands of resistance fighters who immediately set out to join the fight. But on the twenty-third, from half past five o'clock in the morning, a first set of incoming shells had the population on alert. Beginning in the afternoon, from Saint-Pierre and the heights overlooking Elbeuf, the Americans opened fire on St. Aubin, a fire which, in almost uninterrupted salvos, would continue until the evening of the twenty-seventh.

Now the Germans, on their part, had reason to believe that St. Aubin (by now completely evacuated by them) was already occupied by the adversary. From the cliffs of Orival, where they had hidden artillery pieces in the caves which overlook the valley from a height of about two hundred feet, they undertook a systematic and particularly focused artillery fire.

For three long days, several thousand shells fired from the north crushed St. Aubin, whose inhabitants took refuge. From their dominant positions the German guns worked with formidable precision, while the Allied air force swooped down on them.

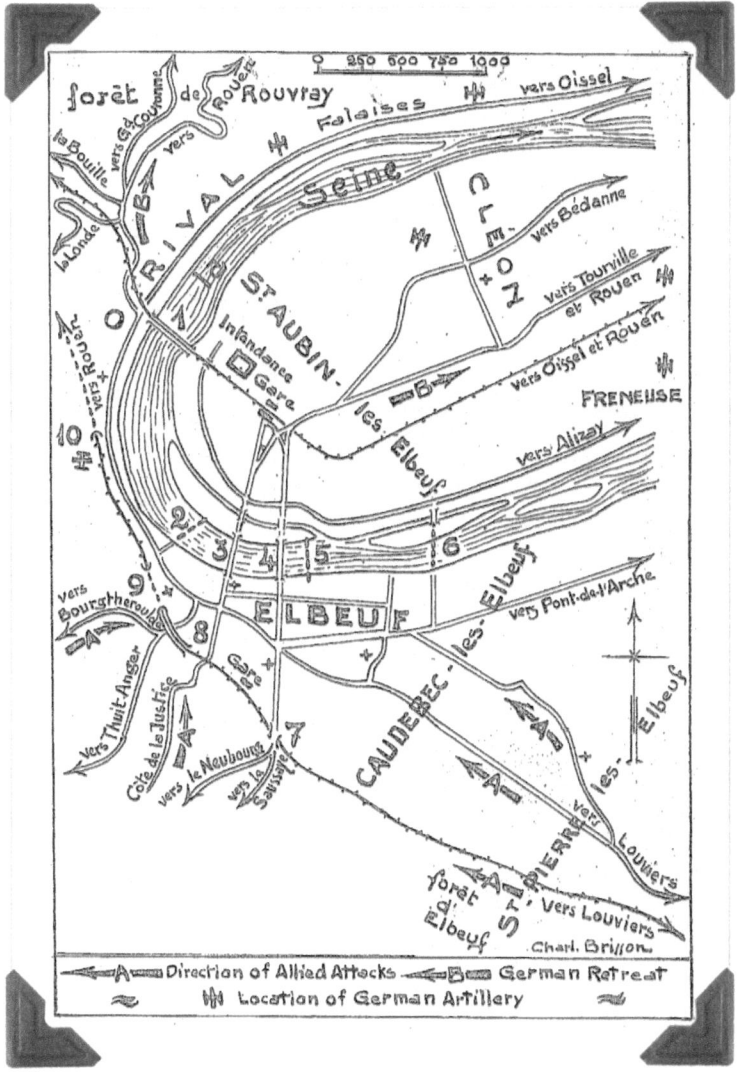

Location of German artillery and Allied Troops During these Three Days

On the evening of the twenty-seventh, finally, the German fire slows down and the Allied fire stops. On the morning of the twenty-eighth, the first Canadian elements cross the Seine, occupy St. Aubin, and spread out in and around the town. They encounter the same enthusiastic, emotional, even passionate reception, as in Elbeuf in the previous days.

*The Canadian troops crossing the Seine from Elbeuf to St. Aubin,
which is finally liberated.*

Already, the "Royal Engineers" are busy on the banks of the Seine, unloading innumerable trucks, carrying dismountable boats out of which they will make three bridges. A few more hours and the first Allied cars will cross the river for days and days by the Gray Bridge and the Roscoë Bridge. Thousands of vehicles, trucks, tanks, and cannons will cross the river and go north and west in pursuit of the enemy and the recapture of France.

Admittedly, the cannonade still rolls in the north toward Rouen and in the east toward the Andelle and the middle Seine. From time to time, we hear distant explosions: mines, structures, or shells that the enemy destroys before abandoning some positions. The battle that continues is no longer the battle in the valley, the battle of the Seine. The sky is now clear, no more of the reddish smoke which swirled above the bombed targets for days. At the windows, the flags are finally unfurled; on the lips, *La Marseillaise* finally released; on all things and in all hearts, great and deep joy.

Of course, the ruins are immense and innumerable, but they can be repaired. These walls will be raised, these houses will be rebuilt, and plumes of smoke will crown the high chimneys of the industrious city. A great silent smile shines in all eyes.

Sometimes a truck passes by crowded with dazed prisoners, the only Germans we will see from now on. The hunt has started for notorious collaborators, who are quickly picked up and now out of commission. In the streets, bizarre processions parade, unleashing insults; a drum followed by women and girls with shaved hair, evil eyes, and bitter mouths, surrounded by armed resistance fighters. Everywhere placards affixed by the occupiers are torn down and on the walls are now displayed very French posters, freshly pasted, speaking of freedom, order, and dignity. The joy expressed in the previous paragraphs is exactly what I feel, even now, more than seventy-five years later.

For the history lover, here are some details about the armed forces that liberated Elbeuf and makes me proud and thankful for their efforts and bravery:

The town of Elbeuf was liberated on August 25, 1944 by the 109th US Infantry Regiment and the 2nd Battalion of the 66th US Armored Regiment, which were relieved on August 26, 1944 by the Armored Group A of the 2nd US Armored Division, to which was attached the 99th Autonomous US Infantry Battalion. The Armored Group A included the 66th Armored Regiment, the 14th Motorized Artillery Group, the 2nd Battalion of the 4th Mobile Infantry Regiment, and Company A of the 4th Motorized Medical Battalion. The Armored Group A was relieved in turn on August 26, 1944 at 7:45 p.m. by the 7th Canadian Infantry Brigade.

The Normandy Campaign was probably the bloodiest of the war: Between June 6 and August 30, 1944, a mere three months, around 425,000 Allied and German soldiers lost their lives. It is also known that around twenty thousand French civilians were killed from errant Allied (American and British) bombing raids or misguided artillery. Whole towns and villages reduced to rubble, collateral damage as we would say now. It is not beyond imagining that this could have been my end. But Providence decided that was not the time.

The history of the war is a long and painful one and did not spare St. Aubin. Sometime after the landing and the Allied armies' advance, St. Aubin became the prize of an artillery duel between the Allies and the Germans that lasted three days, during which thousands of shells crashed on the town.[43]

The air raids previously mentioned were witnessed by my brother, whose location was even closer to the beaches than mine. Only fifteen when he witnessed and "recorded" the scene below. It gives a vivid sense of that reality.

Watercolor by my brother, Simon: The bottom reads "Remembrance of June 6, 1944"

Sometime in August, I saw convoys of German trucks evacuating toward the east, and sometime later, perhaps a few days, a convoy of Allied troops rolling into town. It was the Second Canadian Army Corps, the date was the twenty-eighth of August, 1944,[44] and we were liberated.

I'm not sure how long they stayed nearby, but I remember climbing aboard one of their armored vehicles, along with other boys from the village. In every town and village where Allied troops entered, if they paused at all—perhaps to regroup or refresh—they were swarmed by grateful citizens. And so, the conquering heroes allowed us, the kids, to climb aboard.

Photo of French boys aboard a Canadian armored vehicle
in Elbeuf depicts my experience[45]

On one of the amphibious vehicles, the soldiers also gave us a ride across the river. Along with every other kid in town, I begged for "tchwinggum" and cigarettes pour papa. I vaguely recall being successful. It must have been with cigarettes because I don't know if the Canadians were purveyors of "tchwinggum." This was associated with Americans, but I'm not sure I knew the difference. It may be that American soldiers passed through at another point, as the Allied armies crisscrossed, sometimes exchanging positions. I also remember the sad sight of a number of women with shaved heads passing by in a horse-drawn lorry with the villagers crowding the street, yelling, and gesturing. I was told they were collaborators, but of course, I had no understanding then that their crime was sleeping with the enemy.

Earlier, I speculated that the Lecleres may have presented me as a relative from the city. Or it may be that the Lecleres were a well-respected family in the town, and people knew better than to ask. All of this is conjecture, of course. In a small town, people also tend to know where one's relatives live. St. Aubin wasn't that small at the time, with a population around 4,700,[46] but not large enough to provide the anonymity of a city. It may also be that country people were generally more hospitable and accepting of strangers, and perhaps their hatred of the Boches overrode any suspicion.

At that time, I was unaware of many things concerning my stay with the Lecleres, which I discovered forty-four years later when I reconnected with Gaston. How I wish I had asked him the questions I keep asking myself now. But Gaston told me that besides the Lecleres themselves, only two people knew my real identity—one was Louise Brida, the neighbor who took care of me after school, and the other was the principal of the school. At the time, there were also many non-Jewish refugees from Paris or other urban centers fleeing to the relative safety of the countryside, and I could have been taken as one of those. Nevertheless, it would have taken only one suspicious neighbor to whisper something to the Germans or the Vichy police. I had asked Professor Baldenweck and my friend Dr. Jean-Marc Dreyfus, two scholars of the period, what penalties were imposed on individuals who hid or harbored Jews. The answer was surprising. The following edited excerpt was sent to me by Professor Baldenweck:

> There is a relevant book by Patrick Cabanel, "History of the Righteous in France," published (in French) by Armand Colin in 2012 and in particular the part entitled, "What Were the Risks of the Righteous in France?" He indicates that in France there was no German directive toward those who helped or welcomed Jews. Despite the lack of systematic repression of aid to Jews, "those who were tempted to provide it could fear the worst from the Germans. The British author, Bob Moore, author of many books about the Holocaust, reminds us that families like the Lecleres acted in spite of their fear about possible reprisals.
>
> Nevertheless, the Vichy government had no such constraints, and at times deported those who aided Jews, but their reprisals toward their compatriots did not rise to the level of cruelty imposed by the Germans in Poland or other eastern countries. The Yad Vashem citation to the righteous mentions the risk to their lives. And that was certainly true in certain countries, notably Poland, where the families of the righteous were executed on the spot. In France, many individuals merited righteousness for saving children.

Still, why did the Lecleres choose to take me in? What compels people to risk life and fortune (as far as they knew) to save a stranger? The literature about protectors indicates no simple or single motivational thread or characteristics. "Rescuers were peasants and nannies, aristocrats and clergy, bakers and doctors, social workers and storekeepers, school children and police officers, diplomats and grandmothers"[47] and from many countries and religious persuasions. But I am convinced that all must have shared a sense of morality that underlaid any other individual reason.

After the liberation, my uncle David ascribed to the Lecleres a monetary incentive for taking me in. Having survived the war, the brutal Nazi occupation, and the loss of so many relatives, it's understandable that my uncle would have had a jaundiced view of human nature. He could not accept that some individuals would have acted altruistically. But he would have known that continuing payments would be impossible, even if an initial one had been made.

The best argument against my uncle's supposition is that the penalty for harboring a Jew would have been a powerful deterrent. So, it's hard to believe that the Lecleres took me in for money. They were simply courageous people who did what many others did, unfortunately much too few. It was also in 1989 that I found out from Gaston that Marcel had been in the French underground, though it did not occur to me to ask Gaston in exactly what capacity. I suspect it must have been probably as a courier, or some "desk" job, rather than as an armed fighter.

In one of the many email interchanges I had with Professor Baldenweck, I mentioned the Lecleres' role in shielding me, and that Gaston had said that Marcel had been in the French underground. He proceeded to try to find the Lecleres' names on a list of participants in the resistance.[48] While researching his book, he accumulated a list of over ten thousand individuals who were in the resistance in some capacity. But the Lecleres' name was not on that list.

Whatever the Lecleres' motivation for taking me in, I know they grew very fond of me, for Gaston told me that after the war, his parents had wanted to adopt me.

VI

AFTER THE WAR

BETWEEN FRANCE
AND AMERICA

This adoption might well have taken place were it not for the fact that one day, a slight middle-aged man knocked on the Lecleres' door, announced that he was my uncle, and had come to reclaim me. How did my uncle know where I was? Given that my mother and her brother weren't on speaking terms at the time of the rafle, he wouldn't have known about the Bonneaus. Herein lies a tale. After the war, Oncle David bumped into a fellow watchmaker who happened to also know another watchmaker's family (the Krum family), who had been helped by the Bonneaus as well. It seems that Monsieur Krum had told the aforementioned watchmaker that the Jeruchims had been helped by the Bonneaus and Oncle David tracked the Bonneaus down.

Imagine this unlikely sequence, not to mention that the watchmakers in question were Jewish and had also managed to survive. For some time, I had been under the impression that my uncle's sudden appearance had been as much a surprise for the Lecleres as for me. But, later I learned that my sister met Monsieur Leclere in Paris in the spring of 1945. She remembers having coffee with him in a café. A logical deduction is that after my uncle discovered where I was, he probably wrote a letter to the Lecleres, identifying himself and announcing that he wanted to reclaim me on behalf of the family. Alice remembers someone saying that I should remain with the Lecleres until the end of school, and in fact I was picked up in the summer of 1945, after the end of the school year.

In those days it was not the custom to take children into confidence about any decisions concerning them. So, I did not know what was coming until it came. I sometimes wonder what my life would have been like if my uncle hadn't found us. Perhaps I would have become a French technocrat, perhaps a foreman in a cookware factory? French society does not have the upward mobility available in the U.S., but it's possible that good grades would have propelled me upward.

My wife believes that this sudden uprooting from the Lecleres was a second trauma for me, a second loss of "parents" and a family environment. After all, I had lived with the Lecleres close to half of my life. But I can't remember any outward drama or tears about the separation. Perhaps I had already been hardened by my first, irreparable loss.

I remember that my uncle bribed me with a little bag of fresh apricots, which were a rare delicacy then, and which I still love, dried or fresh. We then took a train to a small town called *Le Grand-Lucé*, close to the city of *Le Mans* (about seventeen miles), the site of the famous auto race, and about 140 miles southwest of Paris, where my uncle and his family vacationed before the war and where they had hidden during the war.

There, my uncle and his wife had assembled their son Raoul, my brother, sister, and me in a modest resort, presumably for all of us to reintroduce ourselves. I have a hazy memory of this reunion, but I don't remember it specifically as a happy one for me. I don't think I really recognized Simon and Alice, I didn't know my uncle's family, and I had just left the family I knew. My most vivid memory is being introduced to a swimming pool, considered a luxury then. This was the first time I had encountered one and I was afraid of the water. I overcame that fear many years later when I spent one summer in my teen years as part of the waterfront staff at a summer camp in upstate New York, and later as the lifeguard at a resort hotel in the Catskills.

Oncle David had serendipitously found Simon and Alice living with the Bonneaus in December 1944. Paris had been liberated half a year before that (August 1944). By the end of June or sometime in July, all German troops had fled Normandy. (Germany finally surrendered unconditionally on May 7, 1945.) So, there would have been no obstacles related to the war to "retrieve" me. While my uncle and the Bonneaus thought it best for me to finish the school year in St. Aubin, I think the real reason was that there was no place for me. The Bonneaus' house was now full and my uncle had a tiny apartment, already too small for his family of three. What must be the case is that in the interim, from December 1944 to July 1945, my uncle was trying to find a place for us to live. At that time, he wanted to undertake the role of guardian since all three of us were minors, and our parents were missing, but he did not officially become so until December of that year. Then, on December 3, 1945, a *Conseil de Famille* (family council) took place in the chambers of a *Juge de Paix* (Justice of the Peace), though that title does not necessarily imply the identical authority as in the States.

This council had been requested by Oncle David to establish who would be in charge of my siblings and me. He had requested this meeting before receiving an answer from the French government to petitions he had filed to determine our parents' whereabouts. At that point, someone had to be legally empowered to make decisions for us, otherwise little could have been done in our name.

It's interesting to read the minutes (in French). There were six individuals, aside from the judge, all of whom purportedly had our welfare at heart. They were divided into two categories, representing the matrilineal line (mother's side) and the patrilineal line (father's side). Four of the attendees were witnesses. One of those should be mentioned by name: Albert Bonneau, whom you have met earlier. After due discussion and citing various articles of the civil code, our uncle who, of course, represented our mother's side, was declared our primary guardian. Monsieur Maurice Pinkowski, a former watchmaker colleague of our father and representing our father's side, was declared a surrogate guardian.

Oncle David, his wife Berthe, and their son Raoul, couldn't insert three more bodies into their small apartment, or even one for that matter. I also don't know whether he could have afforded to feed us all; there may still have been rationing. Still, Joan thinks he was remiss in not making arrangements to take us in. Having grown up in a nurturing nuclear family, away from the chaos of the war, it was not possible for her to understand that circumstances could be so dire that our guardian sent us to an orphanage. I think our uncle simply wanted to reunite us and place us in an environment where we would be taken care of. Indeed, arrangements were made and the three of us moved into a *maison d'enfants*, a "children's home."

Before the war, there had existed a number of Jewish social services/welfare organizations whose *raison d'être* was to assist Jews from foreign lands in France, or those who were poor, or provide assistance in different ways. After the takeover by the Nazis, many of those organizations continued to provide their services, but also created clandestine activities especially to rescue children and find them hiding places. After the war, these organizations' main efforts were to assist the survivors, again mostly children such as me and my siblings.

I resided in three different *maisons d'enfants*, effectively orphanages, but not quite the same; *orphelinat* is the word in French for orphanage. *Maison d'enfants* implies something softer. The first of these was in a town called Cailly-sur-Eure, approximately a hundred kilometers northwest of Paris. This orphanage, named *Maison Juliette*, was supported by an organization called WIZO, standing for Women's International Zionist Organization. However, this was no ordinary orphanage because all of the "residents" were children whose fate mirrored our own, and all the "counselors" were themselves older survivors. The environment at Cailly was more like a large family with a lot of camaraderie and warmth, especially toward the younger children, one of whom I happened to be. All of the kids around my age, about two dozen or so, slept in a dormitory, possibly a converted dance space. I'm sure that this sense of shared history (although we wouldn't have thought of it this way) was of great value in keeping me psychologically grounded, in addition to which, of course, I had my brother and sister close by.

Simon, Alice, and Michel at Versailles, the summer before we left for America

But Simon, Alice, and I stayed together in Cailly only for a relatively short time, probably less than a year. We were settled in Cailly almost immediately after the war, still a time of chaos in France, and the organizing of war orphans had not yet consolidated. After a while, the powers that be decided that it would be better to organize the orphanages around age brackets. So, at some point the children, were resettled in two other orphanages not very far from each other but not in immediate proximity. These two homes were located in a small town, Jouy-en-Josas, located less than twenty miles southwest of Paris. The social organization "sponsoring" these homes was the *Eclaireurs Israélites de France* (EIF), a name which roughly means "Israelite Scouts of France," but was an offshoot of the Jewish scouting organization that had morphed into something different.

Group photo of the child survivors at the maison d'enfants in Cailly-sur-Eure

The two homes were given the fragrant names of *Les Glycines* (wisteria) and *Les Eglantines* (rosebush), the latter being the residence of the older kids. Alice and Simon went to live there. The actual structures at each location were elegant former villas, the latter being quite a bit larger. A picture of *Les Glycines,* where I was relocated, is shown on page 98.

It's likely that these villas had been commandeered by the Nazis, and had now been unoccupied. I speculate that the owners had rented or "loaned" their property to our sponsoring organizations. These villas look elegant from the outside, but of course the interior had been made simply utilitarian. Most rooms were essentially bare except for cots, but these rooms were not gigantic, so there was more of a sense of privacy than in the previous *maison d'enfants*. We had precious few possessions, so closets and dressers were unnecessary.

The acquisition of this photo was unexpected. In May of 2000 there was a reunion in Jouy of the former child residents, which I did not attend, but my brother did. There is a Jouy Historical Society (JHS) which publishes half-yearly local historical "stories" in *Les Cahiers Historiques de Jouy-en-Josas* (in French), something quite surprising to me because one would normally expect such a society to exist only in much larger cities.

Villa "Les Glycines," as it was then
Photo from Les Cahiers Historiques de Jouy, No. 14, July 2012

When we arrived there in 1946–47 the population of Jouy was only about 2,500, and even as late as 1999, it was only about 8,000. I conjecture that this reunion triggered an effort by the JHS to research the maisons d'enfants that had been established in their town. In 2012 the JHS published an issue of their journal devoted to these children's homes. This issue provided minute detail (as is the tendency of the French!) of the creation of these homes, hearkening back to their origins in the south of France before the war.

At *Les Glycines*, life gained a degree of stability. We ate communal meals and amused ourselves in all kinds of ways. Since toys were at a premium, we played games of imagination. I was a little mischievous by that time, which I recall paying for on two occasions. One time I was teasing a rather bigger boy who started running after me. I scrambled up the stairs trying to escape, and while running down a corridor, I turned around to see where he was. When I turned my head back toward the front, lo and behold there was a closed door two inches from my face. I barreled into it and stunned myself into unconsciousness. When I woke up, I was in bed under the concerned looks of a counselor. I did not fully learn my lesson. One day a few of my co-residents and I were gazing out a window on the second floor, when we all more or less simultaneously spied a marble on the ground. To us, that marble was even better than a large diamond. Our group pushed and shoved each other out of the way so we could skedaddle down the stairs to retrieve this treasure. I was on the small side and was easily shoved aside by the bigger kids who were running down the stairs ahead of me. So, I did the only logical thing: I jumped out the window. I broke my arm, but I got the marble!

My last misadventure at the maison d'enfants began with a visit from a friend of my brother's. He had a beautiful racing bike, the type with the curled handlebars. Such a bike was the stuff of dreams. I begged him to let me ride it. Reluctantly, he agreed. It was actually a bit too big. As I started to ride it down a hill, I lost control and crashed into a wall. In this instance, only my ego was bruised, but the bike was mangled. My brother and his friend must have been enraged, but I have blocked out what ensued.

At *Les Glycines* all of the children went to the local public school. In Jouy, I discovered a talent for learning, which had begun in St. Aubin. At the end of each year there was a formal ceremony in the town hall called the *distribution des prix* (awarding of prizes) which was attended by the entire village. The mayor presided in formal dress with sashes and medals across his chest, seconded by other dignitaries including, no doubt, the principal of the school. The awards were books and because I generally did well, I won some of those prizes. My sister remembers attending at least one such ceremony and chuckles when she recalls that practically every name called to receive a prize sounded "foreign": Finkelstein, Menkes, Jeruchim, and so on, all children from our orphanage. I say *foreign* because these were not typical French names, but I ascribe the disproportionate number of prizes awarded to children from the *maison d'enfants* to the emphasis on study that is basic to Jewish culture, not inherent superiority. The preponderance of those names may have stirred some anti-Semitic feelings among the attendees from the village, but if so, I was unaware of it.

In the warm days, we played soccer, marbles, or organized races. Indoors, we played checkers, card games like belote, or games that tested knowledge and memory. In one such game, around fifteen to twenty kids about my age would sit cross-legged in a circle and an elder would name a country, whose capital the first kid to his or her left would have to tell. The next kid would then have to name the capital of a second country, but also repeat the previous country and capital, and so on. If an incorrect answer was given, that child would sit out the remainder of that round. I usually did fairly well in that game.

Sometime in 1947, I was then about ten years old, I received a real entertainment treat. My brother, who by then was on his own, had somehow gotten enough money to take me to Paris for a showing of the movie *Fantasia*. Before the war, my brother had read comic books based on Disney characters, and I was aware of Mickey Mouse. I was thrilled to go into an actual theater. The crowd was excited; sellers of *Eskimo Gervais* (a kind of ice cream bar) carried in an insulated box walked the aisles. Based on my brother's description, I thought this film was going to be a Mickey Mouse "special." Of course, I didn't understand what this film was about. As it progressed, I became restive (*The Sorcerer's Apprentice* was the eighth piece out of thirteen in Fantasia). Où est Mickey (where is Mickey), I kept asking my brother. He finally arrived on screen, holding his broom!

In spite of the circumstances that took me there, my time at *Les Glycines* was a happy one. Such is the resilience of children if they were blessed to have it. And then, in 1947, there came a great deal of excitement and hubbub. Arrangements had been made for emigration to Palestine. A large number, by far the majority of the children in the home went. Or, if they were too young and alone, the decision had been made for them. It is likely that they no longer had any living relatives. In my case, the decision to go to America had already been made because we had relatives there. Thus, most of my contemporaries at *Les Glycines* boarded the now famous ship called the *Exodus* made famous by the author Leon Uris.

Les Glycines was now nearly empty and probably no longer cost-effective to run for so few children. Thus, it was disbanded as an orphanage. I remember feeling somewhat sad and lonely when my fellow survivors departed. Probably many such events were taking place across France. The last of us from *Les Glycines* were sent to another orphanage which was located far to the south in a town called *Moissac*, about 115 miles southeast from Bordeaux, and not that far from the *Pyrénées*. The building there was also elegant, or had been. It was on a somewhat sprawling property, surrounded by open fields and vineyards. The *maitresse*, Fanny, was a severe-looking woman, herself a survivor from Poland who inspired respect if not fear, but had a good heart that she tried to hide. I have little memory of day-to-day life there. I remember frolicking and camping in the fields, but I have no memory of going to school, though it must have been the case. I was initially lonely because Simon and Alice were no longer close by, but after a while I made friends and life settled down again.

By that time, I knew we were going to America, so I looked upon my stay in *Moissac* as a temporary stopover before departing. I had been given the impression by Simon or Alice that the *démarches* (processes) were underway to obtain all the requisite paperwork. That was the case, but as with all such bureaucratic enterprises, progress is slow. Our passage to America was by no means guaranteed for several reasons. First was obtaining an exit visa, which ran into a bit of trouble as I relate later; then, of course, was obtaining an immigration visa into the US. French people were generally looked upon favorably, much more so than people from eastern Europe. Of course, one needed a passport to immigrate, and to be a citizen to get a passport.

Therein lies a tale. My siblings traveled on a French passport, but I did not. I traveled on a stateless "passport." The reason I enclose passport in quotation marks is that a passport must be issued by a country, and "stateless" means without a country!

When we left France in 1949, I may have noticed, or not, that my passport was different from my siblings', but if I had it wouldn't have meant anything to me at that age. My "passport" slept for many years in a tiny suitcase that I had carried with me on my transatlantic voyage. Long after, as I was looking for something in my trove of old documents, I stumbled on that stateless passport. And I was puzzled, as well as irritated.

Why was I without a country? This has to do with the citizenship laws of France, which do not accord citizenship simply for having been born there. So, the document I had was functionally a passport for the purpose of travel, but for nothing else. (For brevity, I will call it a passport.) Why am I spending time on what might be viewed simply as old paperwork? I was offended: I was as French as any French boy my age.

French citizenship laws have changed over time, but among other requirements, a child born of non-French parents must have resided in France for a certain number of years uninterruptedly and be eighteen years old or older. I still don't meet these criteria. Recently, I reapplied for my citizenship and was denied on those grounds. I was puzzled because these rules differ from US laws, but also irritated that but for events I couldn't control, I can't become a French citizen. And why, after so many years, did I want to have my French citizenship?

It's a matter of identity. Much later in life, I realized how important identity is to most people. And what do I mean by identity? A connection with a history, or people, that has an emotional component.

After I had been in the States for a few years, I became fluent in the language but not the culture. I frequently heard people referring to others sometimes like "Oh, he's Irish," or "She's Italian." That puzzled me. Aren't all these people Americans, I wondered? But people who have been in the States for generations also often refer to themselves that way. Identity is more than citizenship. It's a DNA chain that passes values, attitudes, food choices, and traditions from ancestors in foreign lands. Nowadays, it seems relatively common to hyphenate one's roots (e.g., Polish-American, Italian-American, and so on). In the France of my youth, I had never heard people hyphenate their identities. A hyphenated identity is simply proclaiming being American but taking pride in one's heritage. I must say, though, that Franco-American does not seem to be a common hyphenation, except on a can of spaghetti. I am proud of being an American, but also of my French heritage.

In our process to emigrate, another hurdle came from America. We had to obtain affidavits of support before the immigration authorities would let us in, lest we were to feed off public welfare. Milton and Molly (née Kestenbaum) Mandell, who lived in Arlington, Virginia, provided this assurance. It turns out that our grandmother, Tessie Shapiro, was Molly's grandfather's cousin. I had always thought that the Mandells were wealthy, but Alice sent me a copy of the letter they wrote accepting responsibility for us. Milton was just a working stiff, an "examiner" employed by the civil service commission, making about $140 a week. That was enough to mollify the powers that be, but this tells you how poor the rest of our family must have been if the Mandells were considered "well-to-do." Milton generously guaranteed our financial support, although he never paid a dime on our behalf, nor did it turn out to be necessary. Still, he put his neck out for us, and I thank him for it. There was also apparently another individual, by the name of Irving Brackish, who provided an affidavit, but whose record I do not have. He is mentioned in a letter from my grandmother Tessie addressed to my sister at Oncle David's Paris address, dated November 24, 1947, just a month after we left France.

My grandmother's letter raised a bit of a puzzle in my mind, and illustrates the difficulty in reconstructing history. As I said, Tessie's letter is dated November 24, 1947, but the letter from Milton Mandell states his earnings as of December 29, 1948! How can this be? One might conjecture that she mistakenly wrote the wrong year, but a copy of the envelope in which the letter came clearly says November 1947. Although other scenarios could be imagined, some mysteries can't be easily resolved. As a quasi-humorous aside, that letter was initially returned for insufficient postage—two cents short! Here

I must mention that my grandmother is the reason the three of us were able to come to America. She was the prime mover in that effort. It isn't clear that any other members of the family in the States would have been moved to do so. But according to my sister, Tessie was a fighter, and she was fighting for her grandchildren. She did not have the means to guarantee our support, but by the force of her personality she badgered our other relatives until it became a *fait accompli*.

Once the visa was approved in July 1949, passage aboard a ship had to be found, as well as the funds for it. Of course, my siblings and I had hardly a *sou* to our name, and our uncle could not afford anything near the cost of three transatlantic tickets. Our uncle had previously written to our relatives in America, who apparently could not afford the sum in question, and he had beseeched local Jewish agencies for the requisite amount. They apparently were skeptical that our "rich" American relatives could not afford it. Today, it would seem ludicrous that some sort of plan, however tentative, would not have been made for funding a trip whose date was not yet certain, but anticipated. But such were the circumstances then. There was no money, and it was probably felt that nothing should, or could, be done prior to actually obtaining a visa.

Another unexpected hurdle arose in the spring of 1948. My brother received a notice to report for a physical at an army induction center in Paris, for which he dutifully complied. Even though our visa was still relatively far into the future at that time, we already "knew" we were going to America. My passport has one page of legalese dated April 1948. Several pages in my passport show a succession of exit visa dates which had passed and been renewed to a later date. I'm speculating that at each of those exit dates the US immigration visa had not yet been granted. Had my brother actually been inducted into the French military, I'm certain neither Alice nor I would have left for America without him. And life being as fickle as it is, who knows what would have followed?

But here again, fate intervened in the presence of Jean Torrès. Jean Torrès was the stepson of the French politician Léon Blum, the first Jewish man to have become prime minister of France in 1936. Monsieur Blum was a prodigious intellectual and a man of the people. I did not realize until recently how accomplished he was in so many ways—a poet, a writer, a social activist,[49] arguing for the common man. He was later in Buchenwald, the largest Nazi concentration camp in Germany, but survived. After the war he settled in the little town of Jouy-en-Josas where we lived in the *maison d'enfants,* a fortuitous coincidence. Jean Torrès also lived there with his mother and stepfather. Apparently, he became friendly with the director of the *maison d'enfants* and was a frequent visitor. We, my siblings and I, even went to an afternoon garden party at their estate, according to my brother, though I have no recollection of the event. The significance of all this is that shortly after receiving his induction notice, my brother contacted Jean to see if he could help, and indeed he did. Of course, Monsieur Blum had many influential contacts in the government, and they came through. Sometime later, Jean gave Simon a document exempting him from military service.[50] I suppose that's another instance of the saying "it's not what you know, but who you know," and so we were free to leave.

However, one more hurdle needed to be conquered before that could happen. Since I was a minor, I had to obtain "permission" to leave the country. Apparently, Oncle David thought that he had that power, but the French bureaucrats, ever vigilant, said "NON!" As I related earlier, there had been a family council, on December 3, 1945, where my uncle was declared our primary guardian and Maurice Pinkowski the surrogate guardian. The stick-by-the rules French civil service authorities required not only my uncle's permission for me to leave, but also Monsieur Pinkowski's. Below, I have included a copy of a letter to my sister, in French, from the American Jewish Joint

Distribution Committee, the organization that funded our cross-Atlantic voyage, indicating the necessity of Monsieur Pinkowski's permission. Of course, it was given.

Sometime later, relatively close to our departure from France, I was sent from *Moissac* to *Versailles* to join Alice. She was now living in what had been a school for young Jewish women from the Middle East, established there in 1922: *l'Ecole de l'Alliance Israélite Versailles,* which was part of a network of such schools founded in the nineteenth century.

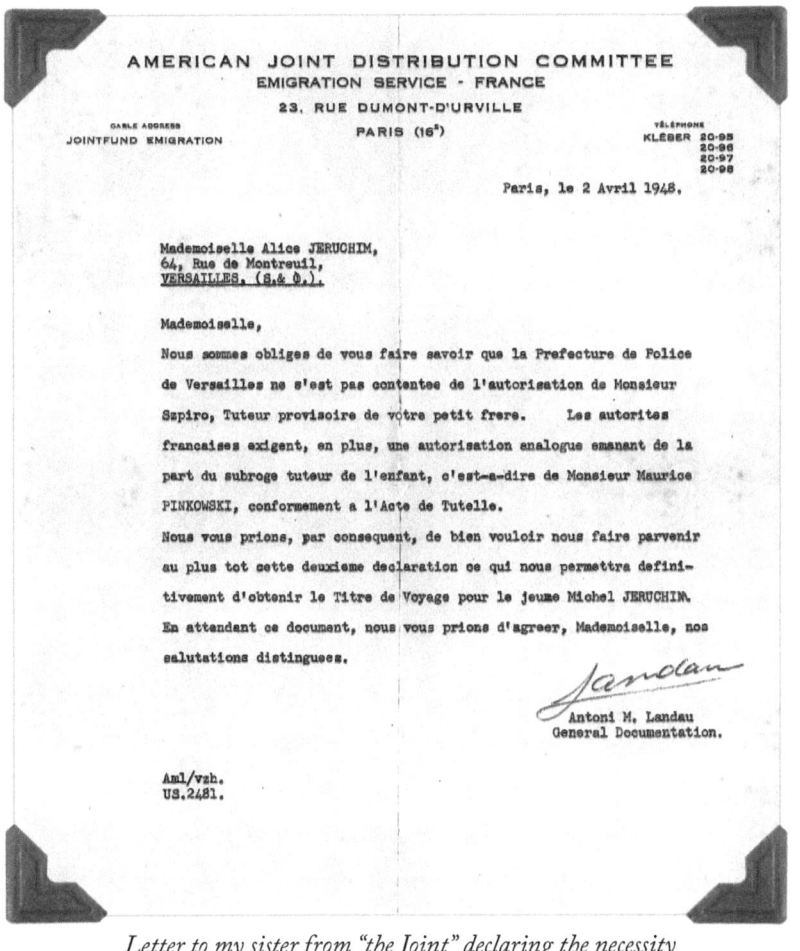

Letter to my sister from "the Joint" declaring the necessity of the surrogate's permission for me to leave

My sister now lived among many other young women who were also survivors. It was, in a sense, a communal home for these young women, who had no other home to go to and were there temporarily until they were able to find somewhere to live on their own. Under the mores of the time, a male would not have been allowed to reside there, but because of the circumstances and my age, I was permitted to live with all those young women. *Malheureusement*, I was too young to profit from this circumstance!

VII

AMERICA!

OCTOBER 1949 – SEPTEMBER 1956

I never realized how close we came to missing the boat. Our visa was set to expire on October 26, 1949, just twenty-four hours after we would land in the United States. Obtaining the funds for a transatlantic voyage was beginning to seem insurmountable, but finally it was arranged and paid for by an American relief organization called the American Jewish Joint Distribution Committee, commonly known as "the Joint" or the JDC, based in New York City. The JDC was founded during WWI, and its mission goes beyond relief in the typical sense, and is not limited to Jews. My sister Alice began making almost daily trips to their Paris office to beg for these funds more than a year before our departure. She still remembers the address: 23 *rue Dumont d' Urville*, Paris 16ème.

Finally, all paperwork issues resolved, we were ready to go. A day or two before we took a last look at Paris, captured in this photo.

My siblings had mixed feelings, especially my brother. Aside from leaving the land they knew, they were wondering about what kind of future awaited them. How would they adapt? What profession could they practice? How would they make a living? I had no such misgivings.

I had the insouciance of a boy. I was looking forward to the land of milk and honey, to borrow a biblical phrase.

Au revoir to France: Alice, Michel, Simon—October 1949

On October 3, 1949, in Cannes we boarded the SS Sobieski, a one-time Polish passenger liner that had been converted to a troop ship during the war. The quarters for the immigrant class, at least, were below deck and probably not changed since the war. However, part of the ship still kept "regular" quarters for some few paying passengers, and it had a bar.

I knew that I was supposed to share my quarters with other men, possibly of all different nationalities, customs, and languages.

The picture that I saw when I entered the "room" however, was quite unexpected. The "cabin" was a huge, bare space dimly lit by four incandescent light bulbs and accommodating about a hundred double-decker bunk beds, army style. When my eyes became accustomed to the darkness I could see four men on the floor, throwing in turn two little white cubes. Just a few feet from them, another group of men was singing songs to the accompaniment of a guitar in a language I did not recognize. The rest were more subdued. Some were praying, some were writing, and the majority were sleeping.

Although I had been a bit shocked initially by my surroundings, it didn't really dismay me since I had lived in a communal environment for the past four years, so in a way this wasn't so different from the children's homes. After contemplating the "accommodations" for a while I went up on deck to get some fresh air. Peering over the railing and daydreaming about what was to come, I was startled into the present by a ship's steward shaking a small bell, calling for dinner in three languages in a voice that would have been the pride of any medieval town crier.

The first day, we were lulled into complacency by the calmness of the Mediterranean. The rough waves of the Atlantic brought us into the reality of ocean travel. I don't remember exactly how long I was seasick, but it was long enough. We settled in for a twelve-day passage. A young man who was trying to get friendly with Alice bought me a Coke at the ship's bar. I thought it tasted awful, like medicine. Many years later, Diet Coke with lemon has become one of my favorite thirst quenchers, an example of how life and taste can change; but I'll never go along with sweet pickles!

We reached New York at night. The illuminated skyscrapers seemed to come out of the night and reach for the sky. In the distance, a long bridge with a multitude of cars rolling appeared as if in a dream.

Around me, everyone was smiling, laughing, crying, or just plain staring. Arrogant little tugboats tooting their horns came to guide our ship through the maze of buoys and floating signs. Somehow, though, amidst all that clamor and movement, we understood that we had finally reached America.

At last, in the morning light, as the ship glided toward the dock, the Statue of Liberty greeted us serenely unaffected by the hustle and bustle of the harbor. Could there be a more apt symbol of welcome than this enduring gift from France? I couldn't yet appreciate how meaningful that might have been to us three émigrés from France, nor did I realize the irony that a symbol of American freedom came from the country that was culpable in my parents' death. But now I prefer to see this statue as a universal message of welcome to all strangers. Our ship was towed in by a red tugboat that led us to a pier on the east side of the Hudson River, somewhere on the west side of Manhattan. Ellis Island had long been closed. We were now officially in America.

At immigration, before disembarking, a fee had to be paid for one of our papers, probably mine because I was not officially a French citizen. My sister had come prepared, having sewn a $100 bill into her garter belt, savings she had scrabbled from her work. She found a ladies' room to undo the stitches and retrieve it and pay the fee.

We disembarked on a long, covered concrete pier with large banners hanging from the ceiling, each bearing a different letter to indicate last names and where we would find our luggage. I had a tiny suitcase with a capital J decal on it. It contained not much more than some of the letters from Simon and Alice that I had received in one or the other of the maison d'enfants. That suitcase, along with the letters, has since been donated to the US Holocaust Museum in Washington, DC.

Our most precious possession was our father's bicycle, which had been crated and shipped at a cost that much exceeded its monetary value, but which represented a priceless tangible connection to him. My sister says that she and my brother would ride their bikes with my father in the *Bois de Vincennes*. I was strapped in a toddler's seat fastened to the rack on the back of my father's bike. I had been puzzled as to how we had managed to recover this precious bicycle, but it appears that some time right after the *rafle*, it had been transferred to the Bonneaus' house for safekeeping.

Me on my father's bike: Brooklyn c. 1950–51

Simon's account of our arrival, written in the French he knew best at the time is reproduced below: its poetry and elegance is not easily imparted in English, so first I'll quote the original, followed by a translation:

Mardi, le 25 Octobre 1949.

Ce matin on est matinal et chacun apprête les étiquettes sur ses bagages. Les escaliers sont pleins, et avec une larme de crocodile on donne un pourboire aux garçons d'étage. Il fait un froid de canard.

Bon Dieu, que le paysage est gris. On commence a se donner des tas d'adresses, et patati et patata.

Bon, le bateau avance tout de même et d'un seul coup nous voila pris entre des batiments d'un gris vert et des docks sensiblement de la même teinte, et l'eau verte, et le ciel gris, et le brouillard, et je me sens pour la premiere fois l'ame triste et le coeur etreint. L'idée de plaisanter ne me vient pas.

Déjà, le bateau est venu sagement se ranger le long du quai et une fanfare idiote fait des siennes. Je n'ai pas le temps d'être abbatu car on est pris dans l'engrenage des ordres et contre-ordres. On regarde avec curiosité ces "Americains" de l'autre côté du quai.

Dans la salle à manger nous sommes devant un inspecteur Americain, tout vêtu de noir, qui compulse nos papiers en silence. Soudain il se met a nous dire que Michel n'est pas en règle.[51]

Après vérifications et la somme de vingt cinq dollars que nous devons verser, alors tout est finalement parfait. L'alerte avait été chaude!

Nous sortons sur le pont et avant de passer sur la passerelle nous donnons une fois de plus nos papiers. Enfin, l'ultime moment est arrivé. Il est onze heures et demi du matin et nous mettons le pied sur le béton americain.

Nous traversons le hall pour rechercher nos bagages. Je regarde avec curiosité des messieurs qui portent des cavattes aux noeuds enormes et aux couleurs perçantes. Ils mangent des sandwich fumants qu'ils ont acheté à un petit comptoir.

Nous avons trouvés la lettre "J," et, là, devant nos bagages, se tient un monsieur d'allure distinguée vêtu d'une gabardine grise. Il nous sourit et demande: "Jeruchim?" Nous comprenons que c'est le fameux Oncle Sam et nous l'embrassons avec enthousiasme.

D'anciens amis qui ont leur bagages nous disent aurevoir. Nous remplissons les formalités douanières et nous descendons dans le hall ou attendaient depuis un bon nombre d'heures notre nouvelle famille.

Tuesday, October 25, 1949

This morning, we're up bright and early, and everyone affixes their luggage tags. The stairs are full, and with crocodile tears we give a tip to the bellboys. It's freezing cold. God, it's so grey outside. We start exchanging lots of addresses, and chit-chat with our fellow passengers.

Well, the ship continues to get closer and all of a sudden we find ourselves wedged between the greenish-grey buildings and the docks, all more or less the same color, and the green water, and the grey sky, and the fog, and for the first time I feel sadness in my soul and a heavy heart. No thought of joking around.

Already the ship has quietly glided alongside the pier, and a brass band is blaring its welcome. I haven't got the time to be depressed because we're caught in the grip of orders and counter-orders. We look at the "Americans" on the other side of the pier with curiosity.

In the dining room, we stand in front of an American inspector, all dressed in black, who's looking over our documents in silence. Suddenly he starts to tell us that Michel's are not in order. After our papers are checked again and after forking over $25, everything is finally perfect. But what an awful scare!

We go out onto the deck, but before getting on the gangway, we have to show our papers one more time. Finally, the ultimate moment has arrived. It's 11:30 in the morning and we're setting foot on American soil, actually concrete.

Next, we walk through a long hall to look for our suitcases. I look with curiosity at men wearing enormous knotted ties in shocking colors. They're eating steaming sandwiches they bought from a little stand.

We find the letter "J" and there, in front of our bags, there's a distinguished looking man wearing a grey overcoat. He smiles at us and asks "Jeruchim?" We realize it's our famous Uncle Sam and we enthusiastically give him a big hug.

Some old friends who've gotten their luggage say goodbye to us. We fill out the customs forms and go down to the entrance where our new family has been waiting for many hours.

After we went through the necessary formalities, we were led to a receiving family group. They were smiling, but I couldn't understand a word they said. I'm sure Alice translated. She had a working knowledge of English, which she had picked up after the Allied landing. She interacted with GIs, or more likely they wanted to interact with her, and little by little she acquired some facility. Some of the GIs gave her books, which she read and somehow absorbed. Alice is a voracious reader and gifted at languages. Then, in 1947, she spent four weeks in England with one of the well-to-do Jewish families who were hosting survivors.

We were to live in Brooklyn with our Uncle Sam (my mother's oldest brother) and his wife Bessie. Bessie was his second wife, his first having died many years prior. Bessie's husband had also died previously, so this was a second marriage for both. Simon and I drove with one of Bessie's daughters, Malvina, and her husband Murray. Their car was a Kaiser, a brand long since deceased, but reasonably large. Just riding in a car was a luxury. I thought to myself, these people are rich, and I smiled inwardly, and probably outwardly, all the way to Brooklyn. Of course, the reality was much different. Malvina and Murray were childless, and Malvina apparently took a liking to me. When we arrived, I had not much more than the clothes on my back and my tiny suitcase. But soon after, Malvina took me shopping for clothes and outfitted me so that I could go to school looking "normal." But the style was foreign to me, and I felt the winter cap with ear flaps made me look like a clown.

Sam and Bessie lived in a third-floor walk-up apartment of a three-story brick building at 320 Cortelyou Road, on the corner of East Fourth Street in Brooklyn. Living with them were Harold, Bessie's bachelor son from her first marriage; Sylvia, Bessie's daughter from her first marriage; Sylvia's husband Louis; and their children, Randy and Gary, who were two years apart, the older about three years younger than me. The apartment was a "railroad" apartment in analogy to a railroad car, where an aisle separates living quarters on either side. Upon entering this apartment, the kitchen lay immediately to the left. To the right was a bathroom, the only one, and Sam and Bessie's bedroom. Forward from the kitchen was the "aisle," the subsequent spaces separated by arched openings. The next room was a small alcove which contained a sleep sofa. The living room followed, and to the right of the living room there was a small bedroom, the domain of Sylvia and Louis.

The first night, Simon and I and Sylvia's kids shared the convertible sofa. I was no stranger to crowded conditions so this cozy arrangement didn't register as unusual. Alice slept on a convertible sofa in the living room. Alice thinks Harold slept in the tiny bedroom at the end of the railroad car, but I thought that his sister Sylvia slept there. Our arrival must surely have put a crimp in their lifestyle and generated resentment, although I was oblivious to it at the time. They knew our story and would no doubt have felt guilty had they outwardly shown their resentment, but now I can understand their frustration at the crowding due to our presence.

In many families, when children have lost their parents, other members of the family step in, typically the closest of kin. In this case, it was my grandmother Tessie, the only grandparent I would ever know, but not before we arrived in the States. It is an unfortunate fact of my life that I never had any grandparents to spoil me, and this might have been an opportunity had I been placed in her household, but it was not to be; by then she was too old for such a task, nor would she have had sufficient funds for it. I'm not sure what image I had of her when I arrived; I think at that point she was just a name. She had been brought over from Poland by her son Sam after he had immigrated in the early 1920s, and she promptly set to apply her inventive skills. Among others she invented a recipe for blond hair, which she bottled and sold, long before it became widely popular. She kept busy in other ways. She had a stall in an outdoor market where she sold embroidery kits for aprons, tablecloths, towels, and so on. I related in Chapter III how she had created an eatery in Warsaw, and she put her cooking skills to work here also. She was in demand for parties, bar mitzvahs, and weddings. She knew she needed to have some income.

By the time we arrived in the States all of her activities had long ceased. In 1949, she was eighty years old, in poor health, and a shadow of the resourceful young woman she had been. She passed away four years later, and I'm sad that I never really had the chance to get to know her as a person. She couldn't speak English or French and I couldn't speak Yiddish or Polish. Still, I hope my granddaughters have inherited the strength and resourcefulness of this remarkable woman.

Uncle Sam and Bessie were of modest means. Sam had not worked for some time. He had been a house painter, and paint in those days had lead as an ingredient. Sam contracted lung disease, which was eventually resolved, but left him permanently debilitated. Thus, Alice and Simon felt pressure to earn money to help support the additional expense we represented. Soon after we arrived, Alice landed a job as a photo retoucher with the help of *Rachelle*, an old friend who had been with us in the *maison d'enfants*. Rachelle had been living in the States for some time and was already "wise" to the way of doing things. My brother's search for work was more difficult, until he received an unanticipated letter from Jean Torrès, Léon Blum's stepson whom I mentioned earlier. During the war, Jean had studied law in New York and had made a number of influential friends with influential acquaintances. One of those was Mr. Schick, a Frenchman of Alsatian origin. Jean had asked Mr. Schick to help us get acclimated.

A few months after we arrived, Mr. and Mrs. Schick invited us to dinner. Their town house on the Upper East Side of Manhattan was a level of posh that we had never seen. A maid in uniform opened the door ushering us in; footsteps were quieted by the plush Persian carpets. At some point, the question of employment came up, and Simon related his disappointment at the difficulty of finding a job. Mr. Schick subsequently contacted the owner of the Morton Freund advertising agency, which led to Simon's first job, a minor position delivering finished artwork to customers. After attending an art school in Paris, this was a frustrating development. But Simon learned a lot by observing the senior designers and later became a top cosmetics packaging artist himself.

After the meal we made our departure, and Mr. Schick handed my brother a book, dedicated to "Simon Jerry." My brother's puzzlement was clarified: Mr. Schick was of the opinion that we needed to change our name to something more "American," and Jerry was his suggestion, I assume because it matches the first three letters of our name. Apparently, he wasn't aware that Jerry was a derogatory term for a German soldier. But even if the suggested name had been Smith, we wouldn't have accepted it. Without articulating it, we felt our name was the only thing that was left of our parents.

The crowding situation at 320 Cortelyou Road resolved itself little by little. At some point relatively soon after our arrival, Sylvia and her family moved out and that created a lot of available space. In May of 1951, Simon was drafted in the US Army, and sometime in the fall of 1951 my sister, herself finding the situation less than desirable, moved to Rochester, New York. She had been trained in France to retouch photos. Since Kodak, then the center of gravity of the photographic world, was headquartered in Rochester, it was a natural place to go. That left Sam, Bessie, Harold, and me in the apartment. Harold tried to act as a big brother, but he wasn't a natural at it. During the three years that I lived there, I tried to make myself inconspicuous. It was my nature, my European upbringing, and a sense that I was in a culture whose mores and standards I did not fully understand. So, I did not want to make a *faux pas* that would have embarrassed me.

Simon's departure for the army was an emotional shock, as we were very close and he had been a father figure. When Alice left not long after, I felt somewhat at sea for some time; but, of course, I had to adjust. It may be that my wartime experience had taught me, too early, to accept loss and to adapt. I was not mistreated by the Shapiro family, but there was no real warmth. Simon and I, realizing that we were second-class citizens, used to joke wryly about it, in French, of course. Sam and Bessie had family visitors on a more or less regular basis. It seemed when visitors arrived that bowls of fruit and other goodies materialized out of thin air. At that time, fresh fruit were a special treat, at least for us, but as soon as the company departed, the cornucopia vanished, presumably to prevent the hungry foreigners from devouring this precious offering. One pair of relatively frequent visitors were Milton, Bessie and Sam's own son, and his fiancée Renée. Milton seemed unlike the rest in personality and demeanor; he was friendly, laid-back, and open.

Also, he was educated, the first member of the clan to attend college at the City College of New York (CCNY).

Other visitors were Sam's children by his first wife (Rebecca), Irving and Ida, and their families. Here, I have to interpose a small story. It turns out that Rebecca's family lived in New York but had emigrated from Poland after WWI. On a trip back to Poland to visit relatives, sometime in the 1920s, they encountered my family, meaning my grandmother and her children. How this encounter took place is left to our imagination. Perhaps there was a gathering at Rebecca's relatives' house where the neighborhood was invited. Somehow, Sam and Rebecca must have been in proximity some place at some time, and they fell in love on the spot.

My cousin Ida's family's visits were more frequent, and many times they took me back to their house. They were the successful branch of the family. Ida was married to Larry Hochberg who had a clothing manufacturing business, and they had two children, Richard, about my age, and Marsha, a few years younger. They were much more genteel and kind than Bessie's offspring. Marsha and I connected on and off over time and reconnected in 2003 when the Holocaust Museum[52] celebrated its tenth anniversary with a "tribute to survivors" theme, and invited survivors to attend. The occasion was covered by *The New York Times*, one of whose reporters asked to interview me and a few others as well. The reporter, Joe Berger, is himself a distinguished writer with a family history connected to the Holocaust. Marsha read the article and wrote me a letter. It had been a very long time since we had communicated, but I was glad to hear from her. I responded, and for the next ten years or so we saw each other as much as possible, until her untimely death from ovarian cancer.

Sometime in late 1951, my Uncle Sam decided that I should be bar mitzvah. After all, I was already past thirteen, the traditional age when this ceremony takes place. I'm not sure that I really knew what it meant then, because my religious education had been close to nil. Our parents had not been religious, and I'm not sure they would have made it a requirement for Simon and me, had life proceeded "normally." It's true that in the *maison d'enfants* we were taught Hebrew, we celebrated the major holidays (Passover, Rosh Hashanah, Purim, and Chanukah) but I don't recall specific religious instruction, and the orientation in the orphanage was more on Jewish identity than on religion *per se*. One fine morning, my uncle told me to dress nicely, and we walked to the local synagogue. He must have discussed my situation with the rabbi, who no doubt gave dispensation from having to recite or read the customary liturgy for this occasion. At the synagogue, I went up to the bimah (the podium) and read about twenty seconds worth of something in Hebrew and I was declared a bar mitzvah. The whole procedure did not take more than a few minutes; then we went home, had some sweet wine and sponge cake. And that was that!

My brother was already a young man when we arrived, and much more tuned in to spoken or unspoken messages and body language from others than I. In his second book of memoirs[53] he gives a detailed description of his impressions, the dynamics of the Shapiro household after we moved in, and the emanations from the other occupants of the apartment, of which I was at the time blissfully unaware or chose to be so. He confirms that there was a certain degree of resentment.

With zero English at my command, very soon after I arrived, I was enrolled in PS (Public School) 179, just a few blocks from where we lived. In those days, there were no special programs to integrate immigrants into the schools; no pampering, no language tutoring, or any other kind for that matter. I was a bit small for my age, about 4'5." The powers that be at PS 179 probably just looked at me and said he looks tall enough to be in fourth grade, which is where they stuck me. I would have un-

The building into which we moved after arriving; we lived on the top floor.

derstood as much at the Institute for Advanced Study in Princeton. I sat mutely in class where no special effort was made to include me. Gradually, I learned English by osmosis, and by making friends. One boy in particular, Joel, lived in an apartment house not too far from us. He often invited me to his place, which was palatial by comparison, and I remember him pointing to one or another object, speaking its name in English. As my English improved, it became more obvious that I was misplaced in fourth grade, and I was "promoted" up, first one year then the next.

By December 1949, I had already acquired some listening, but not speaking, proficiency in English. Still, I figured out that the teacher in my class was asking the students what they were doing during the

Christmas recess. After several classmates appeared to say they were going to "my ami," I began to feel good that they were trying to include me by saying they were going to visit a friend. I made a mental note to tell them that the proper construction in French was *mon ami*, (my friend) not "my ami" but I don't think I ever followed through.

During the two and a half years that I attended PS 179, I slowly absorbed American culture and I started to make money. Across from 320 Cortelyou Road was a series of stores. On the left was the greengrocer, owned by an Italian man everyone called Joe, who was as big and strong as an ox. Next to Joe's was the grocery store, owned by Mr. Eisenfeld, who was never seen without an unlit cigar in his mouth and flecks of tobacco dotting his lips. Soon enough, Bessie would ask me to run errands, perhaps pick something up at the butcher or the baker. One time, she asked me to go to Mr. Eisenfeld's store and get a half-sour pickle. When I returned with the precious pickle, I told Bessie that they did not have half pickles, so I got a whole one! She roared in laughter. At the time, it was common to find barrels of pickles in local groceries. There were typically two barrels, one of which held *really* sour pickles and the other less sour, or "half" sour. There were no half pickles. Aunt Bessie was very amused at this young immigrant's innocent malapropism.

I became the delivery boy for both Joe and Mr. Eisenfeld. They shared a bicycle with a basket in front of the handlebars, into which went the packages that I would deliver. It was never very far. I worked for tips, and with these I would treat myself to candy bars, comic books (I loved Batman and Superman), movies, and my favorite: a plate of whipped cream at the candy store/soda shop, which was to the right of the grocery store. One might think that coming from the land of crème Chantilly I would have been well acquainted with whipped cream. Not so! I discovered it in the candy store, and to the owner's amusement I would go in every so often and order simply a plate of whipped cream.

Not long after we arrived, perhaps a few months, my brother and I were given a regular task. Our grandmother was unable to shop for herself. We were asked to go to lower Manhattan where she lived and do that for her. By then, we had developed a working knowledge of English and of the New York City subway system. Thus, we took periodic trips to visit her and go to the store. When we would visit her, we also delivered meat to her from the kosher butcher in our neighborhood. Although she had initially been relatively well off in her family of origin as well as with the family of my grandfather (recall Alice's memories in Chapter III), by the time I got to know her she was essentially destitute and her son, my Uncle Sam, regularly bought a couple of pounds of lamb stew for her from that neighborhood kosher butcher, which it was our job to deliver. I suspect the meat was more mutton than lamb, and Tessie cooked this stew to oblivion. The odor pervaded her little apartment to nauseous heights. I think this is where I learned to dislike lamb until I was properly introduced to it by Madame Goldberg—but more about this later. Simon and I usually, or often, made this trip together before he was drafted in the Army, where he served on the front lines in Korea. I used to say about this, that he went from the fire into the frying pan. After he left for basic training, I made the trip to my grandmother's apartment by myself.

As I entered eighth grade, it was time to think about high school. Normally in New York City one would go to a "district" high school, that is, a high school designated for all residents within a certain boundary around it. I don't remember who suggested that I take an entrance exam for Brooklyn Technical High School (Brooklyn Tech). Perhaps it was Harold or Milton, the college graduate, who was more attuned to education. There were then several non-district high schools in New York City: Bronx High School of Science, Stuyvesant High School, High School for the Performing Arts, and Brooklyn Tech. Acceptance into these "elite" high schools required passing an entrance exam. The first two were (and still are) more abstractly oriented but would also have meant much more commuting. In any case, Harold or Milton thought engineering would be a very fine profession, and this was Brooklyn Tech's orientation. After barely more than two years in the United States I took the entrance exam. I passed, and entered Brooklyn Tech in September 1952.

High school was an emancipation of sorts. I felt very grown up taking the subway on my own. Brooklyn Tech was not a totally academic institution. It offered several tracks, all but one of which, today, would be called vocational: aircraft engines, chemical industry, metallurgical, and others. But I chose to enroll in the college prep (CP) track. In a way, the more lasting influence of Brooklyn Tech may have been the caliber of the classmates I encountered. At PS 179 I never really felt challenged, but Brooklyn Tech was an eye-opener, and perhaps for the first time I realized, if I had ever thought about it, that there were many people much smarter than I was. The teachers were excellent, something that I intuitively appreciated then, but even more so much later.

Mingling with all those other "smart guys" rubbed off. Even after more than sixty years, I still remember some of them: Paul Feldman, Herbert Einbeinder, Ciro Petti, and especially Marty Sapsowitz, with whom I became good friends, as we both loved classical music. I was challenged to keep up. My mind and outlook expanded from that of a PS 179 bumpkin to an almost wiseass New York City teenager. There was an honor roll at Brooklyn Tech, published in the school's newspaper, *The Survey*, every semester. An average of eighty-five was needed to appear there. My average at the end of the first semester was eighty-nine, which I thought pretty special, until I read the list and saw how many had better numbers, up to ninety-nine! That put me in my place, but I worked all the harder to catch up. Little by little, camaraderie developed with like-minded others. Lunchtime was especially enjoyable, schmoozing with the guys in the cafeteria. I made many friends at Brooklyn Tech, many of whom I continued to be friends with during my college years, and some into the very present.

In 1953, not long after I entered Brooklyn Tech, Simon came back from serving in the Korean War.[54] The army was a maturing experience for him, and he realized that staying at the Shapiros' apartment would not be a welcome lifestyle. So, we looked for a place to live, and within a short time we left 320 Cortelyou Road. We found a basement apartment in a private home owned by the Horowitz family, at 1403 E 48th Street, Brooklyn, NY. I went to school and Simon went to work. I came home from school much earlier than Simon did, and it was natural for me to contribute to the "household," which took the form of making supper. With no cooking experience, I probably opened a can of sardines for the main, and perhaps, only course. Still, it was my first step in the art of cooking, one which I fully embraced as time passed by.

We did not stay very long at the Horowitz's apartment. Soon after Simon returned, he reconnected with an army acquaintance, Sidney Goldman, who offered us a better deal. It turns out that Sid's mother owned a sizable house, or so it seemed then, at 5690 Kings Highway in Brooklyn, and it had an unoccupied basement apartment which was offered to us. We took it. Sometime that year, 1953, Alice came to visit us from Rochester and met Sidney. Later, in 1954, she married him.

Alice and Sid, now a couple, were moving to Long Island to share a house with Sid's mother. It was time for another move for me and Simon. We searched for a place and found an ad for another basement apartment at 9209 Avenue B in Brooklyn. The house was owned by the Schwartz family: George, Ruth, and their children Wendy, five, and Marc, three. We quickly bonded. Ruth was the emotional engine of the family, and accepted us without reservation. The door to the higher floor from the basement apartment was always open and soon I would go in and out. I played with the kids, who were adorable, often romping with Marc on the floor. When I went upstairs after school, Ruth would ply me with food. The bond we initially formed has lasted a lifetime, and the Schwartzs became family. Wendy referred to us as her older brothers, and, much later, our own kids called Ruth "Aunt Ruth." Marc eventually moved to California where we visited him with our young boys, and I have a photo of Marc carrying Kenny on his shoulders just as I had done with him two decades earlier. Sadly, George, Ruth, and Wendy have passed away, but we still keep in touch with Marc, and visit as often as we can.

At Brooklyn Tech, I became aware that I had a penchant for writing. I wrote some pieces for *Horizon*, the school's literary "magazine," a once-a-semester booklet with poems, short stories, and essays. I joined the staff of the school newspaper, *The Survey*, in my sophomore year, 1954. The paper had four large-size pages, and four editors in charge of different subject matter, overseen by a faculty advisor, Mr. Flaumenhaft, a kindly and intelligent elderly man. By the spring semester of my junior year, I had become the assistant features editor, and by the fall semester of my senior year I had become the features editor. In the spring semester I was kicked upstairs to be one of two advisory editors. There was a lot of camaraderie in the "newsroom," and an atmosphere that made us feel that we were doing something worthwhile. This was likely the source of my early attraction to the field of journalism, as I relate later, but as with many other dreams, that did not happen.

I had also earlier joined a "service" organization called the SOS. Our job was to keep order in the hallways during change of class or dismissal. Besides looking good on one's résumé, the special badge we wore allowed us to roam the halls at will and cut in the lunch line at the cafeteria.

My junior year creative writing class was led by Mary Heslin, a young energetic woman who had probably not been out of college for more than a few years, but seemed so much older than we. Inspiring and also a stickler, she took a liking to me, which resulted in extra attention but extra challenges. She gave me a term assignment, fairly unusual at the time. It was to read and write a report on a medieval book, *The Art of Courtly Love*, written by Andreas Capellanus in the twelfth century. I'm not sure why she chose that book. Perhaps she thought any male born in France was genetically predisposed to amorous enterprise. The book laid out thirty-one "Rules of Love" espoused by troubadours, traveling musicians, and storytellers who serenaded the ladies with (presumably) nothing but chaste intent. According to the troubadours, love was not appropriate for marriage, but only as an unattainable goal to be strived for. I was too young to pay much attention to those rules, and in any case, I didn't play the lute. What counts is that I got an A for my report.

Part of Ms. Heslin's class was devoted to preparing us for the New York State Regents Exam. At the time this exam was given across all of New York state. If you "passed" you were awarded a "scholarship" for college. Only a certain number of such scholarships were given, and one simply had to have a high enough score within the whole of New York state to be within that number. I was fortunate to receive that scholarship, as it was one of my main sources of income in college. It amounted to $1,200 a year, worth more than $10,000 now, and was just enough to pay for most of my expenses. As part of the preparation for the Regents Exam, Ms. Heslin gave us an enormous list of words, synonyms, antonyms, and definitions that we had to memorize. That very process honed my vocabulary, sharpening my consciousness of language, and certainly contributed to passing the Regents Exam.

Less challenging at Brooklyn Tech was language class. At the time, France and Germany were the acknowledged foreign countries that were the most advanced in the sciences and mathematics. In the college prep track, one had to take one or the other language. I wanted nothing to do with anything German, so I took French. Monsieur Tron was the instructor, and of course he soon learned that I was slightly ahead of the others. I became his informal "assistant," grading his exams. Perfection doesn't exist, so I only got ninety-nines on my report card.

In junior year, as is typical, we started thinking about college. Competition was strong but friendly, nothing like today's no-holds barred battle for admission to even mediocre schools. I was still somewhat naïve about the process, but I was learning from my schoolmates. Like most of them I was dreaming of MIT or some Ivy League university. I hadn't yet decided what I really wanted to do. I was very attracted by the idea of becoming a writer of some kind, and I was thinking about entering a school of journalism. It happens that Columbia University was well-known for its school of journalism and for most everything else. I applied to Columbia and was accepted. However, they offered me a rather small scholarship, which couldn't begin to pay for tuition, let alone board. Columbia was out.

I was fortunate to live in New York City, which at the time had one of the best public university systems in the country.[55] It included Brooklyn College, Queens College, Hunter College, and the City College of New York. CCNY harbored the engineering schools, which is the direction that reality and practicality pushed me toward. Before admittance to CCNY one also had to take an entrance exam. The exam was moderately difficult, but not too much so, because that would have been politically awkward for the city fathers. The consequence was that many more students were admitted into the engineering schools than could really be accommodated. The solution, possibly intentional, was to make the curriculum sufficiently difficult that natural selection would adjust the student count to a number that would fit the available classrooms and faculty. I took and passed the entrance exam and was admitted into the freshman class of September 1956.

At the end of high school, I was given a recognition that surprises me to this day, in the certificate below which I had completely forgotten about, but recently discovered in a pile of papers. It gives me a good feeling to gaze at this certificate because, in a way, my high school years were some of the best four years of my life. Even though I was penniless, I was happy.

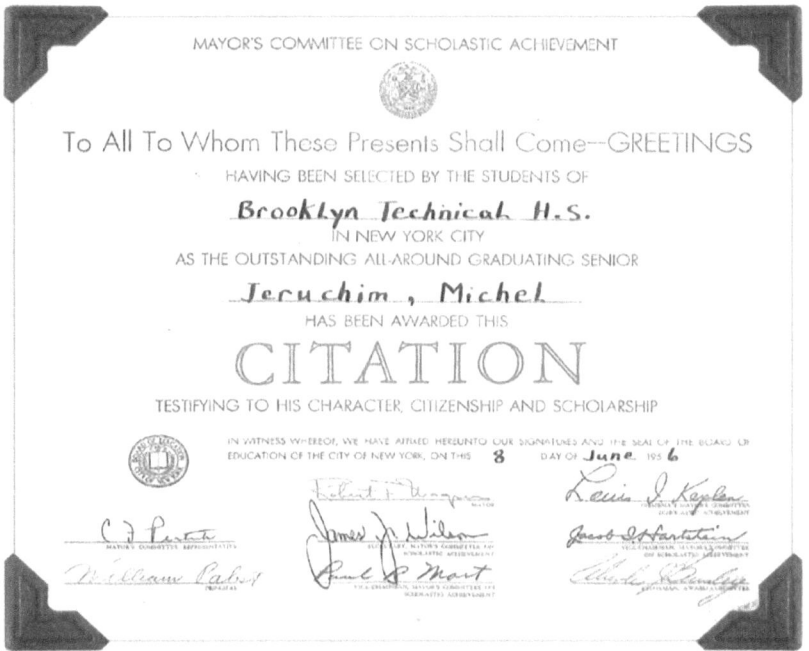

One aspect of American life that was totally unexpected and unwelcome was the stifling summer heat, something I had never experienced in France. Air-conditioning was not widespread and we certainly didn't have it at 320 Cortelyou Road. I was fortunate to spend several summers, or part of them, in "the mountains" as they were referred to, meaning somewhere north of New York City in New York state. The first or second summer after I arrived, I was sent for a couple of weeks, or possibly more, to a camp in Harriman State Park. I believe that this sojourn was arranged by my uncle through a Jewish charity. Later, while still in high school, I was introduced to a rabbi who ran a camp in the Pocono Mountains area, near a town called Honesdale. At the time this seemed far away. I was not a counselor, but a hired hand. I worked there for two years in the summer. I was a *factotum*. There was a large guest house on the grounds, almost a small hotel, where parents would stay when they visited their children. I carried their luggage to their rooms and ran whatever errands they required. During the day I worked at a little concession stand in the guest house, where they sold candy and cigarettes. At night, I assisted in the coffee shop, a little enterprise in one of the buildings where people could come and get coffee, tea, hot dogs, hamburgers, and sweets. I didn't make much money, but I had room and board and country air.

These summers would not have been especially memorable, except for one thing—my introduction to classical music. I became friendly with one of the senior counselors, whose first name I remember to be Yale—or was it he was *going* to Yale? No matter. One day we were talking about music. At the time, I loved the big band sound, especially Glenn Miller. Yale said to me something like "that's good music, but you can't compare that to classical music." He had a portable victrola in his bunk and several long-playing records. He started me off with Rossini's "William Tell Overture," a bit of which I already knew from having watched *The Lone Ranger* series on television, which I loved. Yale then upped the ante, perhaps a few days later, and put on Beethoven's "Seventh Symphony." It was an immediate revelation. It opened up a whole new world that I've been exploring ever since, and takes me to a place of joy beyond words, which is what music is. When I hear certain works, like Beethoven's "Ninth Symphony," or Bach's "Goldberg Variations," and many other sublime inspirations, it's the closest I ever come to rapture. I had a hi-fi system, as it was known then, with a speaker enclosure the size of a small dresser. I often stood in from of it, baton in hand, "conducting" whatever was playing on the turntable. My hero was Arturo Toscanini, one of the greatest conductors of all time. I imagined myself on the podium, a pipe dream, of course. But who knows where life could have taken me, had I been able to get a musical education.

During a later summer, I went back again to a summer camp in upstate New York to be an assistant to the head of the waterfront, which was on a lake. During that summer, I took the Red Cross water safety class and passed the exam to be a *bona fide* lifeguard. This served me well because the following summer I got a job as the lifeguard of the pool at a Catskills hotel. That was close to *la dolce vita*, as I didn't have much to do except admire those bodies deserving of it—I'm not talking about the men! I also gave swimming lessons to a couple. They were the dance instructors at the hotel, but did not know how to swim and were fearful of the water. So, we made a barter agreement: They would give me dance lessons in exchange for swimming lessons. That's how I became a good dancer.

On December 8, 1955, at the United States District Court in Brooklyn, in a room full of new citizens raising our hands together, I recited The Oath of Allegience and became an American citizen. I was already a thoroughly American boy, but those citizenship papers confirmed it. Alice and Simon had already become naturalized earlier in 1955. November 6, 1955, Simon married Cécile Rojer, herself a hidden child during the war in a Belgian convent, and whose parents perished in Auschwitz as did ours. Initially I regarded Cécile as an interloper, but by and by we got along.

We were still living in the basement apartment at the Schwartz house, and Cécile moved in. The apartment was much too small for a threesome, and in any case inappropriate for a couple at that stage of their marriage. As it happened, the house next door to the Schwartz residence was inhabited by a widow, Mrs. Newman, who lived by herself in a house of the same size. Ruth Schwartz spoke to her and she agreed to take me in as a boarder. I was given a sizeable room of my own, and space in the refrigerator. I went next door frequently to visit with Ruth and her family, and Simon and Cécile, with whom I would occasionally share dinner. But by that time, I think I was becoming mature enough not to overdo it. I continued living at Mrs. Newman's house until the end of my first semester in college, when events transpired for still another move.

VIII

SCHOOL AND WORK

SEPTEMBER 1956 – MAY 1967

In September 1956, I entered CCNY. Depending on one's major, there were certain prerequisites that had to be taken. Class registration was not conducted by computer. All of these "prereqs" were probably the same for all engineering students, not just those electing electrical engineering. I had a list of courses to take. Registration today is in a different universe, calmly done on a device of one's choosing. At that time, computers were in their infancy. The first electronic computer dubbed *ENIAC* was developed at the Moore School of Electrical Engineering, University of Pennsylvania, in 1946, a mere ten years before I entered CCNY! Personal computing was unknown, and only behemoth mainframes, taking up half a football field, were commercially operational. Registration at CCNY was done by hand and was chaotic. Imagine arranging a compatible schedule for one thousand people in this fashion. We entered a large room, where a number of young men, who looked like they may have been seniors or graduate students, sat at a long table. A queue formed, and by and by one approached the table. I think we knew ahead of time which professors taught which courses. Most professors had a reputation, one way or another, which skewed the selection, but the hour for one's preferred teacher may have conflicted with other constraints. In any case, if your preference could not be matched, the gatekeepers at the table assigned a professor and a time for a particular subject. Getting through registration was a major accomplishment.

When classes started my sense of place in the hierarchy of intelligence was challenged once again. At Brooklyn Tech I had encountered some really smart guys, and here I met even smarter ones, although there seemed to be relatively fewer, as a percentage. The reason for this, as I alluded to earlier, was that the entrance exam could not be made overly difficult for political reasons. Thus, some milk came in with the cream. As had happened at Brooklyn Tech, it took me some time to get my balance, as it were. My grades the first year were okay but not spectacular. I found my rhythm during the second year, the first semester in which I earned all As. I was very pleased with myself!

When I started attending CCNY, I was still living next door to the Schwartzes and Simon and Cécile in East Flatbush. The trip to CCNY in upper Manhattan was a schlep, as they say in French. I had to take a bus to the subway and from there to 139th Street, with a change of line in between. It dawned on me that I needed to live closer to CCNY. I could not afford to rent my own place, so I started looking at newspaper ads for people who wanted to share an apartment. By and by I stumbled on an ad that offered to share an apartment on West 72nd Street, right off Central Park West, a much swankier neighborhood than where I had been living. I don't remember offhand whether an amount was mentioned in the ad, but the location was so good that I decided I had nothing to lose; and so I called and made an appointment with the tenant to see what could be arranged.

At the appointed time I rang the bell and a burly guy sporting a shoulder holster answered the door and introduced himself as Stanley. He quickly tried to put me at ease by informing me that he was a private detective and had just gotten home from work. His manner seemed gentle enough, and soon we were negotiating. He said that it was companionship that he was looking for and offered me an unbelievably low rental rate, $25 a month. I jumped at it and gave him six months' worth right off the bat, lest he change his mind, and I promptly moved in. It was not a large apartment, and the bedroom had two beds, a large one and a single bed, more like a cot, which was to be mine. The first night after I moved in, Stanley told me that there was something wrong with my cot, and that I should share his bed until he could get it fixed. Of course, there was nothing wrong with the cot. Stanley wanted me to be his "boyfriend." Perhaps I should have realized from the beginning that his generous offer came with a price, but I was still naïve in many ways. Maybe Stanley thought I had understood that a "bargain" had been made. In any case, I made it clear that I was not interested and there were no recriminations. I went on to explain my monetary circumstance and that I wanted to stay the length of time I had paid for. And so, I did. Stanley managed to be away much of the time, and I made dinner for myself and studied.

Sometime during my stay, Providence arrived again. In my high school French class I had become friends with a classmate named Bob Goldberg, whose mother, *Berthe*, was French, and *plus royaliste que le roi*.[56] She was a GI bride who had met her husband, an American soldier, during World War I. Through Bob, she often invited me to their home for dinner. Berthe and I enjoyed bantering in French, though to be polite we would switch back to English. And, it goes without saying,

I loved her cooking. My palate had already been primed by Suzanne Leclere's cooking, but the limitedness of ingredients in wartime had no doubt constrained what she could "cook up." Berthe Goldberg offered the full range of French cuisine, specializing in delicious sauces. But more than that, I observed her technique, which was essentially: There's no shortcut to doing things the "right" way, which she knew instinctively and had probably been taught as a young girl in France.

Bob also started his college career at CCNY. Around that time, he fell under the spell of a young woman and all thoughts of studying evaporated. As one would expect, this caught up to him. He flunked out of CCNY the first semester. I remember staying up most of a night, trying to tutor him in calculus prior to the final exam. It was too little, too late. However, he was given the opportunity to redeem himself by going to night school. If his grades were above a certain level for a semester or two, he would be readmitted as a full-time student. Bob accepted his fate, and obtained a job during the day at a company whose business was in the line of work he wanted in the first place: civil engineering.[57] It transpired then, that on the days that he had class, Bob would come to the apartment on 72nd Street, more or less on a weekly basis, and I would make a simple dinner for the two of us. At some point during a conversation, I told him about the "situation" I was in. A week or two later, to my surprise, Bob told me that he had told his parents about that situation and that they were inviting me to come and live with them. It took me about a microsecond to accept, and I moved into the Goldberg home at the beginning of my third semester.

If going from Brooklyn to CCNY was a schlep, going from the Goldbergs' house to CCNY was a trek that took about an hour and a half. The Goldbergs lived on 232nd Street in Cambria Heights, in the borough of Queens, just a few blocks from the border between

New York City and Nassau County on Long Island. I first had to walk to a bus stop, which was not too near, to be transported to the subway which took me to midtown Manhattan where I changed to a different line for uptown Manhattan. The only saving grace about this trip was that both the bus and subway stops near the Goldbergs were the terminus of their respective lines. This meant that the bus and subway cars were nearly empty in the morning and I could get a seat. This allowed me to supplement my sleep time or study, whichever was more crucial on any particular day.

I lived with the Goldbergs for about three and a half years, and this was the closest to a stable family environment that I had had since the Lecleres. It was a smallish house, but the attic space had been converted into a bedroom, which was spacious, and there I settled. Madame Goldberg, as I said, was a quintessential French woman. My stay at her house was to be influential for the rest of my life in the culinary sphere. She was a superb cook. Her style was probably what would be called *cuisine bourgeoise,* but it was refined. *Cuisine bourgeoise* originated as everyday cooking for the middle class, though that description has now faded away. It is not *haute cuisine*, fancy cooking, that was once developed for the upper classes and now offered in certain restaurants, but at its best it rivals the finest dishes. Berthe changed my mind about lamb; her *gigot d'agneau* (roasted leg of lamb), encrusted with garlic, was succulent. Its aroma wafted out of the oven, and could lift you off your feet. Observing Berthe in the kitchen for several years was equivalent to cooking school, though not quite so formal. After all, I had another school to attend which was more pressing.

If there was anything to break the pleasant and quiet atmosphere at the Goldberg home, it was Berthe's railing at Bob about his study habits: "Why can't you be more like Michel?" she would say, and whenever she said it, I felt embarrassed and wanted to disappear. Bob good-naturedly ignored her; it did not affect our relationship, and we have remained lifelong friends. We enjoyed going out together, and we had a winter ritual. After all the rides had been shut down for the winter in Coney Island, we hopped on Bob's Vespa scooter late in the evening and drove about twenty miles to Nathan's on the beach. If you had a bird's eye view a mile above Coney Island, it would have been pitch black except for a lighted spot with dozens of people waiting in line for a hot dog or a lobster roll.

Three summers came and went while living with the Goldbergs, and I needed to find summer jobs that paid a little more than free food and fresh air. One summer, through a connection of Mr. Goldberg's, I landed a temporary job at a mail sorting facility at Idlewild Airport (now Kennedy). The mail came in sacks from overseas, and it had to be put in bins according to destination. It was boring, except if there were postcards. They tended to elicit chuckles around the room, as some of the men would occasionally read the postcards out loud if they were sufficiently entertaining. The following summer was drudgery.

Again, Mr. Goldberg came through with a job at a plastic factory. I sat in front of a machine into which raw plastic material was fed, compressed at high temperature, and extruded into small objects, like plastic lids for salt shakers. When these objects exited the machine, I had to pull them off and throw them into a bin. The only saving grace of this job, besides the pay, was the lunch prepared by Madame Goldberg. Before my final summer prior to graduating from CCNY, I wanted a job that was more respectably engineering-like. The appropriate office at CCNY directed me to the New York City Transit Authority, who gave me a job for the summer. I had to read blueprints about locations of power cables and verify where they were and that they were not damaged. It was probably make-work, but it entailed walking in the tunnels and elevated tracks, though I was with a senior employee who ensured my safety. Still, in this case, I might have preferred free food and plastic lids instead.

The courses at CCNY in the first year and part of the second year were all prerequisites: mathematics (calculus and differential equations), physics, English, and humanities. I must admit that the course I liked best was humanities. I was lucky to have had an inspiring professor, who, among other subjects, opened me up to Greek and Roman myths. I could almost visualize myself in the marketplace listening to Socrates. The technical subjects were too difficult to be fun. However, I actually started to enjoy the electrical engineering courses in the second year. The subjects, by and large, were abstract, but I could somehow connect them to real-world applications. Courses were arranged in sequences of related subjects in increasingly complex fashion. The course sequence that seemed to resonate the most in my brain dealt with circuits and electromagnetic theory. The subject matter that turned out later to be the one most compatible with my way of thinking, communication theory, was then considered graduate school material, and was introduced only in a one-semester course in senior year and at a relatively elementary level.

As time went by, I did not continue to have straight As, but I did reasonably well, eventually graduating *cum laude*. As I recall, only a small fraction of the freshmen who entered with me in the engineering schools graduated with an engineering degree. This does not mean that the remainder did not graduate college at all. I think most did, after having transferred to a different major, perhaps business. Probably a lot of those did much better financially than their engineering colleagues!

Although I was firmly focused on doing as well as possible in my courses, because graduating and finding work thereafter were essential goals for survival, I did find time for social activities. At CCNY, I encountered many of my classmates from Brooklyn Tech who were there because they were almost as poor as I was, though they had not had the same dramatic childhood, and we hung out together. At some point we collectively decided to form a social club (later absorbed by a national fraternity) and rented space in a somewhat dilapidated house somewhere in Brooklyn, where we had regular Friday night socials. Sororities or clubs from different colleges were invited; there was dancing but no hard drinking. It was very reserved by today's standards, but it allowed us to let off a little steam.

The curriculum for an engineering degree at CCNY was a five-year program. I loaded up a bit each semester and took a summer course so that I could finish in four and a half years. I was chomping at the bit to get out in the world and make some money. I graduated in February of 1961: sixth in my class of ninety-one Electrical Engineers and tenth in the school of engineering. Representatives from industry would visit campus and some office would set up interview appointments. I interviewed with a few companies: Airborne Instruments Laboratory, on Long Island; IBM; and General Electric (GE). IBM invited me to visit their headquarters, then in Poughkeepsie, New York. I felt that I was in a factory of drones: Every man wore black slacks, a white shirt, and a thin black tie, or so it seemed. I felt uncomfortable and did not pursue employment there.

GE thought I might fit in with their relatively newly created department, called MSVD (Missiles and Space Vehicle Department), located at 32nd and Chestnut Streets in Philadelphia. An interview was set up and I took the train to Philadelphia. I accepted an offer from them because space and satellites were very glamorous at that time, just a few years after Sputnik, and because they also offered me a nice (at that time) starting salary ($6,900), an option to have four six-month rotations in different groups of my choosing, and fully paid tuition to graduate school at the University of Pennsylvania (Penn). Generous

Electric (as we employees sometimes liked to say) permitted me to take whichever courses I wanted to during the day or whenever the courses were given. It was an offer I couldn't refuse. The rotational assignments were especially attractive because I didn't really know what I would find satisfying as a career, and this afforded me some exploration. And my snobbish side was secretly pleased with the opportunity to attend Penn—at last, an Ivy League school! Naturally, Penn first had to declare me a suitable candidate, and after an interview with the chairman of the electrical engineering department I was accepted. Thus, I was enrolled in the Moore School of Electrical Engineering. Because I was entering mid-year, the chairman suggested I take a single course to get acclimated, and this course was a brain opener.

Cécile had an uncle, Bernard, who lived in the northeast section of Philadelphia with his wife and two daughters, Eliane and Yvette. Cécile had asked Bernard to put me up until I found my own place, which he graciously granted. I did not stay there very long, perhaps two or three months at the most. For one thing, Bernard lived inconveniently far from my workplace. For another, I was not totally comfortable there, psychologically. Bernard had a strong personality, and seemed to require frequent acknowledgment of his magnanimity. He had complained to Cécile that I was remote, but he didn't understand that I felt I was intruding in that household, and wanted to make myself as unobtrusive as possible. So, after dinner I would exchange pleasantries for a few minutes and then retire to my room, not much more than a closet but adequate under the circumstances.

There was a more compelling reason for absenting myself. I had started graduate school. As had happened every time that my education went up a level, it opened new intellectual doors and it took me time to adjust. The first course I took treated probability and random processes. I'm glad this was the only course I had to deal with, because I hadn't been prepared for this type of thinking. These notions were then not taught at the undergraduate level and were a revelation. Although in our daily lives physical processes appear to be deterministic, in fact, at a microscopic or atomic level, they are not. This was one of the great discoveries of the quantum physicists. But I have since also come to realize that randomness is ever present in our lives. A long time ago, I read a book titled *The Crime of Julian Wells*,[58] and a phrase there captures the essence of my view about the randomness of life:

> *"... For here was Julian's sense of life's cruel randomness, life a lottery upon whose uncontrollable outcome everything depended, how because this streetcar stopped on this particular corner at this particular moment, nothing for this particular human being would ever be the same."*

For us, my siblings and me, it was the chance event that our mother had a dental appointment the day before the raid that would have ended our lives, and for me other unexpected encounters that I describe elsewhere in this memoir.

When I started working (and beginning graduate school) in February 1961, I was still boarding at the home of Cécile's uncle. I had to take a bus, then a subway, which reminded me of the long commute I once took to go to CCNY from the Goldbergs' house. So, sometime in the early spring, I started looking for an apartment nearer to work. I found an ad for a third-floor apartment at 1331 Chestnut Street, on the corner of 34th Street, near the center of Philadelphia. It was an ideal location, and the rent was reasonable. I called the phone number listed in the newspaper, and was informed that, unfortunately, the apartment in question had just been rented to someone else. The building owner, however, asked for my number, and said he would call me if something opened up in one of his other buildings.

One day later, that gentleman called me to say that the apartment I had called about was now available; the person who had initially wanted it was backing out. I jumped at it. This is another case of the randomness of life because living on the first floor of this three-story building were two Penn students, Dave Pollack and Steve Wolfgang. If the person originally wanting my apartment had indeed rented it, the odds are minuscule that I would ever have met Steve and, therefore, would not have met his sister Joan. Such are the dice that Fortune rolls for us.

Steve was a New Yorker. In my mind this was an immediate reason for a connection. One day soon after I had moved in, I knocked on their door to ask for a cup of sugar. This was a standard pretext for saying hello, but Steve, who answered the door, promptly made a beeline for the kitchen before I could say this was just a way of introducing myself. It turned out, of course, that we were compatible in many ways, and we became good friends. And eventually, I met his sister.

IX

A BIT ABOUT MY PROFESSIONAL HISTORY

FEBRUARY 1, 1961 – JUNE 30, 2000

The building where I initially worked was located at 32nd and Chestnut Streets, just two blocks from where I was now living. I could practically roll out of bed to get there. Since I was given the opportunity to choose four different work assignments, the first was the *Navigation and Control Systems* group, one of whose specialties was controlling the "attitude" of a spacecraft, meaning its orientation in space so that the antennas would point in the correct direction and the same for the solar panels from which the spacecraft draws its energy. Nowadays, people don't make too much of a distinction in terminology between satellite and spacecraft. Then, technical people liked to think of something in space as a "craft" navigating in space as opposed to water, but satellite would be proper for an object circling the Earth, and spacecraft for outer space exploration.

As in earlier experiences going from one educational level to another, it took some time for my brain to make the necessary adjustments, but this time on two fronts. If I had met increasingly smart guys (in those days they were only guys) going from public school to high school to college, here *all* the guys were smart, and the subject matter was difficult. There were no more idealizing assumptions commonly made for homework problems—this was real life, and errors had consequences other than a low grade. Because I was in a learning mode, I'm not sure that whatever problems I was asked to deal with were useful for anyone but me. And while I found the discipline challenging, it didn't quite register as something that I wanted to spend my career doing.

After my six-month stint in the Controls group, I decided to join the *Communication and Instrumentation Systems* group. I had taken one introductory course in my last semester of college, which had been made interesting by the professor, Mauro Zambuto, a voluble and extroverted Italian. His enthusiasm for the subject was contagious. And so, I decided to make it one of my choices for a six-month assignment. It set the pattern for the rest of my professional life. It turns out that the subject matter of "communication" is both abstract and practical, and the nature of the abstractions somehow engaged my brain in a satisfying fashion. I really enjoyed grappling and solving problems related to the subject matter. How to describe why that is so; it's difficult, but basically it has structure and logic of a kind that I find satisfying, like some foods one likes, there is no explanation, it just is.

When I chose this second six-month assignment, there was a significant catch. The group's office location was in King of Prussia, about twenty-five miles or so west of the center of Philadelphia, with no possibility of public transportation. At that time, GE was moving most of its Space Division operations there, and was in the process of completing a large center of operation. It had rented a number of small buildings in the area, pending completion of that headquarters. It was in one of those buildings that I was supposed to go to next. I needed a car to get there. That was my first major financial decision. I bought a Ford Falcon, even before I had a license, or knew how to drive, because I needed a practice car. One of my acquaintances at the time—Steve Wolfgang's initial roommate, Dave Pollack—gave me driving lessons. Within a few weeks I had a license and I could join all the other drivers on the way out of town. At that time, I considered it fun! It gave me a sense of freedom and traffic was a walk in the park, compared to today.

For my third six-month assignment, I joined the *Antennas and Propagation Engineering* group, which was also located in King of Prussia. Coming out of college this was the subject to which I had the most exposure and which seemed the most intellectually appealing. Of course, communicating to and from satellites implies "propagation," namely the transmission of information on electromagnetic ("radio") waves. Antennas are the "mouths" and "ears" of such transmissions. During my assignment I submitted a patent application for the following: When an object from space reenters the atmosphere, it does so at such high velocity that it "heats" the atmospheric medium through which it travels (which is not "empty" space) by friction with the particles in that medium, and creates what is called *reentry plasma*, a sort of ionized cloud around itself. You can perhaps get a sense of such a thing by visualizing a campfire and the shimmering air above it. The reentry plasma would block out communication to the space object. I proposed a device that would allow electromagnetic waves to pierce through. I'm not sure whether GE pursued a patent because, among other possible reasons, the legal cost might not have been worthwhile, given a relatively small market. But I was starting to think independently.

By the end of this rotation, I realized that this discipline was not quite what I had imagined. Although it was very mathematically based, it became clear that it required a good bit of intuition as well, and here I use intuition as it is often used in this context, namely as a natural feel for the physical manifestation of the equations. It may surprise some readers that there is such a thing as intuition in the sciences or mathematics, as these fields are probably viewed as "objective," but in fact the incredible diversity of subjects in math/science strike different chords in the brains of different people, and depending on how one's brain is "wired," one or another of these subjects will strike the right chord in a particular individual.

A year and a half had passed, and I needed to choose one more assignment. I chose a group called *Electronic Physics*. I really didn't know what it meant but it sounded good. The location was back in Philadelphia. I'm not sure what the full breadth of the group's activities was, but I was mostly involved with something called radar cross section. What I worked on, under the group leader's supervision, a PhD physicist, dealt with properties of materials that would absorb rather than reflect electromagnetic waves, with the ultimate aim of using such materials on aircraft or other airborne objects so that they would be more difficult to detect by radar. And again, while the subject matter was interesting and challenging, I didn't fall in love with it.

During my second assignment, in the Communication and Instrumentation Systems group, I had had two excellent mentors: the manager of the group, Ed Niemann, and the senior engineer in the group, Tom Sayer, who became my role model for analytical thinking and eventually my friend. The relationships I forged with these men no doubt influenced me in choosing the Communication Systems group for my "permanent" position, though I would probably have chosen it in any case.

In May 1962, Steve Wolfgang graduated from Penn and was about to enter its medical school in the fall. His roommate at 3331 Market Street, Dave, had applied for veterinary school but had not been accepted, for which he was sorely disappointed. So, he returned to the countryside, Pottsville, to his father's mink farm. In the intervening year and a half, Steve and I had become good friends and we decided to rent a place together. The landlord of 3331 Market Street also had a building at 3514 Market Street, which had been empty and he was looking to get something out of it. The ground floor had been a deli but the top two floors were available and were offered to us for a song. We promptly took them and set up house there for the next five years.

I started work as a communications engineer in a group of really smart guys. In pretty short order I came to the conclusion that I had a lot to learn, much more than I had learned in the preceding two years. This was one reason that I made up my mind that I needed to return to school. A second reason was that soon after I started in this group, a large contract that many members of the group were working on was cancelled by the government. This was 1963–1964. The word "layoffs" was flying around. I'm not sure if I would have been on that layoff list, but I decided to do everything I could to insulate myself from such a future possibility, which was to get a PhD.

I reasoned (and I wasn't far off) that if I had such a degree, implying deeper knowledge in a particular discipline than (perhaps most of) my coworkers and capitalizing on the aura of "doctor," it would be much more difficult for management to lay me off. You have to remember that I was self-supporting and I could not afford to be out of work. However, the first step was to get a master's degree, for which I had been taking courses during the preceding two years. I was also fortunate that one of the problems I was asked to work on could be turned into my master's thesis at Penn. So, in May of 1963 I received my master's degree (MSEE).

Then, I told my manager that I intended to apply to a PhD program at Penn, which I started in the fall semester, 1964. Here serendipity helped me out again, due I think to the "space race" which had been elevated to a national priority. First of all, and perhaps unexpectedly, the management was enthusiastic about the idea and my manager submitted a request to higher management for a stipend, probably unheard of today. Then out of the blue, I received a letter from Penn, offering me a fellowship from the Ford Foundation. But my good luck didn't stop there. Two months later I received a second letter from Penn (see below), which offered me a different fellowship, this one from NASA, with a significantly higher stipend. Of course, I quickly accepted it, instead of the original offer. So, I could study for the next two years without financial worries.

Those two years of full-time graduate school were two of the best years of my life. I was essentially worry-free, except perhaps before tests but I generally took those in stride. I had no one to worry about except myself. I had enough money to support my lifestyle. I had a car, I dated, I went out with Steve and other friends. What could be better? The most stressful period of this time was "the orals," the oral examination by a committee of professors to grill you, to see if you were worthy of the title of "doctor." Some professors had reputations as nasty interrogators and everyone dreaded having them on their committee.

Through the grapevine, I learned of a study group of students preparing for the PhD orals and I joined that group. While in one way it highlighted the stress, it was actually very useful in revealing one's weaknesses, as we took turns to quiz one another individually in a mock examination. One unexpected and felicitous side effect is that one of my fellow preparers, Len Weinberg, became a lifelong friend. I don't quite remember all the subjects on which we were quizzed, but I do remember mathematics, electromagnetic theory, and electric circuit theory. Finally, the day came. It was sometime after the end of the spring semester, and I may have thought a painless death would be preferable, but I showed up anyway and passed.

Now, I needed to find a dissertation topic, the last hurdle to overcome before a degree. I solicited suggestions from different professors, but ultimately chose one from Professor Aravind Joshi, whose course in coding theory I was taking at the time. He made a suggestion which I found attractive. It dealt with a particular approach to encoding digital information with a high degree of self-correcting capability. Professor Joshi was very helpful along the way, inviting me to come to his house multiple times to discuss one idea or another. By this time, fall 1966, my fellowship had expired and I returned to work.

However, I was given free rein to work on my dissertation during work hours. I completed it in relatively short order, and the last hurdle was to appear before another committee to "defend" my dissertation. For this I was not nervous at all, because my mind was so steeped in the subject matter that I was completely confident in explaining and "defending" what I had done. Finally, in May of 1967 I was awarded the PhD degree from the University of Pennsylvania. I was proud that I had completed all coursework since starting graduate school with nothing but an A. I attended graduation, a ceremony with much pomp and circumstance, and I found myself thinking how much I would have loved my parents to be there.

I celebrated my new "status" by buying a Buick Skylark, a lively hardtop sedan. By then, I was still commuting to King of Prussia and starting to work on "real" problems. By and large, I was given problems requiring *analysis*, which in this context implies the use of abstract reasoning and mathematical application, as opposed to implementation, such as circuit design. Around this time, my impulse to write surfaced again and finally I found an outlet in technical writing, documenting my work.

A consequence of writing, and being published, is that it puts one's name in front of people's eyes, and so I started to get a small reputation at work. I also had the impulse to expose my work outside the company by submitting papers to professional or scholarly journals. At this point, however, I didn't have much to offer, but my first publication appeared in the Proceedings of the IEEE[59] in June of 1968. It was a small piece, but it was a start. It turns out the management was all in favor of publishing because it burnished the reputation of the company, as well as mine. By the time I retired, I had published or presented at professional conferences some forty papers, contributed chapters to two books, and cowritten two books, each with a second edition. (Appendix 2 lists the publications or presentations that I authored or coauthored.)

In the Communications and Instrumentation group[60] I worked on a number of projects, but one in particular led to other things. Sometime in 1968, one of our marketing specialists landed a small six-month study contract with the Office of Telecommunications Policy[61] (OTP). My mentor Tom Sayer and I were assigned to work on it, but very soon after Tom was reassigned to another project, so I became the principal investigator. The study was about the burgeoning communication satellite industry, and how many satellites could share a certain arc of the geostationary orbit visible from the continental US and the frequency spectrum allocated for that purpose. The basic constraint is interference, which allows only so many satellites to be visible from Earth and be relatively interference-free. An analogous situation exists on Earth with radio stations, which must be located sufficiently distant from one another to avoid interference (i.e., receiving both stations with the same intensity on your radio dial).

At the end of the contract period, I wrote a final report and submitted it to the government contracting officer (CO). The CO, Don Jansky, an enthusiastic young engineer, had an illustrious uncle, Karl Jansky, who is considered one of the founding figures of radio astronomy. The review of the final report by Don and his colleagues was very favorable. So, they renewed the contract for another six months, but passed the contract supervision to NASA. By then, NASA had been appointed to advise the FCC on the technical parameters for operating commercial satellites. In fact, our contract was renewed two more times for a total of two years, ending sometime in 1970. After the initial contract, I "acquired" another colleague to assist me, as it became more than a one-man job. His name was Dave Kane, with whom (and his wife) Joan and I later became good friends. The four volumes that were published over the life of the contract and the accompanying computer program were major elements in helping NASA make recommendations to the FCC. An important reason that the study was started in the first place was an impending international regulatory conference (World Administrative Radio Conference, or WARC) which for the first time was to set technical rules for satellite communication for the world at large. Of course, I didn't know at the time that this study would be the start of one of my two career-long tracks.

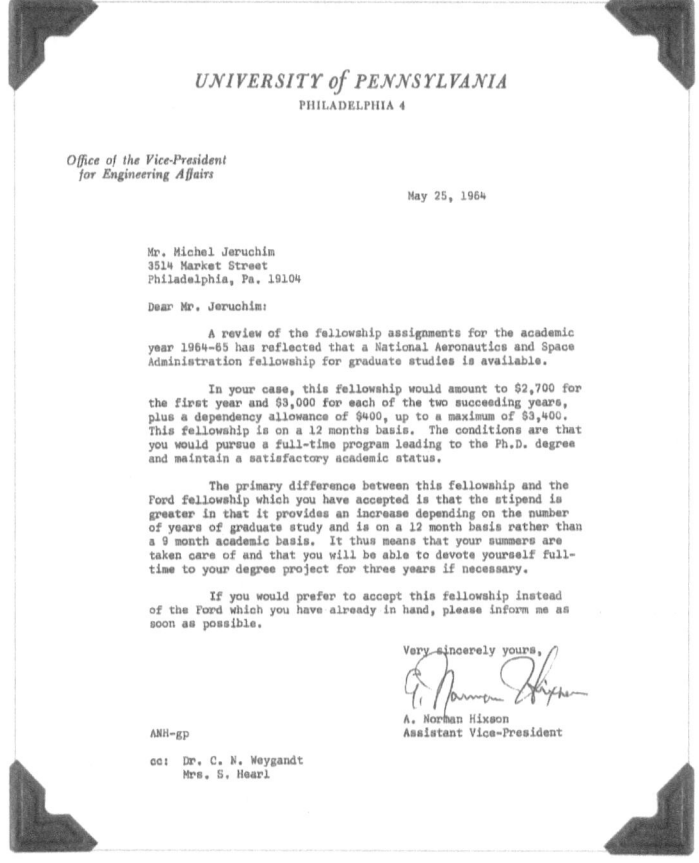

A copy of the second fellowship I was offered

A SHORT DETOUR INTO THE REGULATORY WORLD OF COMMUNICATION

You have no doubt heard of the Federal Communications Commission (FCC), whose job is to "regulate" commercial communication. There are both technical and non-technical aspects to this job, the first one being unrelated to content, and this is the part that my work related to. The technical aspects are basically geared to ensuring interference-free (or almost so) operation of licensed operators.

A simple illustration of what this means, that I alluded to earlier, concerns the assigned frequency of radio station transmitters and their geographical separation so that when you turn on your radio you hear only the station you want. You've probably experienced receiving a signal from two different stations when traveling by car and approaching the boundary where the signal strength from both stations is weak and approximately equal. Then what you hear sounds like someone speaking under water.

Every country has an FCC equivalent, typically called the Ministry of Communications. The US is peculiar in this respect, in that it has two regulatory agencies: the FCC, which regulates commercial operators, and the National Telecommunications and Information Administration (NTIA), which regulates communications for all federal agencies.

The International Telecommunication Union (ITU), a specialized agency of the United Nations, headquartered in Geneva, supersedes the individual countries' rules for satellite communication. Because (for practical and theoretical reasons) satellite emissions cannot be strictly limited to the territory of the country for which the signal is intended, there must be international agreements on limiting unwanted and unintentional interference to those other countries. These agreements are drafted at conferences (now called the World Radio Communication Conference or WRC since 1992) held at different intervals, now every three or four years. The reason why such conferences are recurring is that the evolution of technology requires (or may require) changing the rules in order to accommodate new technology. These "agreements" have the status of a treaty, and according to US law the Senate must ratify any such agreements.

◇◇

I participated in the space WARC in 1971 as a member of the US delegation and this established a bit of reputation in the subject matter of that world. My company was subsequently solicited to provide my services to the government at other regulatory conferences. Some of my publications also relate to this subject and this eventually led to my election as a fellow of the IEEE. The IEEE that I alluded to is a professional organization but it confers different levels of membership, depending on recognized achievements. I joined the organization as a plain "member" soon after I became employed.

To achieve higher levels, one has to be sponsored by a member who already has a higher level and submit an application that is reviewed by a committee who decides if the elevation is warranted. Thus, I next became a senior member based on whatever I had done up to that time, and eventually I was sponsored for the grade of fellow in 1986, which only a small percentage of IEEE members ever become. I was elected a fellow on the basis of my contributions to the regulatory development for communication satellites, and, short of a revolutionary invention, professionally speaking that was about as high as I could go in terms of recognition, and I was just fine with that.

When I first started working at GE, it seemed generally accepted that the desirable career path was management. After all, managers were paid more, there was prestige associated with being a manager and there was the possibility of climbing the management ladder and making even more money. There were three management levels under the general manager labeled C, B, and A. A C-level manager might supervise ten to twenty engineers, a B-level might oversee three level C groups, and an A-level could have maybe six to ten B-level groups under him. Joining this club was my initial goal. At different occasions I was "deputized" by my manager, Don Hagen, to be acting manager when he had to be out of town or on vacation. At some point in the early seventies, I was offered the C-level position, managing the communications group.

By that time, however, my goals and outlook on life had evolved. I had had sufficient opportunity to observe that stepping on the management track was akin to joining a religious order—your personal life was subordinate to the good of the order. When the offer was made, I had been married for about four years, and we had the near-term expectation of a third member of the family. Loyalty to the family, and being present, felt more important to me than managerial elevation. So, I declined the offer—there were no hard feelings. In this decision I was partly motivated by the fact that I did not feel managing was a natural position for me. So, I decided that I preferred to try "climbing" up a much smaller technical ladder. And in this enterprise, I did climb as high as it was possible. In 1993, the management of the division I was working in decided to create a special recognition for individuals who had a long track of significant technical contributions. These individuals, about half a dozen or so at the time, were dubbed "fellows" and I was one of them. The title came with a few perks, like a private office, and I must say I did not object.

Luck struck again sometime in early 1972. I was transferred to another group doing advanced planning for a satellite system that needed a more modern analytical tool to assist in the design process. This fairly new tool was called *simulation*[62] and I was tasked with developing one. Initially I had no idea of what simulation was. It was a steep learning curve. Although the term simulation has a generic meaning, in this context it means imitating or emulating the functioning of real hardware with equations that model all the pieces of equipment in the communication chain of a satellite, and then letting a computer "solve" this string of equations to produce an estimate of the quality of what it is that the satellite transmits. In this fashion one can view the quality of that transmission without having to build actual hardware, which is very expensive, especially if it doesn't work. If the simulated observation shows inadequate quality, one then "tweaks" one or another property of the models until acceptable performance is observed. In this way one can "home in" on a set of design parameters that will satisfy the performance requirements, a much more efficient and cost-effective approach to building hardware. Of course, what the simulation produces is only as good as the verisimilitude (true to life) of the models, which is something that requires fairly accurate understanding of the components of a system.

Within six months of the beginning of my assignment, I had a working simulation with the help of an excellent programmer. We (the company) had been given a challenge from the customer. They would provide a hefty bonus (to the company, unfortunately) if the simulation prediction was "close" to the observation of real hardware that was set up in a laboratory. The application of computer simulation to system design was quite new at the time and not necessarily trusted. This was why the customer elected to spend money to set up an entire chain of equipment in a laboratory and make measurements which could then be compared to the corresponding software measurements. The laboratory experiment was supervised by my lifelong colleague John Moore. Of course, this was constructed as a "blind" study. There was a $100,000 bonus (still a lot at that time) if the two sets of measurements were within the inevitable measurement uncertainty. To make a short story long, we succeeded.

This launched the simulation phase of my career for the next thirty years or so, although I was still engaged with regulatory work. Over the next few years, I kept refining the simulation in different ways. In 1975–76 my management thought that the simulation I had developed might be commercially viable. The marketing department set up a "sales" meeting with some individuals at Bell Laboratories, then by far the premier technical organization in the US if not the world. But there was no sale because my management did not want to provide the source code, only the compiled version. It's something like selling a car without permitting the buyer to lift the hood. However, this too was a serendipitous meeting for me personally because one of the Bell Labs attendees was one Philip (Phil) Balaban, a PhD engineer who was impressed with the work. It also happens that around that time Phil was mentoring a young Indian educator who was on sabbatical from the University of Kansas, by the name of K. Sam Shanmugan (Sam), with whom I also developed a professional collaboration.

In the seventies and eighties and even part of the nineties my company[63] was generous in allowing me to attend professional conferences. In many of those conferences I presented papers, but it was an opportunity to mingle with engineers and scientists from all over the country and the world. In those conferences I kept running into Phil and Sam, and we slowly became professional friends. I also was introduced early on to some of the luminaries in the field. Eventually these connections pulled me into the world of scholarly technical publications. The main publication in the communications field was (is) the IEEE Transactions on Communication. I began to be solicited to review papers submitted to this journal, and eventually I was talked into becoming one of the editors of the journal for the specific area of "computer-aided design and analysis," a position that I held for about three years. It was a lot of additional work and responsibility but I felt it would be good for me professionally.

In 1987 I was invited to present a paper at a workshop in Sedona, Arizona. Phil and Sam were there also, and it was during that workshop that the three of us agreed to write a book together on simulation of communication systems. At that time, to my knowledge, there had not yet been any book-length text on the subject. It was an all-consuming endeavor. For the next five years or so, I sat at the kitchen table researching and writing in the evening, but not until after I had read stories to my boys while they had apple slices or milk and cookies before going to bed. We read all kinds of stories, but those that stand out in my mind were by Isaac Bashevis Singer, whom I mentioned earlier. Many of his stories included zany characters that could be appreciated by a child as well as an adult. And I must mention one more book, discovered by Joan: *When Hitler Stole the Pink Rabbit*, by Judith Kerr. Although I always hesitated to talk to my boys about the Holocaust, this book, intended for children, does a masterful job of imparting the tension and danger without being too frightening.

The simulation book we were writing was published in 1992. As most everyone is aware, technology marches on and in the year 2000, we published a second edition, 907 pages of hard labor. The citations are given in Appendix 2.

By that time my distrust of fate had mostly disappeared. With a house and two children out of college, I had fulfilled my major obligations. I felt financially free and I was ready to retire, which I did on June 30, 2000, without giving much thought about how I would fill in the time. However, that question was quickly answered, at least in part, when my manager asked if I wanted to consult part-time. This was just what the doctor (engineer) ordered.

X

HOW I MET MY CHILDREN'S MOTHER

COOKING UP A LIFE

In May of 1962, Steve Wolfgang had graduated from Penn and was about to enter medical school, and we had moved to 3514 Market Street. Little by little I began to know Steve's family. Philadelphia at that time was, or at least felt, very provincial, especially coming from New York. We needed to breathe in the New York air, so once a month or every other month we took a road trip. New York wasn't that far, and, as I alluded to earlier, I enjoyed driving. We would always go to Steve's parents' house in Forest Hills. I'm not sure if Steve's sister, Joan, was still living there when Steve and I were taking those trips, because she would have been at the University of Wisconsin–Madison, beginning sometime in the summer or fall of 1962. She would come home on holidays, but at those times I would visit my brother or my sister.

For six or seven years I had known Joan's mother, Paula, and her father, Ernst, and I had become very fond of and comfortable with them, not only because they were wonderful individuals, but I felt a kinship with their European origins. Joan's mother used to say, "I only have sons, no sons-in-law; I only have daughters, no daughters-in-law." She was very generous with her affection and her acceptance, as was Ernst, who was much less demonstrative. I was fortunate that Paula and Ernst "adopted" me without reservation. Ernst had the grace of a nineteenth century gentleman: intelligent, well-read, always polite, with a wry sense of humor that his wife sometimes derided as *frankfurter witz*, an uncomplimentary allusion to the wit of people from Frankfurt. Ernst was a superb speech writer and speaker. In 1990 he gave a speech at Kenny's bar mitzvah honoring my parents, which left no dry eyes in the congregation.

But the kinship had deeper roots because both Ernst's and Paula's lives were also affected by the rise of the Nazis. Ernst was born in Frankfurt, Germany, on September 23, 1903. I indicated earlier that Ernst was a meticulous note-taker, and between the late 1980s and early 1990s he wrote an unpublished biography, relating information about his own family as well as Paula's. A remarkable fact in this biography is that his grandfather was born in 1800, the beginning of Napoleonic times. Imagine, just two generations in over a century! This unusual succession occurred because both his grandfather and father had long lives, married late and consequently had children late. But what is perhaps even more interesting is that his grandfather was the first in Ernst's line to have a last name.[64] But, what's in a name? History, of course, of a people, not the dry history of dates and battles. My brother and I, and my son Kenny, always wondered where our own name came from and what meaning might it have. Briefly, Jeruchim means "he who receives compassion." An explanation appears in the endnotes.

Ernst had earned a doctorate in economics at the University of Frankfurt, and worked in a bank owned by Jews as their bond specialist. When the Nazis came along, unlike most other German Jews who thought "that would pass," Ernst thought otherwise. In 1933, along with several other members of the bank, he departed for Palestine. His father was ill and could not travel, so his mother stayed behind to care for him. While Ernst's father died before the Nazis could murder him, his mother died in the Theresienstadt concentration camp. In Palestine, Ernst's foresight surfaced again. After he was forced to carry a rifle and take guard duty against possible Arab attacks, he said "there will never be peace in Palestine." His words were prophetic. So, in 1937, the same year I was born, he immigrated to the USA.

Joan's mother, Paula, was born on November 11, 1911, in Kolomea, a city whose country shifted with the never-ending wars in Europe. It was part of the Austro-Hungarian Empire, then Poland, later annexed by Russia after WWII, and now in Ukraine. When WWI erupted, the Russians quickly occupied Galicia, the province where Paula lived, and she and her family fled to Vienna. Paula was then only about three or four years old. She preferred to say she was Austrian, and considered Vienna her hometown and German her native language as she had never learned Polish. Paula's move to Vienna was beneficial to me decades later. In Vienna, she had absorbed the techniques of the justly famous Viennese pastries, which I love. When Steve and I visited in New York, and later Joan and I, she would always have a batch of Linzer cookies, sometimes a flourless torte or a Sachertorte waiting. I had difficulty controlling myself with these goodies.

Theodor Herzl, the driving force behind a movement to create a Jewish homeland in Palestine, was then a resident of Vienna and his presence and stature were influential. As a young woman, not even out of her teens, Paula joined a youth Zionist organization. There she met Hans Altschul, the leader of the group, five years older than she, with whom she fell in love. The same happened to him as well and they decided to marry and follow the ideals of Zionism by immigrating to Palestine, in spite of Paula's parents' opposition. Paula had a bit of a daring spirit, logic notwithstanding, and they settled in a kibbutz. This was in 1929: Paula was eighteen years old. But Paula and Hans became disillusioned with the kibbutz and moved to Tel Aviv. Tragically, three years later Hans developed cancer and died.

Curiously, Ernst does not describe how he met Paula in Tel Aviv, but Paula described herself as a woman of the Earth, a pioneer, and Ernst as a capitalist, a union unlikely to be consummated. Nevertheless, it was. After overcoming several bureaucratic obstacles, Paula was able to come to the States and married Ernst in New York on August 11, 1939. Their union produced a son, Steven, and a daughter, Joan, who was born on the same day as her father, but exactly forty-two years later. It must have been Ernst's best birthday gift, but as a young girl, Joan wasn't so pleased that she had to share her birthday!

If those events hadn't happened, Joan's and my life would have been different. Like DNA, history's twists and turns propagate through the ages.

The spark between Joan and me ignited during one particular visit to New York which coincided with Joan's visit to her parents. It may have been just after she had graduated with a BA in English from the University of Wisconsin (1966). She was taking a break before beginning a special program to obtain her master's degree in English literature as well as doing a student teaching assignment to complete a teaching certification.

The last time I had seen her, she was "just" a girl, but now she had grown into a young woman, and I felt an immediate attraction. During the evening we arrived, or possibly the next one, Steve went out, and Joan and I stayed behind. We stayed up for much of the evening and into the night in her parents' living room, talking and doing other things until her mother came down the stairs to ask, wasn't it time to go to bed?

It's of course trite to say that a spark can light a fire, but the flame goes out unless more fuel is put on it. The fuel for Joan and me was frequent telephone conversations. Long distance calls were expensive, actually quite usurious, and because I was working and could afford it, I almost always initiated them. We also communicated by mail, *real* mail, but Joan was more assiduous about it. At some point we agreed to meet in Chicago, which isn't all that far from Madison. We met and spent a weekend together. Subsequently, maybe a few months later, I flew to Madison and again spent the weekend with Joan.

Over the telephone, we would say we missed each other, but otherwise our conversations generally consisted of "chit-chat" about everyday goings-on. We both knew if we said too much it might have been awkward and too emotional. Instead, we revealed ourselves in our correspondence. We wrote a lot, not as voluminously as Elizabeth Barrett and Robert Browning, but over a period of about two years we exchanged dozens of letters. Here is a very small sample, written after our meeting in Chicago:

October 27, 1967

Dear Joan,

After we separated, I didn't quite know what to do with myself. I felt such a gulf of emptiness that my immediate reaction was to question if our meeting had actually happened. It's difficult to believe that the absence of one person can cause such a vacuum. It's funny how speechless we were when we were leaving, or when we had just arrived. It's as if, in both cases the emotional impact of the situation made words extraneous.

Back at my desk, now, I'm trying not to be too analytical, but it's hard: My emotions are involved. Without a tangible trace of you, the whole episode seems like a dream. You know I was afraid at the beginning, but little-by-little you "broke me down," so to speak. I was primed and ready to love and be open, and then you were gone. I know that I am difficult to really get to know, but I'm glad that you've pierced a little deeper into my "dark recesses." It will be easier from now on.

Excerpt from Joan's letter: November 15, 1967

Dear Pumpkin,

I have just reread your letter. I was very touched when I received it. When I read the part that said: "I don't think I could ever love you as much if you didn't understand me so well," I felt an instant pang of emotionalism. It is this that I tried to describe to you in my last letter. Without relying on triteness I will attempt again to explain to you what this is like. Perhaps it might be helpful if I told you the way the romantics felt during artistic creation, as if I were slowly soaring away from the mundane world. Also there is the blissful happiness. Yet what predominates is the intensity which seems to bubble inside me until I think it might explode. And the love reaches out to you; it is centered on the realization of you even though you are far away, even though it is a feeling within myself...

◇◇

It was clearer to Joan than to me that no future would develop unless we lived in the same town and we made a joint decision to see only each other and see how the relationship would develop. So, after graduating with her master's degree in the spring of 1968, Joan moved to Philadelphia. At first, she rented an apartment in a student neighborhood, and we began our real courtship, though I should remind the reader of Shakespeare's line, "the course of true love never did run smooth."

It was a bit stormy, at least at the beginning. Joan is an intense person, and I resisted being pulled in for some time. I don't remember just how much of my story I had told her but she was insightful about my resistance, a skill she has put to use professionally as a psychologist. Much of my earlier life had been beset by a sense of "abandonment," which of course had not been intentional, but a child does not make such distinctions. So, I was wary of forming close relationships lest they were taken from me. But, by and by, I came to trust Joan. It's difficult to pinpoint when that trust came about, but she was steadfast, in spite of all my unconscious attempts to distance myself. After about five months we decided to get engaged and set a date for a wedding.

On August 3, 1969, in the afternoon, we were married in my brother's house in Pomona, New York. We were not religious (and still are not), nor were Simon and Cécile, nor Joan's parents. Nevertheless, we had a Jewish ceremony. Someone had found a rabbi willing to perform it, and Marc Schwartz played Mendelssohn's "Wedding March" on the piano as Joan walked into the living room where family and the very closest friends had gathered. Joan looked radiant, although she said she was very nervous, but probably not half as nervous as I was, though I tried hard not to show it.

Paula, Joan's mother, arranged the reception at The Motel on the Mountain in Suffern, New York, where we had a re-creation of the wedding ceremony, officiated by Michael Barenbaum, the relatively new husband of Joan's beloved cousin, Hannah. Michael had just graduated as a rabbi from the Hebrew Union College in Cincinnati. My brother's daughters, Vivian and Linda, were the flower girls.

Paula, who was a good cook, an excellent baker, and a wonderful hostess designed the menu: fresh fruit cup supreme; quiche aux fruits de mer; prime rib, spinach, sauce Chef Karl; tomates grillées aux champignons; salad verdi; crème glacée, walnut torte aux fraises. There was a band and lots of dancing until it was time to depart for our honeymoon.

At that time, it was fashionable to travel to Europe, although still not very common. But I really wanted to show Joan something of France. As our minds had been filled with wedding planning, and we were too inexperienced to plan such a trip on our own, we booked with a tour company. Joan's brother (Steve) and his wife (Terry) drove us to Kennedy Airport where we took off for London, the first stop on our tour. London was followed by Rome, Florence, and Venice in Italy; next stops were Salzburg, Austria; Lucerne, Switzerland; and then Paris. As sacrilegious as it may sound, I recall the food in Italy to have been better than in France. Upon our return we settled down to an apartment in Wayne, Pennsylvania, which was not too far from where I worked in King of Prussia, and Joan started a job as an English teacher at a suburban school district.

For the next four years we enjoyed life without any sense of burden or obligations. Joan studied Julia Child's *The Art of French Cooking*, practically cover to cover. Of course, Joan was aware of my culinary tendencies and wanted to cater to them. I should say that had the war not happened I might not have developed that French palate.

As I alluded to earlier, my sister says that my mother's home cooking was Polish-Jewish; chicken soup, potato soup, leek and potato soup, borscht, and occasionally gefilte fish made from scratch. The only French influence was salad, flavored as it should be with oil and vinegar. I wonder if my love of salad is an unconscious remnant of that time. As I remarked earlier, my acquaintance with French cooking developed initially during my stay with the Lecleres and reinforced later on by Madame Goldberg.

Joan could have starred in the 2009 film *Julie and Julia*, about a young woman who cooked every recipe in Julia Child's famous tome. I assisted in many of the recipes, which served me well in further understanding the principles and techniques of French cooking. We gave many dinner parties to test out Julia's recipes. During these years, and for many years thereafter, we didn't particularly celebrate holidays of any sort, religious or secular, except for one—Thanksgiving. It happens that on the occasion of Thanksgiving, 1955, my sister-in-law Cécile received a turkey from her boss at a little company she was working for. At that time, I think we were more or less oblivious of that holiday, but after some reflection, we (Simon, Alice, and I) adopted it as the most meaningful celebration for us.

Around the table, at some point during the meal, each of us told everyone else what we were thankful for. We were thankful for the bounty that America had allowed us to receive, although we worked for it. Implicitly, we were thankful for the "greatest generation" to have liberated Europe, something which was still fresh in our psyches, but we didn't talk about our parents. For the next thirty years or so, we rotated the venue of the feast, Simon, Alice, and me, although Joan and I didn't actually host until we were married. My brother used his artistic talent and sense of humor to create a new menu card each year. Following is the first one.

Once our children came along, we observed other holidays, as our interactions with their schools and their friends opened us to other celebrations, and we also started to "observe" in a secular way the traditional Jewish holidays. Joan and I did not want to have our children's *tabula rasa* filled with "isms" or other cultures' mores and practices. So, we thought it appropriate to introduce them to Judaism. We later joined a synagogue, but we were okay to let the future take them where they wanted to go. Many Jewish households follow a biblical injunction in Deuteronomy "... thou shall write them upon the door-posts of thy house..." Here, "them" refers to God's laws. The implementation of this command is a *mezuzah*, a small rectangular or semi-cylindrical vessel holding a parchment inscribed with specific Hebrew verses from the Torah. Although not religious, Joan had been inclined to attach one on the side of the front door. I was unable to agree. This is where the rational and irrational collide. I could not shake the residue of the Jewish registration edict I mentioned earlier, which allowed the French police (under orders from the Nazis) to know exactly where Jews could be collected. I know this is America, but we also know too well how quickly things can change.

Joan and Michel shortly after their wedding day

We took our time having children, because we liked our lives as a couple. Our first child, Claude (my middle name[65]) was born on January 30, 1974. It will not be news to any parent how their lives were transformed after their first child came along. There is something deeply fundamental to humanness about children and the instant bond from the parents' side that overtakes prior doubts.

Almost immediately after Claude's birth, Joan started writing a chronicle about his development, following in her father's footsteps. From the moment his children were born Joan's father had kept detailed records of their development well into their adulthood. He called these record his "chronic" which term we always used to chuckle about, not recognizing that this is the German word for chronicle. For several of the weeks following Claude's birth Joan kept nudging me to write something as well. Finally, I succumbed and this is what I wrote while my memory of the event was still crystal clear:

◇◇

February 25, 1974

Joan is making me write a small section of this journal because she feels it will somehow be enriched for having my hand in it. Though I didn't see the logic of it, I acquiesce. Actually, I perhaps got a clearer view—or at least a different and probably more objective perspective—of the whole process. On Tuesday night, January 29, we went to bed about 11 p.m. The house was full of the odor of cinnamon, Joan having just baked four loaves of coffee cake, recipe from James Beard. This was actually the end of a productive day for Joan since she had also, earlier in the day, gone to the Y and swam a dozen laps in the big pool. Is the theory of a spurt of energy before labor correct, or was it a coincidence? Anyway, at about half-past midnight Joan rouses me and says she's leaking. We ask ourselves is this the breaking of the "bag of water" which occurs not infrequently. The leaking, however, is a mere trickle of droplets, nothing like the inundation expected under the hypothesis. The trickle was tinged with blood, however, which worried us. I called Terry and explained the situation. She said not to worry, as leaking was not uncommon days, even a week, before delivery, due to increasing distention of the cervix. We tried to go back to sleep, somewhat, but not completely reassured. Joan could not sleep at all. She sat on the floor in yoga position and read a novel of light fiction by the light of a small lamp so as not to disturb me. I slept fitfully and not well. At about 6 a.m. we decided to call Joan's OB/ GYN, Doctor Chasteney. He was on vacation, as we knew. His answering service took our message. Half an hour later, Dr. Kaighn Smith, who was taking over for Chasteney, called back and Joan explained the circumstances. He told Joan that she was just "flirting with labor," and to call back when the contractions were regular and five minutes apart. Joan said what if they don't get regular? He said, then, come in if we want at 1:30 p.m. and he would look into it, so to speak, and see what's going on. At about 7:30 Steve called to see what was happening. Terry offered to come over and help Joan pass the time. She came at ten. I took the opportunity to go to the office as I had a lot of things to do. I came back at noon, as Terry had to go home. Even though Terry was convinced it was false labor, Joan was less sure of it and didn't want to be alone. Joan timed her contractions which were irregular in spacing as well as intensity. Finally, we decided to take the OB up on his offer and go in to have Joan examined. We arrived at Lankenau at 1:30 p.m., January 30, and went to Smith's office. About ten minutes after she went in, he came out and said "she's 3 cm dilated, you're going to have a baby this afternoon." This was probably only slightly less of a shock to me than to the receptionist who, upon our entrance, had originally asked Joan if she were pregnant! We then proceeded to Maternity, after losing our way a couple of times, and Joan checked into the baby factory.[66] *I then went down, got the suitcase, which we had had the vision to pack, and went to Admissions to tell them Joan had come in to deliver. Meanwhile Joan was being prepped by a very sweet but apparently forgetful nurse who lost Joan's underwear.*

While this was going on, also, I went up to the fifth floor and changed into scrubs. Joan was brought into the labor room where the fetal heart monitors were installed and a sugar-water IV was inserted. I was admitted into the labor room, and then the fun started. I sat on a stool near the bed so I could see the heart rate meter and the chart recording in analog fashion Joan's contractions. In the beginning the contractions weren't too bad and Joan got by them quite well with "normal complete breathing." Between contractions she wasn't too social but never got downright mean. All this time the OB nurse came in and out, checking Joan's blood pressure and various other things. A couple of times an alarm buzzer rang, which brought the nurse in—the IV was somehow not working and she fixed it. The place was well-run with up-to-date equipment. As time passed the contractions became more severe and now Joan began to ask me specifically to coach her. There were some complications. From the beginning, Dr. Apostolides, who was taking over the evening duty for Chasteney, didn't quite like the way things were developing. To begin with, the baby hadn't descended. So, he ordered an injection (oxytocin) to stimulate the contractions so as to expel the baby downward. From the way things were going, Dr. A began to suspect that the baby was in a breach position. To confirm his suspicions, he ordered X-rays to be taken. So, Joan was put on a rolling stretcher, notwithstanding her complaints at being moved, and taken down two floors to the X-ray department. The X-rays indeed confirmed that Claude was in a breach position, in fact so-called frank breach, even though a week earlier Dr. Chasteney had stated that he was in the proper position. At this point, Dr. A told me that the delivery would involve an obstetrical procedure (turning the baby) and that, therefore, I would not be permitted in the delivery room during the actual delivery but I would be called in as soon as Claude was delivered. Another complication was Joan's blood pressure—it was uncomfortably high. If left unchecked it could have induced toxemia, so Joan was given injections of magnesium sulphate to mitigate it. Finally, the expulsion stage arrived. When the contractions came, I, together with Dr. A or the nurse, held up Joan's head and raised her legs while she pushed. She was very tired but with verbal encouragement she pushed mightily and valiantly. Finally, Dr. A said the time had come. Joan was put on a stretcher and wheeled to the delivery room. I went to a side room to wait and whiled away the time by taking pictures of myself looking in the mirror and reading Newsweek. I did not time it but it seemed only about ten minutes before the nurse came in and said "okay Papa, you can come in now." I was very relieved that Joan and the baby were fine.

I was surprised, but pleased, that we had a son. For some reason everyone had predicted a girl. I went into the delivery room and sat near Joan's head. The "crew" was busying itself delivering the afterbirth, while Dr. A and the nurse tended to Claude, cutting the umbilical cord and cleaning him up. I had the camera and from my somewhat limited vantage point took a few pictures. Finally, they weighed and measured Claude, took his footprint, put a name tag on him, and took him to the nursery. Joan and I were left by ourselves.

*I congratulated her and vice versa. I don't remember exactly what
we talked about, but mostly I praised her for her performance. She
was too tired to talk. Finally, Joan's room was prepared, she was
brought to it, and I left. I stopped at Steve and Terry's house where
Terry made me dinner. I was hungry. I called Joan's parents and
Grandma went bananas. I then went home, called Simon and
Alice, went to bed and slept the sleep of the just.*

◇◇

As I said, a child transforms a household. At that time, it was still
unusual for newly minted mothers to work, so Joan quit her teaching
job, which was a great sacrifice. She is not domestically oriented in the
"traditional" way, but she did the dutiful things with Claude and she
greatly enjoyed being with him at playdates and the rest of the typical
activities.

Joan believed that a child should have a sibling, and after some
time, the seed was planted, emerging in another boy—Kenneth Alan
W. (Kenny), born June 2nd, 1977. The "W" is simply an initial to
remember his grandfather Wolf (my father), and his other grandfather
(by his last name) Wolfgang. Here, as with Claude, I recorded the late
stages of pregnancy, up to the day of birth.

◇◇

June 22, 1977

*As Joan has written elsewhere, the two weeks or so before Kenneth's
arrival were somewhat of a strain. Aside from the baby's "lateness,"
not the least frustrating aspect was the fact that Joan's Braxton Hicks*

contractions seemed to occur predominantly at night, which meant that our sleep for those two weeks was constantly interrupted; Joan's for obvious reasons and mine because I was unconsciously prepared for instant action, and every time Joan stirred, I awakened. So, I was hoping that when Kenny decided to come, he would do so in the morning, after I had had some measure of rest. Need I say it didn't happen that way? At about 7 p.m. on June 1, Joan had some contractions and we decided to time them, possibly out of wishful thinking since similar contractions had occurred countless times. We had done some timing on a couple of previous occasions, obviously to no avail. At any rate, by 11 p.m. the contractions seemed regular enough to cause us to call Dr. Chasteney, our obstetrician. He wasn't on call that night but his associate Dr. Harrer, who was, called us back shortly. Upon hearing the symptoms, he advised us to come to the hospital. We called Steve and Terry and arrived at their house at about midnight. Claude awakened on the trip but did not ask a single question. We are convinced he knew what was happening, with that sixth sense children have, and with the same sense that tells them a serious situation is at hand, he behaved in exemplary fashion. No tears, no whining, no fussing. I carried him into the Wolfgangs' guest bed, told him I had to take Mommy to the hospital, and that he was loved in this house and would be cared for as in his own. Not a peep. We stayed in the outer room for perhaps half an hour to make certain there would be no eruption, and there wasn't. (Terry later told me that he was very good, woke up once and cried from disorientation, but went back to sleep when she comforted him.) We got to Lankenau at about 1 a.m. and I brought Joan in through the emergency entrance because one can drive right up to the door. She was taken up and I went back to park the car. I checked in with Admissions and then brought Joan's suitcase upstairs. After a short wait in the "Fathers' Room" (where "conventional" daddies pace the floor to await the news), I was called in and given a set of "whites," which I changed into. I thus took a picture of myself in the mirror, for the record, which the interested reader may see elsewhere in this book.[67] Joan in the meantime had been "prepped" and was in the labor room, into which I was ushered. What ensued was one of the longest nights I've had. I was already tired and I had a hard time staying awake. I was sitting in a chair next to Joan's bed and dozed off several times. Once, Joan admonished me to stay awake "because I need you."

Fortunately, she needed my presence more than my coaching. She was a real trooper. She breathed right through her contractions, literally, like an old pro. Actually, she slept through perhaps half of them, due probably to the medication and her fatigue. I tried to keep myself awake by looking at the monitors—the uterine contraction graph and the digital display of the fetal heartbeat. There were welcome distractions when the nurse would come in to check on things. The night passed. Sometime in the early morning the resident in attendance gave Joan her epidural. Dr. Harrer came in at about 7 a.m. and coaxed Joan into pushing, most of which was supervised by the nurse, with my assistance. At about 7:30 I noticed the fetal heart rate was dropping. Before I could ask about it, we were informed that Joan was now going to the delivery room. (It turns out that the umbilical cord was wrapped around Kenny's head, and Dr. Harrer decided to precipitate matters rather than let the baby come down on his own devices, which would have taken perhaps another hour.) Inside the delivery room, Joan was transferred to a table and I sat near her head. The attending staff was serious about its work, but there was an air of lightness, almost casual. Of course, they'd done it hundreds of times. Dr. Harrer used an instrument

best described as a shoehorn with a long handle, which he seemed
to use (from my angle) to pry Kenny out, assisted by his mother,
who was pushing, who was assisted by the nurse, who was pushing
down on Joan. As he worked, Dr. Harrer was calmly teaching and
explaining to the resident. As the baby was nearing the exit sign,
Dr. Harrer invited me to come around and look, I went behind him,
like an umpire behind a catcher. Seeing the baby's head crown was
an incredible sight. It was hard to believe that I was actually seeing
it happen. Fortunately, I was not so thunderstruck into inaction.
I clicked away with my camera (thereby gaining approbation from
Dr. Harrer for my cool professionalism!) as Kenny came out (at
7:49 a.m.), and subsequently as the action unfolded (finding time
to reload), resulting in some beautiful pictures. It was thrilling to
be there and made me feel very close to Joan and the baby. After a
while, Joan was wheeled to the recovery room where I stayed with
her for an hour or so and then I left to pick up Claude.

I suspect my own experience led me to feel very strongly that
I should be present as much as possible in my children's lives, which is
one reason I chose a career track that would not require constant traveling, as I related earlier. Joan gives me credit for being ahead of my time,
being a hands-on father and sharing the parenting responsibilities.

However, there is one thing I wish to add here connected to
our children. Many, if not most, Holocaust survivors have difficulty
relating their experiences, even to those closest to them. This is a
known phenomenon for anyone who has undergone extreme trauma.
I was the same. When our children were young, I steered away from
the subject, not only because it was personally painful, but also to shield
them from a story that would have been incomprehensible to them. But
it seems, from what I've read, that somehow that experience seems to
exude through our pores, and younger generations "know" something

tragic has happened. An obvious gateway to that "knowledge" is the absence of grandparents. My younger son used to ask me about his grandma and grandpa on my side. He knew his grandparents from his mother's side very well, so where were the other grandparents? I tried to tell him that my mommy and daddy were no longer alive, without details. At one of the few times the subject came up, he declared, at the age of five, "When I grow up, I'll be your daddy." Such is the sensitivity and generosity of small children.

Small children, of course, become bigger children and, as is natural, they are curious and want to know more about who came before them. This happened gradually, in part from my brother and sister, with whom we met on a more or less regular basis at their homes or ours, on holidays or for no particular occasion. Although we did not learn the specific circumstances of my parents' disappearance until our boys were in their twenties, we all understood that they could not be alive. But at different times when Joan and I and the boys were with my siblings and their families, my sister would sit down with Claude or Kenny and tell them stories of my childhood, and about my parents and where we lived. Those memories were inaccessible to me.

When Kenny became thirteen, the traditional age to become bar mitzvah, Kenny led the Friday evening and Saturday morning services and read his portion of the Torah, all in exemplary manner. He declared, after the celebration party, that this had been the best day of his life. Perhaps this was a sign we didn't see then that he would later become very observant. We asked Kenny, what would he like as a gift to celebrate this passage into manhood.[68] Kenny had been keen on seeing where I had lived with my parents. So, we offered him a trip to Paris. Claude, then sixteen, had always indicated an interest to visit Europe, and we offered him a "bonus," which was to go to Amsterdam where he could meet his pal Wilko-Jan Balkema, the son of a Dutch family whose "breadwinner" had been on assignment in the States, and who then lived near us. So, in August 1990, the four of us took a trip to Paris. This trip didn't make as much of a cultural dent on the boys as I had hoped, as the first thing they wanted to do in Paris was to find a McDonald's!

However, I too wanted to see where my family and I had lived before the roundup, as I hadn't ever done so after 1942. The address was 71 rue Colmet Lépinay, in Montreuil. We took the *métro* to the *Croix de Chavaux* station and a short walk to the building, a plain brick structure. I hoped to see the actual apartment. I knocked on the door of the concierge to request entry, explaining that I lived there many years ago, prior to the war. Unfortunately, we were gruffly rebuffed by the territorial concierge. Sensing my disappointment, my boys put their arms around me. All we could do then was drown our disappointment in confections, which we did at a nearby *pâtisserie*.

While in the neighborhood, we visited the primary school my brother had attended. It was not far from my family's former apartment, and my boys and I entered the school. I thought of my brother walking in those hallways, knowing it was perhaps the closest tangible indication that the Jeruchim family had lived and thrived *there*. And the "smell," of polished wood also gave me a bittersweet reminder of my own days in school.

For Joan and me, traveling continued for the next thirty years or so, as I relate in the next chapter. Many people like to travel, to discover the world. For us, though, it was more; it was also discovering the world as our parents knew it.

XI

TEACHING AND TRAVELING THE WORLD

Over many decades, Joan and I went on numerous travels, usually together but sometimes individually, and our lives have been greatly enriched by them. We did not look at these trips simply as "vacation." They were voyages of adventure and discovery about cultures, food, art, customs, and scenery that gave us much pleasure and satisfaction. We consider ourselves "citizens of the world," since we both have European roots. The majority of these trips were occasioned by professional activity on my part, after which Joan would often join me and we would start our exploration. However, without any prior intention, some of those trips unexpectedly triggered echoes of the Holocaust.

In the summer of 1963, I returned to Europe with a friend for my first significant trip as an American. We visited London, Amsterdam, Copenhagen, Rome, Florence, and finally Paris. I had saved Paris for last, as a sort of trip "dessert." Fourteen years after leaving France, I reveled breathing in the French air. There was much of me that was still pulled by "Frenchness." Hearing French spoken all around me gave me a surge of well-being that almost felt like being "home." But, of course, at that time I was unaware of the French complicity in arresting Jews, including my mother and father.

Oddly enough, I did not contact the Leclere family. I don't think it even occurred to me. What kept me from doing so, I can't really articulate, although today I'm still angry at myself for having lost that opportunity. I was too young or immature to recognize how significant that would have been to both of us.

I did, however, contact *Oncle* David and his family, *Tante* Berthe, his wife, and their son, my cousin Raoul. I don't remember much of that visit, except for an afternoon outing with Raoul, visiting art galleries. Around that time, I had begun to be more aware of, and appreciate, art. I was also aware of the rich heritage of art in France. Before I left, I had asked my brother for the names of French artists whose works I should look for. I didn't know much, but I knew what I liked, and I liked abstract art. Thus it was that I bought a limited edition etching by Georges Braque, entitled "Homage à JS Bach," which combines both art and music—I love Bach! We have since seen the original from which the limited edition was made in the MOMA. I suppose that first trip back whetted my appetite for traveling in Europe, for I returned the following year in the summer.

It was some years before travel resumed, and that was for Joan's and my honeymoon in 1969. Although I had been to various European cities in the earlier trips I just mentioned, I hadn't really absorbed much about the different cultures. But it was different on our honeymoon, perhaps because Joan and I had guides. Our three-week trip was an eye opener into the European way of doing things, even for me who was familiar with the French way. We visited all the obligatory sites, but being herded through galleries and museums on shortened visits made us realize that to see and appreciate places required setting our own pace and making our own independent arrangements And this is what we did for the next forty years, except for countries like China, Japan, and Vietnam where we would likely have been lost without guides. Everywhere we went in Europe, we would try to visit landmark synagogues. Most of them had now become inactive, or with a sliver of members. It wasn't because we wanted to pray or join a service—I've indicated this wasn't our leaning. Rather, it was akin to visiting a gravestone, a silent reminder of what was once, not only in that particular place, not just in that particular edifice, but in all of Europe. Without having articulated it to ourselves, we were instinctively paying respect to all who had vanished in mounds of ashes.

It was not too long before I traveled again, but this time for professional reasons. My involvement with regulatory activities led the government to request my services from GE to attend an international regulatory conference on satellite communication in Geneva, the WARC that I mentioned earlier. Naturally, I couldn't just skip work for six weeks, but the government sent a letter to the general manager of the GE Space Division asking for my release. GE was flattered and "released" me to join them (i.e., allowed me to go and paid my salary while gone). This was the beginning of my involvement with the regulatory world which until that time I didn't even know existed. I was duly "accredited" as a member of the US delegation, which meant that, for the duration of the conference, I was technically a diplomat.

As a technical person I was assigned to a committee charged with developing rules to allow satellites in the geostationary orbit to operate without undue interference. The chairman of the group was a Frenchman, which delighted both of us. I had a few occasions to act as a translator for the corresponding technical terms in French or English. The final documents were at that time issued in three "official" languages: English, French, and Spanish. That has now changed to Arabic, Chinese, English, French, Russian, and Spanish.

This process matured me. I hobnobbed with "important" people. I later developed a professional relationship with some of them. Heady stuff! Of course, I was proud. I felt I was in the middle of where the world was going. And while it burnished my budding reputation, I didn't puff my chest. I knew all too well how life can change suddenly.

In Geneva, I loved walking around the lake, stopping at a café or restaurant where I splurged on huge plates of mussels, washed down by a glass of white wine, followed of course by a Swiss pastry. As a quasi-diplomat I had minor privileges, the most important one from my perspective was access to the tax-free United Nations store, which stocked shelves of all the Swiss chocolates. I probably came home with half a suitcase of them. Relative to the instant communication we have today, it was the dark ages. Every so often I would speak to Joan over an amateur radio link set up by one of the men in our delegation. Normal telephone rates would have been exorbitant. Of course, Joan was not happy about such a long absence, six weeks, and she cried when I returned. We never again had such a long separation.

In conjunction with regulatory activities, I returned to Geneva in 1977, 1978, and 1979. That last trip foreshadowed what was to come. It set the rules for broadcasting satellites which now send programs to millions of people whose little antennas dot the surface or roofs of buildings. On an earlier trip to Geneva, in 1972, Joan joined me afterward in Paris, where we visited Oncle David for a few days. I acted as translator. He had not previously met Joan and was enchanted with her. He gave us the master bedroom in his apartment for the visit, and loved to make us "French" toast for breakfast—the real McCoy!

He also gave Joan a beautiful gold necklace that had belonged to his wife. I could have asked my uncle so many questions about my parents. But I didn't, and he didn't bring up the subject either. It was as if we both had a blind spot. The visit was in the summer, and afterward we left for Madrid, then Lisbon, and finally a beach resort in southern Portugal where we met Marc Schwartz (who played the piano at our wedding) and his then-girlfriend, who were touring Europe.

As a "reward" for the work that I had done, I was offered a position in Geneva at the ITU, sponsored by the US government. Presumably such offers were looked upon as a "perk," a partial vacation, and it was to have been temporary. However, Joan and I were thinking of having children at the time, and we felt uncomfortable about moving away from family. So, I asked my colleague Dave Kane if he were interested in the position. He was, so I recommended him. He got the job, remained in Geneva for the next twenty years, and retired from the ITU with a great pension. Every time I went to Geneva on one of the work trips, I would visit Dave. In 1976, Joan joined me: This was also our first experience leaving a child behind, generally an uncomfortable feeling, but this time we were at peace. Claude, then about two years old, stayed with his grandmother, Paula, who "danced" around him, as she liked to say. Over those ten days he became so bonded with her that he cried when we retrieved him after our return.

During the decade roughly between 1980 and 1990, our travels were mostly restricted to vacations with the boys, typically in New England. There were two exceptions. The first was the 1989 trip to France that I described in the beginning and with the boys in 1990.

To close out the decade, I went to Torino for a week in September. This was a pure boondoggle. I chaired an international workshop on simulation, and all I had to do was make some introductory remarks. Meanwhile, for a week, I pampered myself with northern Italian food, which is closer to French cuisine than most Italian regions, like tagliatelle alla bolognese, risotto alla milanese, and agnolotti.

In 1990, another chance encounter led to "serious" traveling for the next fourteen years. In the early seventies, I had begun work in simulation and developed associated software that my management tried to sell to Bell Labs. In a meeting at the Labs, I met a member of the staff, Phil Balaban, and through him a then-young professor on sabbatical there, Sam Shanmugan, both of whom were also doing similar work. Over the decade of the seventies, we kept meeting at various technical conferences and eventually interacted as reviewers and editors for technical journals. One day in 1990, Phil called me and asked if I wanted to join him in co-teaching a three-day seminar in Stockholm. I was flattered but a bit uncomfortable, knowing that Scandinavians are technically sophisticated. However, I was swayed by the generous fee, all expenses included, and so I agreed. This was in September and already Stockholm was practically dark from noon!

One of Phil's colleagues at Bell Labs had started teaching one-week seminars for a young Swedish company called Continuing Education Institute-Europe (CEI-Europe). This company was headed by Dr. Birgit Jacobson, a professor in materials science. In 1980, Dr. Jacobson had returned to Sweden after four years as a senior research associate at Stanford University. She became aware of the notion of "continuing education," relatively common in the States but not so in Europe. She saw an opportunity and founded CEI-Europe, handpicking instructors who were known in their respective disciplines. She created seminars in various technical areas, but in 1990 she did not have any courses in simulation. Phil's colleague at Bell Labs suggested making a proposal to Birgit about offering a seminar on simulation. She accepted, and Phil, Sam, and I rotated in pairs over the next fourteen years. (Appendix 1 lists the location and dates of our courses.) Initially we gave a five-day seminar, which proved too much material to absorb for the "students" who were all professionals, many with master's degrees and a number who had a PhD, some of whom were professors wanting to educate themselves in this then-nascent field.

Birgit liked to create what she called a mini-campus. That is, she would offer courses in different, but related, disciplines at the same venue, which made for a very stimulating environment. The locations were all over Europe, and Joan and I took advantage of these teaching trips for further exploration. Birgit took good care of her instructors. All expenses were paid for, including airfare, plus a generous sharing of the fees that CEI-Europe charged the students. In the evenings she took all her instructors out to dinner in excellent restaurants. Wine flowed and conversation thrived about all sorts of topics.

Except perhaps for the earlier dates, Joan usually joined me at the end of the course. During the course week I would have been much too tired to be good company, as the teaching schedule was strenuous and I needed to review my notes each evening. The daily schedule started at eight o'clock in the morning and concluded at five o'clock in the evening. Of course, there were breaks, which the students complained were too short, and lunch was always served at the site and was generous.

The September 2001 teaching trip to Dublin took place right after 9/11. The course was scheduled to begin on Monday, September 24, but I usually traveled the preceding Friday to have a few days to adjust to the jetlag. Joan was worried about my flight, but this was probably the safest period to fly. Security was blanketing air travel. My flight was almost empty. Joan joined me at the end of that week. We took the opportunity to hire a driver and explore a good deal of southern Ireland, spending the last few days in Dublin. Upon our return, we flew from Dublin to Manchester which was the departing airport to the States. Security was unbelievably tight. Joan had to be escorted to the ladies' room. Agents held our passports until departure. We were wondering what was going on. Then we learned that President Bush had just ordered the first air raids on Afghanistan.

In August of 1996 we spent a week at a Club Med on Paradise Island, the Bahamas. Club Med is a French firm, and its resorts are mostly frequented by Europeans. During that week we made friends with a French couple, Sylvie and Michel Lamarque and an Italian gentleman by the name of Marco, whose last name I don't remember. As it happens, in October 1996 we taught one of our CEI courses in Baveno, Italy, on the shores of *Lago Maggiore*.

On this trip, Joan came with me from the beginning. Since we were already in northern Italy we decided to spend time in Milan after the course. It turns out that Marco lived in Milan, so we contacted him. He invited us to dinner and took us to one of the reportedly most prestigious restaurants in that city, one he said that had been operating for hundreds of years, and generally not known to outsiders.[69] You might miss it if you walked by, but going through the door was entering another world: A subdued hubbub of elegantly dressed ladies and gentlemen, whose posture and appearance bespoke elegance and means.

After a lovely dinner, Marco insisted on paying and handed the waiter his credit card. The waiter's face almost betrayed embarrassment, "I'm sorry, sir, but we do not accept credit cards." The tone implied we didn't take credit cards three hundred years ago, and we still don't. Marco did not have enough cash. We had enough to advance Marco, but he wouldn't hear of it. What transpired next would only happen in movies. Marco handed the waiter his business card and said he would return the next day with the money. And then we calmly walked out.

In February 1999, we taught in Nice, France. After the Bahamas, we had kept in touch with Sylvie Lamarque whose home was in Provence. Sometime after we first met, it might have been a year or more, she came to Philadelphia to attend a professional conference. She was a pediatric dentist and the conference was sponsored by her professional organization. We met with her several times during her stay, took her out to dinner, and to local sights. Before her departure, we informed her that we would be in Nice for my next course, and she invited us to stay with her for a few days following the end of the course. This, we did, and we discovered Provence. I had been used to the relatively flat and bucolic areas surrounding Paris and the flat plains and gentle hills of Normandy, and I was stunned by the ruggedness of the countryside in Provence. After we arrived in *Le Tholonet*, where Sylvie and her husband Michel lived, they kindly chauffeured us around, to Aix-en-Provence, and as far as Marseille, among other places. It was a delightful visit, but we were also unpleasantly surprised by the chilliness which was brought on by the famous wind called *le Mistral*. I had associated Provence with plentiful sunshine, perhaps "fooled" by Van Gogh's colorful paintings of sunflowers, so I didn't expect to be shivering. Nevertheless, it was another discovery for me of a part of France that I hadn't known.

The following year, in October, I was again teaching in Barcelona, and perhaps because of the relative proximity, we decided to venture to Morocco for about four days. We flew from Barcelona to Casablanca, where we were met by our driver, Khalid Nidaazzi, who was recommended to us by our travel agent. Khalid was supposed to be fluent in English, and although he did have more than a rudimentary command, he was actually fluent in French, the language in which we communicated, while I translated for Joan. From Casablanca, we drove to Rabat, the capital, where we stayed overnight. We then toured Rabat and Meknes for one day and then drove to Fez, where we stayed till our departure. We toured the general area around Fez, including some ancient Roman ruins, but nothing much else stands out about this trip, other than the souk that Khalid took us to, trying of course to get us to buy as much as possible from merchants from whom he undoubtedly got a kickback. I must say that during the trip I did not quite feel at ease, no doubt a consequence of the never-ending Israeli-Palestinian conflict which was always lurking in the back of my mind. There had been no threatening situations, but when we finally returned to Madrid, I felt like kissing the ground when we alighted.

At the end of February, beginning of March, 2001, I had an experience for which I need to give a little background. I mentioned that Birgit Jacobson liked to group courses whose subjects were related in the same location within the same week. Thus, whenever we lectured, there was almost always another course given by two French professors, Gérard Maral and Michel Bousquet, who taught a course in satellite technology. They were on the faculty of the *École Nationale Supérieure de l'Aéronautique et de l'Espace*, the prestigious French aerospace engineering school in Toulouse, part of the University of Toulouse. Since the name of the school is a bit of a mouthful it is typically referred to as *SUPAERO*. Gérard and Michel were engaging fellows and we often schmoozed during the breaks, mixing French and English. Somehow in a conversation with Michel, the idea arose of my giving an abbreviated version of our CEI course in one of his graduate classes. I wouldn't have to do any special preparation, just select part of what I had already used in my own course.

So, it was agreed that I would give a mini seminar at SUPAERO, following our normal CEI seminar in Nice. Joan had arrived at the end of that week in Nice and we took the train to Toulouse, where we were put up by Bousquet in an apartment, functional but basic, although we did have to struggle with the heating system. So, for the ensuing four days I lectured to a graduate class about simulation and communication, but only for about two hours or so each morning.

I was initially hesitant because I didn't think my French was sufficiently fluent for the purpose, but Michel laid my fears to rest—he wanted me to lecture in English! He said that he wanted his students to have a working knowledge of English because so much of the current literature was (is) now in that language. It turns out that only a few of the students were at ease in English, so, with their help I went from English to French or vice versa, as the moment required. Somehow, I felt triumphant. I had left France as a penniless refugee, and here I was lecturing in one of their elite schools.

My final teaching trip was in May 2004, in Copenhagen. From there we decided to go east, specifically to Prague and Budapest, and explore the cultures, art, food, and beer (in Prague). We visited several synagogues in Prague, and the Great Synagogue in Budapest, works of art, beautifully restored, yet depressing. I could appreciate their beauty but I could not enjoy it. They are basically museums and, to me, mausoleums, somber reminders of the once-flourishing Jewish communities that lived there and were murdered.

In the spring of 2005, Joan and I took a land tour in Greece. Our itinerary started in Athens, then to Kalambaka, Delphi, Olympia, Kalavrita, Nauplia, Mycenae, Epidaurus, Corinth, all places with remnants of the glorious ancient Greek culture, and then back to Athens. This trip revealed beautiful and rugged landscapes, and the spectacular monasteries perched on top of almost needlelike rock formations. In my humanities class at CCNY decades earlier, I fell in love with ancient Greek civilization. I read Homer and the great philosophers. I had written a paper on the Socratic method. The logical thinking and probing of Socrates tickled my brain and may well have shaped my own way of thinking. Seeing remnants of ancient Greek temples and the Parthenon in particular, I could close my eyes and almost touch life as it was then in the *agora*.

In October 2006, we took our first cruise. We had always been reluctant to do so, having had the impression that cruises were floating excesses of food and drink shared with one's closest three hundred or three thousand friends (as people were wont to say). So, we looked for something a bit more intimate and signed up for a Windstar cruise from Istanbul to Athens. The ship accommodated about 150 passengers and was beautiful to look at, sleek with four sails that were unfurled when wind was present, but otherwise motor powered. We began our trip with a "pre-trip" of three days in Istanbul. We felt completely at ease there and the east/west combination was surprisingly satisfying. The ship, it turns out, was a little too intimate for our taste. We realized after the cruise ended that a ship of that (small) size has little else to offer than sun and sky.

In 2007 we spent an emotional week in Paris. For the first time, we visited *le Mur des Noms*, the wall of names of French victims of the Nazis that I mentioned earlier. The sheer number of etched names, even a small fraction of all the martyrs in Europe has a sense of unreality.

For the last part of this mini-pilgrimage we went to 92 *Boulevard de la Révolution*, the house of the Bonneaus in Vincennes, which long ago had been sold. We were guided there by my brother's friend, Malvine, who lives in Paris. A middle-aged woman answered the doorbell. She was Jeannine Surel, the current owner. After Malvine explained why we were there, Jeannine couldn't have been more sympathetic and hospitable. She invited us in, offered us a drink, and we sat down in her living room to talk. Very soon after, I burst out in tears. The thought that this was the spot where I had last seen my parents overtook me.

On a more prosaic note, we found the quality of the food in Paris wanting. Once upon a time, one could stop spontaneously in the most humble-looking establishment and have a satisfying meal. It happens that our observation was not singular. Sometime after our return, Joan discovered a book that confirmed our observations, *Au Revoir to All That: Food, Wine, and the End of France* (first published in January 2009), by Michael Steinberger, who begins by saying "Twenty-five years ago it was hard to have a bad meal in France..." Our more recent trips, however, seem to indicate a reversal.

In 2008, we broke out of our western mold and went to China. We booked with a tour organized by the Wisconsin Alumni Association, Joan's alma mater. We may have been reluctant previously because of the long trip, but we found a nonstop flight from Dulles Airport to Beijing, a mere fourteen to fifteen hours. China was a discovery, although of course it was only a tiny sample. We stayed at the Hilton Beijing, which shattered any illusion about backwardness in China.

Although it hardly says much otherwise about China, I was surprised and delighted that, at the lavish breakfast buffet, there were croissants that were as good as any I'd had in France. One little episode of our stay in Beijing stands out: At work I had been assigned to tutor a young Chinese-American who had just been starting out, Desong Yu, whose parents still lived in Beijing. Before leaving for this trip, I had of course mentioned it to Desong, and coincidentally he was going to be visiting his parents at the same time we would be there. So, he and his then-fiancée insisted on taking us out to dinner for the best meal we had while in China. Desong also gave us a gift of a memorial coin set about the Olympics, which had just concluded there, a most generous gesture.

After Beijing we went, in succession, to Xian, famous for its terra cotta soldiers, which is a sight worth seeing. We then boarded a boat for several days' ride down the Yangtze, stopping or passing at Chongqing, Fengdu, Badong, Yangtze Gorges, and Yichang. Along the river, we were reminded by what we saw from the boat that a great deal of China is still rural and undeveloped. From Yichang we flew to

Shanghai, where we stayed for a few days. Aside from the smog, the best thing about Shanghai was its very modern museum, which had some lovely pieces of ancient pottery and other crafts, but precious little otherwise. Joan likes to point out that so much of China's patrimony was destroyed during the Cultural Revolution that little of its "bourgeois" heritage remains.

In August 2010, friends convinced us to join them on a cruise. We were initially skeptical because of our earlier experience on the Windstar. However, the description of the cruise line was so appealing that we agreed. The ship we would take was considerably larger than the Windstar but not the mega-size of many cruise lines—its capacity was in the five hundred to six hundred range, and was luxurious, offering several restaurants with sophisticated cuisine. Besides, we liked the itinerary, which was a cruise around the Baltic Sea, and we especially liked the opportunity to visit St. Petersburg. We first stayed in Copenhagen for a couple of days prior to the departure, a city I was quite familiar with, having taught there several times with CEI. While there we ordered three dozen Orrefors wine glasses that we still have, except maybe for a broken one or two!

The ports of call were Visby, a Swedish island that was quaint but otherwise unremarkable; then Tallinn, Estonia, which I don't remember much about, except a distinct sense of dislike of the Russians imparted by the local guide; then the highlight of the cruise, St. Petersburg, Russia. There the ship docked for several days and we had the opportunity to visit palaces and museums of unbelievable splendor. Upon seeing these sites, we would say to each other, no wonder there was a revolution! The most memorable visit was to the Hermitage, a splendid structure in itself but with a world-class collection that must be seen to be believed. Our next stop was Helsinki, Finland, which lasted less than a day. Then the cruise ended in Stockholm, where we spent a couple of uneventful but pleasant days before flying home.

During our trip to China, we had had the option for a side trip to Hong Kong, which we declined because we didn't have the time. But we promised ourselves then that we would do so sometime. That time came in April 2011. We stayed in Hong Kong for a week, which was actually a bit too long. Like mainland China, there was relatively little cultural activity, at least of the kind that appeals to us. Curiously it seemed that very little English was spoken, except in the very developed business center, contrary to our expectation because it had been ruled by the British for quite some time. Probably the best part of that stay was the high-class restaurants which seemed to abound, located atop skyscrapers overlooking the entire peninsula. One of the more memorable and somewhat humorous experiences in Hong Kong has to do with massage. I love massages, and before departing for Hong Kong I had read in a guide book about the availability of massages of different styles being offered there: reflexology, Swedish, and Chinese. The article warned that the latter could verge on the painful and reported signs in massage rooms reading "no screaming allowed." I thought at the time that was intended to be tongue-in-cheek, but I found out the hard way it was meant to be literal. While there, I did want to try a "local" version, and went to an establishment that had been recommended in the guide book—it wasn't kidding about screaming!

Around the end of 2011, friends mentioned a trip to Cuba, taking place early in 2012. We were intrigued but were aware that travel to that island was restricted. We learned, however, that "religiously" oriented groups could get a waiver from the Treasury Department. It was (perhaps still is) one of the quirks of lawmaking. It wasn't the State Department putting obstacles, but the Treasury, ostensibly because

Congress hadn't wanted Cuba to receive any monetary benefits (as in tourism) from American citizens. Religion was exempted with proper documentation. The tour being offered was led by a rabbi and its agenda was bringing relief to the small and beleaguered remnant of the Jewish community. This would be done by making a monetary contribution and bringing along clothing and medicine.

Although we were a bit uncertain, we decided to join this tour because it would be something quite different from any of our previous travels. Indeed it was! We were rewarded with the warmth of the Cuban people. One day, the tour took us to a small Jewish cemetery[70] in Santa Clara, located about 160 miles southeast of Havana. Although the cemetery was somewhat in disrepair, there, totally unexpectedly, was a small Holocaust memorial, bright and clean with some small flowers planted around an engraved cobblestone from the Warsaw ghetto. My mind couldn't get around the fact of this monument, in a land religiously neutered by Castro. But there it was. The rabbi who led the tour recited the Kaddish. Joan had previously told the rabbi about my own story, and he asked me to speak. It was difficult but through tears I gave a small speech, following which all the other tour members came to me with hugs. Somehow this small humble memorial, in such a seemingly unlikely place, affected me as much as any grand monuments I had previously seen.

In the spring of 2015, we again ventured out of our comfort zone. We booked a two-week tour with Smithsonian Journeys to Japan. It was fantastic! We started in Tokyo, a very impressive megalopolis, followed by Kanazawa and Mount Fuji, then Takayama, and finally Kyoto. Our guide Oka was a fountain of information and helpful beyond expectation. Japan was a revelation in several ways, its culture, its art, its cuisine, and its landscapes, with a pervasive sense of structure and esthetic sensibilities. It seems that no structure or landscape is done without careful attention to order and form. If only American cities were as clean!

Our next Asian discovery was Vietnam, in the winter of 2016. Here again, we were very pleasantly surprised. We traveled more or less the entire eastern length of the country, starting in Hanoi, then in succession to Danang, Hue, Can Tho, and Saigon. We first flew to Seoul, Korea, and then to Hanoi via Korean Air and returned from Saigon through Seoul again. The people were very friendly, as though the war never happened. Of course, it had been over for more than forty years, but in the scheme of things that's a very short time. I don't know whether their friendliness is just something "Asian" or whether the monetary incentive was stronger than the resentment. We took a boat excursion on a tributary of the Mekong delta, and then the delta itself, a truly impressive body of water. On the tributary we made a stop at a tropical fruit farm. The vegetation was so dense that we couldn't see each other just a few feet away. This gave us a sense of what it must have been like fighting in the jungle, decades ago.

XII

OUR PARENTS

REST IN PEACE

When Alice, Simon, and I were reminiscing about our parents at the Gathering of Hidden Children in New York in 1991, I had virtually no memory of them. For some years after the war, there were many stories of people reuniting with "lost" relatives who had somehow survived in places distant from their homes. As late as my high school years, as I mentioned earlier, I harbored the fantasy that my parents would miraculously appear, though I kept that to myself for fear of jinxing it, and for fear of disappointment. By the time I entered college, I had pushed such hopes to the back of my mind and stopped myself from further anguish. But I also mentioned that, when Simon, Alice, and I were talking at the Gathering of Hidden Children, we still hadn't known their fates, although the passage of time and the circumstances of the occupation all but assured that they had died somehow, and we didn't even want to articulate how that might have been.

The Nazis' systematic plan to annihilate the Jewish people in Europe was aided and abetted by local militias in different countries who participated in murders and killing squads, often even more enthusiastically than the Germans. In Lithuania it was various paramilitary groups; in Hungary it was the Arrow Cross Party; in

Ukraine it was the local collaborators; in Croatia it was the Ustasha. The staggering toll of murdered Jews was gladly assisted by collaborationist governments and their agencies, which identified Jews within their boundaries, collected them, interned them, and eventually transported them to the death camps. Although less virulent than other countries, even in "enlightened" France the Vichy government was complicit. This was how my parents were murdered.

My mother, Syma (née Szpiro),[71] was born on August 18, 1899 in Garwolin, Poland, a town on the Wilga River in eastern Poland, situated in the southeastern part of the Garwolin plateau, about forty miles southeast of Warsaw. My father, Wolf Samuel, was born on December 24, 1898 in Ostrów Mazowiecka, Poland, a small city roughly sixty miles northeast of Warsaw. It must have been a wonderful birthday present when my brother was born on December 25.

It was through my brother's unrelenting search that we finally learned our parents' fate. In the late nineties, when my brother was writing his own memoir, the question of what happened to our parents would not let him rest. He wrote letters to many organizations looking for answers: Yad Vashem in Israel, the American Gathering of Jewish Holocaust Survivors in New York, the National Federation of Deportation in Paris, the United States Holocaust Museum in Washington, DC, the International Red Cross through the American Red Cross, and the International Tracing Service. None had answers.

Shortly after the war, our Uncle David petitioned the French government for information, and had received only the forms copied below from the Ministry of Veterans and War Victims, which say only that our parents were arrested in August 1942 and were "political deportees" defined as deported, interned, imprisoned, or (forced) worker. And they had not been repatriated to that day, March 29, 1946.

I don't know how hard the French looked, but I suppose due

regard must be given that so soon after the war, things were chaotic and many archives were still to be found. So, that's where things stood until Simon started his quest.

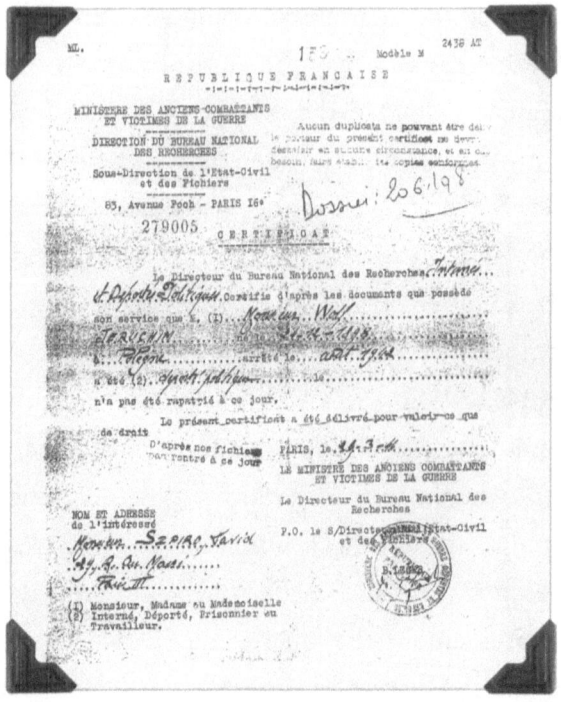

Reproduction of the response from the French Ministry of Veterans and War Victims to my uncle's query about my father's fate

As a last resort, Simon contacted Serge Klarsfeld, a French secular Jew who had made it his mission to document the fate of every Jew deported from France, not all of whom were French citizens; in fact most were foreign residents, as were our parents. This population was targeted initially, but if the war had lasted longer, it is certain that every Jew, French or not, would have met the same fate. In addition to this research, Klarsfeld dedicated his life to hunting Nazis and bringing these killers to justice, most notably the notorious gestapo chief in France, Klaus Barbie. This last piece of information is a paraphrase of a *New York Times* article on Maître (honorific in France for a lawyer)

Klarsfeld, who was born two years before me. He was greatly abetted by his wife Beate, a German, and exposed them both to great danger, vividly pictured in a film called *Nazi Hunter: The Beate Klarsfeld Story* (1986) featuring Farah Fawcett. Mr. Klarsfeld has also been involved in a number of other films and documentaries.

In 1978, Serge Klarsfeld published a monumental volume, *Mémorial de la déportation des Juifs de France*, noting their date of birth, place of birth, last known address, and the number and date of the convoy taking them to Auschwitz, a 1,500-kilometer trip of misery in sealed cattle cars.[72] The magnitude of Klarsfeld's effort is mind-numbing. But, realizing that such an all-encompassing task was bound to have errors and gaps, Klarsfeld spent the next fifteen years revising his tome, as large as a phone book, and published a revised version in 2012.

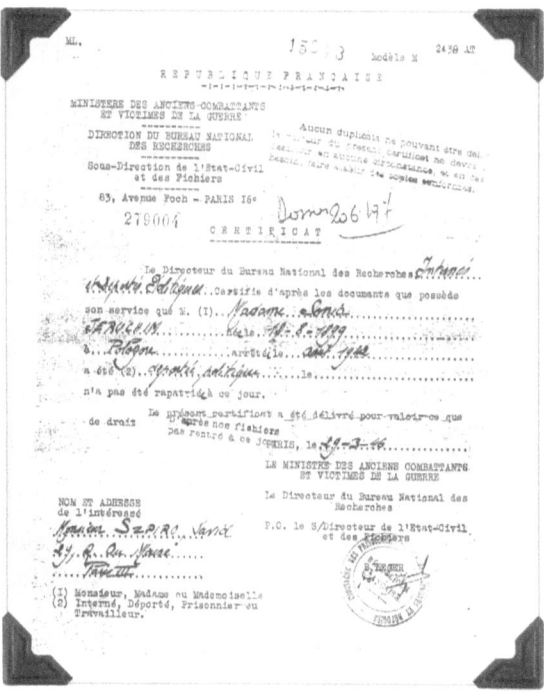

Reproduction of the response from the French Ministry of Veterans and War Victims to my uncle's query about my mother's fate

When Simon initially contacted Klarsfeld, the latter responded that he had located our parents, and that they had been transported on Convoy No. 34 on September 11, 1942. I can understand the anguish of parents whose soldier sons or daughters were missing in action and their desire for the bodies or bones of their children. There is something primitive and deep about knowing what happened to someone close and having something tangible of their being. Of course, in our case the tangible part was impossible. But knowledge was better than uncertainty.

Sometime later, Klarsfeld wrote to Simon with a correction, and with this letter we can put together the final facts about the fate of my parents. After my siblings and I had been secreted out of the Bonneaus' house, either our parents knew, or the Bonneaus told our parents, to try to go to the unoccupied zone, which for a time was safer but not really safe. That part of France was controlled by the Vichy collaborationist government, which operated its own internment camps. It's interesting to note how the French and Germans looked upon that region. The term "unoccupied" is a translation from the German, while the French called it the *zone libre* (free zone), neither term really giving the correct sense of what it was.

The German term is more objectively accurate. There was no significant military presence, hence "unoccupied." But of course, they could have done so anytime they wanted to, and indeed took control in November 1942 when Allied troops landed in North Africa. Till then, the *zone libre* was free only in a certain sense. The government there had jurisdiction only over civil matters, and Jews who sought refuge there were free only if they could avoid arrest. The Vichy régime was openly anti-Semitic. It enacted anti-Jewish laws even before the Nazis might have asked. It operated its own internment camps. They were not extermination camps, although many people died there because of the abject conditions. But once interned, Jews would be sent east to Auschwitz. So, it would be correct to say that Vichy was an accessory to murder.[73] I expand a bit on the Vichy role in the endnotes.

Any trip was a risk. Knowing that Jews would attempt to flee the occupied zone, the French police were very watchful near the line of demarcation between the two zones. Guides were often hired to find a safe path, but some of them delivered their charge to the police or the gestapo and may have collected a bounty.

After my siblings and I had been transported to the relative safety of the Norman countryside in the summer of 1942, it would have been nearly impossible to gain any information about our parents. Then, about six months later, in March 1943, my brother received a visit from Mme Mounier whom I introduced in Chapter 4: She had been the conduit from the OSE to take my siblings to their farms in Normandy. She told Simon that the Bonneaus had received word from our parents that they were imprisoned in Drancy. The Bonneaus' daughter, Madeleine, had gone there to bring them food, and in the process learned from our parents that the guide who was to take them to safety had betrayed them to the border guards.

Wherever and however they were intending to get there, my parents never made it to their destination. They were arrested trying to cross the demarcation line in or near Poitiers (the map that follows shows its location, on the border between the occupied/unoccupied zones). They were then sent to the internment camp at Drancy, near Paris, and on September 11, 1942 they were put on a train, Convoy No. 31, to Auschwitz where they were gassed and burned upon arrival. All this, however, was unknown to us at the time Mme Mounier visited my brother.

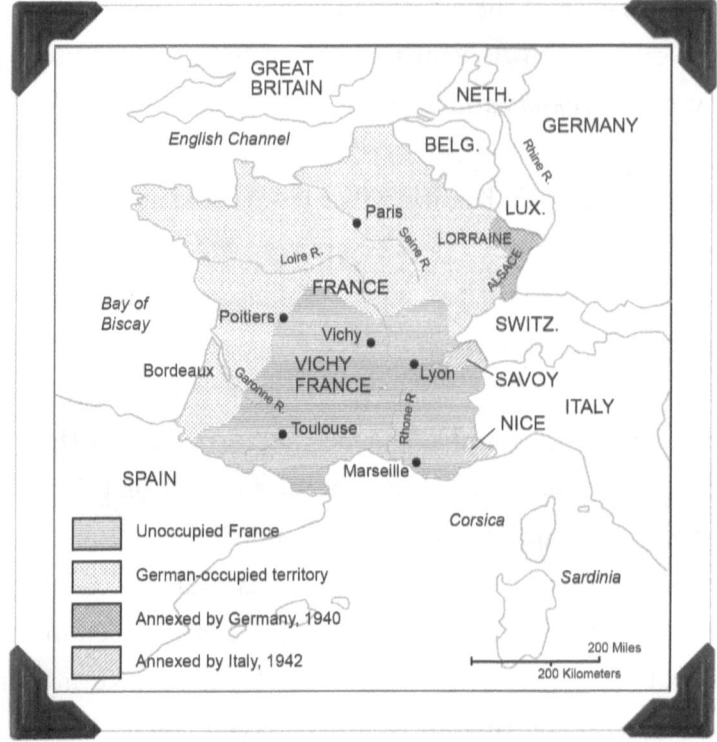

My brother's version of the occupied/unoccupied territories of France.

It took so long to discover these facts, unearthed by Monsieur Klarsfeld, because our parents' last names were misspelled on the deportation index cards (the *"fiches de Drancy"*) in Drancy. I'm told that my parents spoke French with an accent, and in that stressful and nerve-wracking environment they might have stumbled over the words. In any case, they were listed under the name Zernebin, seemingly a long way from Jeruchim. The policeman who was writing this down had first started spelling it correctly, but then crossed it out and entered what he thought he heard.

The photocopy below of the arrest cards shows where they were arrested, Poitiers, their (our) home address, 71 rue Colmet Lépinay, Montreuil, my father's profession, *horloger* (watchmaker), his date of birth, place of birth and his nationality, *Polonais* (Polish). At the bottom of these cards, is written an abbreviation, *dép. 11 Sept. 42*: deported 11 September, 1942.

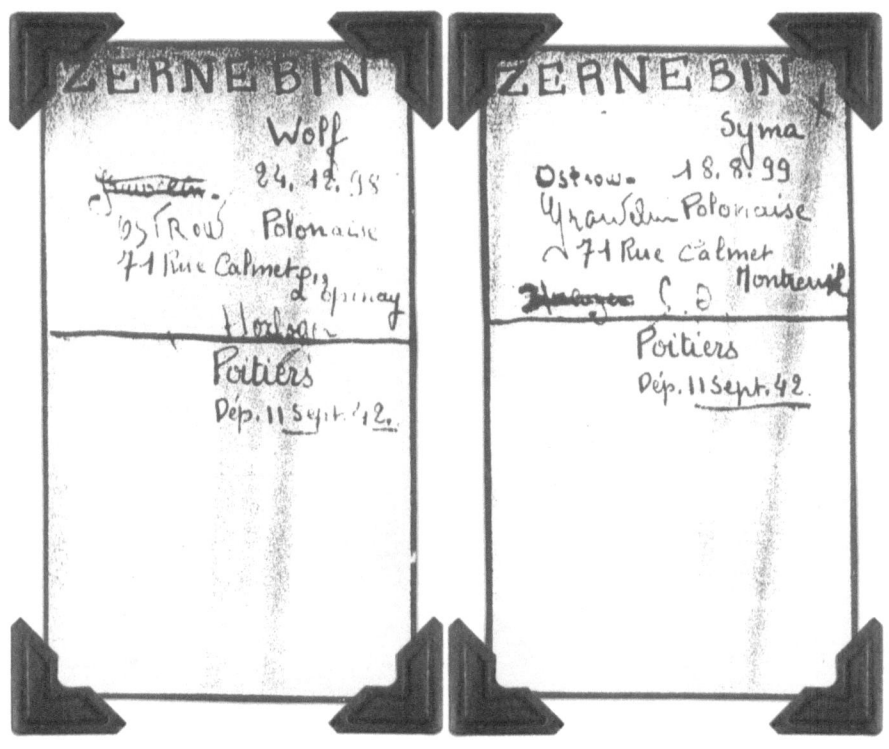

These are the index cards (fiches de Drancy) showing the information collected about my parents before they were sent to Auschwitz

This is the information that set Serge Klarsfeld on the right course. He started to search for data (that Simon gave him) other than the last name—namely, date of birth, place of birth, address, and profession, as related above. And when he found that information in the records it was coupled with Zernebin. That solved the riddle. In early 2015, I contacted the *Mémorial de la Shoah*, the equivalent of the Holocaust Museum in Paris, and asked them to check if our parents' names were properly spelled and located in Klarsfeld's revision: Indeed, it was so, on page 322, they said. I asked for a copy, but they said it was too difficult to physically handle the book. I emailed Klarsfeld himself, and his wife Beate responded, but not more helpfully. Finally, I contacted the Holocaust Museum in Washington, and they were very obliging. Below is a copy of that page. Now we have a documented resting place for our parents.

35	JELINEK	SIMONE	AMAOUA	31	23/07/1911	PARIS	25, r. de Levis	Paris 17
30	JELINEK	BRUNO		41	25/08/1901	VIENNE	Chez M. Chabardes-Pont de Laroque	Lacaune(Tarn)
30	JELINEK	JEANNA	HEDTIC	41	27/08/1901	VIENNE	Chez M. Chabardes-Pont de Laroque	Lacaune(Tarn)
30	JELINEK	ADOLPHE		30	12/11/1911	VIENNE		(Hérault)
30	JELINEK	ERNST		33	12/08/1909	VIENNE		(Hérault)
55	JELLINEK	PAUL		33	17/04/1910	VIENNE	11, r. Paulet	Nîmes(Gard)
69	JELLINEK	FREDERIC		69	31/05/1875	VARSOVIE	135, av. de la Lanterne	Nice(Alpes Maritimes)
70	JELLINEK	FRITZ		38	16/02/1906	VIENNE	19, bd du Moulin	Monaco
72	JELLINEK	ALICE		43	30/06/1900	BADEN	26, av. Saint Augustin	Nice(Alpes Maritimes)
72	JELLINEK	ANNA		38	24/02/1906	VIENNE	26, av. Saint Augustin	Nice(Alpes Maritimes)
72	JELLINEK	MARIE		47	28/05/1897	VIENNE	26, av. Saint Augustin	Nice(Alpes Maritimes)
51	JELLINEK	PAUL		44	30/03/1899	WICA	Camp d'internement	Gurs(Basses Pyrénées)
25	JELLINEK	OTTO		43	17/04/1899	BADEN	Camp d'internement	Les Milles(Bouches du Rhône)
29	JELLINEK	JULIUS		31	17/07/1911	VIENNE	Quartier Mathy	Beaumont de Pertuis(Vaucluse)
29	JELLINEK	RICHARD		49	09/07/1893	VIENNE	Quartier Mathy	Beaumont de Pertuis(Vaucluse)
18	JENSEN	ERICH		28	21/08/1913	VIENNE	Camp d'internement	Gurs(Basses Pyrénées)
48	JERACHAMOVICZ	ABRAHAM		45	20/12/1898	VARSOVIE	39, r. des Graviliers	Paris 03
34	JERACHAMOWICZ	LIBA	ROZENZWAJG	42	04/05/1900	MIEDNYOWICE	39, r. des Graviliers	Paris 03
69	JERAMEC	GEORGES		72	17/04/1872	PARIS	17, r. Louis Blanc	Gien(Loiret)
20	JEREMIAS	HANS		39	02/10/1902	MAYENCE	Camp d'internement	Les Milles(Bouches du Rhône)
22	JEREMIASZ	FRAJDA	CYMMERMAN	46	10/06/1896	NAVARZYN	32, r. de Meaux	Paris 19
32	JEROSCHEWSKY	LEON		63	15/05/1879	NICOLAIEFF	61, r. de Clichy	Paris 09
70	JEROSZCHINSKI	SARAH	MINKOFF	50	18/08/1894	SCHERKAS	9, r. de la Monnaie	Lyon(Rhône)
14	JEROUCHEMSON	ESTHER	GARBOUS	43	25/11/1899	WEGROW	8, r. des Cendriers	Paris 20
16	JEROUCHEMSON	SIMONE		14	08/05/1928	PARIS 20	8, r. des Cendriers	Paris 20
49	JEROWINSKI	SALOMON		75	12/01/1868	TCHERKASS	120, bd de la Chapelle	Paris 18
11	JEROZOLIMSKA	PERLA	ZANGIER	49	15/12/1893	JEDLINSK	31, r. du Renard	Paris 04
51	JEROZOLIMSKI	JOSEPH		47	15/09/1896	LODZ		Marteaux(Corrèze)
10	JEROZOLINSKI	ESTERA	SCHOTTLAND	38	25/07/1903	BRZEZINY	106, av. de Paris	Villejuif(Seine)
22	JEROZOLINSKI	HERSZ		46	01/01/1896	SARDEK	2, r. des Guillemites	Paris 04
50	JEROZOLINSKI	DAVID		44	10/03/1899	RAWA-RUSKA	48, r. de Passy	Paris 16
13	JERSTEIN	JOSEF		48	23/06/1894	EKATERINOSLAV	20, r. Paul Déroulède	Bois Colombes(Seine)
58	JERUCHEMSOHN	SARAH		76	29/10/1867	VARSOVIE	11, r. des Couronnes	Paris 20
58	JERUCHEMSOHN	HERSZ		75	01/05/1868	VARSOVIE	32, r. Ramponneau	Paris 20
57	JERUCHEMSOHN	HINDA		47	15/11/1896	SCHERKAS		Paris
5	JERUCHEMSON	JESZALA		41	06/06/1901	VARSOVIE	57, r. de Lancry	Paris 10
29	JERUCHEMSON	ADOLF		11	03/10/1930	BORGERHOUT	Venant d'Anvers(Belgique)	Camaret/Aigues(Vaucluse)
29	JERUCHEMSON	BLUMA	BEREMBLIT	46	27/03/1896	VARSOVIE	Venant d'Anvers(Belgique)	Camaret/Aigues(Vaucluse)
29	JERUCHEMSON	HELENE		15	15/10/1926	ANVERS	Venant d'Anvers(Belgique)	Camaret/Aigues(Vaucluse)
29	JERUCHEMSON	SZLAMA		40	22/10/1901	KUTNO	Venant d'Anvers(Belgique)	Camaret/Aigues(Vaucluse)
34	JERUCHIM	SAMUEL		44	24/12/1898	OSTROW	71, r. Colmet Lépinay	Montreuil(Seine)-Ligne déma.
34	JERUCHIM	SONIA	SZPIRO	43	18/08/1899	GARWOLIN	71, r. Colmet Lépinay	Montreuil(Seine)-Ligne déma.
5	JERUCHIMOWICZ	BAJNIUZ		30	26/02/1912	VARSOVIE	21, r. Duris	Paris 20
32	JERUENBERGER	WLADIMIR						
52	JERUSALEMI	ROSE	ISRAEL	40	29/05/1902	MARSEILLE	29, r. de la Caisserie	Marseille(Bouches du Rhône)
73	JERUSALINSKI	SAMUEL		39	27/01/1905	BELFORT	19, pl. de la Cité	Rodez(Aveyron)
6	JERUSALMI	SAMI		32	01/10/1909	CONSTANTINOPLE	1, sq. des Partants	Paris 20

Copy of page 322 of Klarsfeld's Mémorial de la Shoah

We also have a physical resting place, as it were, for our parents on *le Mur des Noms* (the Wall of Names) in Paris, at *le Mémorial de la Shoah*, located at 17 Rue Geoffroy l'Asnier, 75004 Paris. Sometime around the year 2000 or 2001, a project was initiated by this organization to erect a wall where the names of every known victim from

France would be inscribed. Simon and I contributed to that project, which was completed in 2003.

Joan and I visited the *Mémorial*, more than once, the first time in 2007 when we took a week's vacation in Paris. The photos below give a perspective of the courtyard and a close-up shows our parents' names. This, at last, will serve as the closest thing possible to a gravestone and a reminder of their lives. It gives me the satisfying sense that my children, grandchildren, great grandchildren, and future generations would be able to visit and pay their respects.

Partial view of the Mur des Noms, Wall of Names

Close up, Mur des Noms, Wall of Names, showing my parents' names

R. . SS
Sicherheits-Dienst
Nachrichten-Uebermittlung

XXVI - 162

Aufgenommen				Befördert				Raum für Eingangsstempel
Tag	Monat	Jahr	Zeit	Tag	Monat	Jahr	Zeit	
von		durch		11 SEPT 1942 durch				
				Verzögerungsvermerk				
Nr. 20491								

Telegramm — Funkspruch — Fernschreiben — Fernspruch

IV J SA 225 a.   Paris, den 11.9.1942
He/Bir

          Dringend, sofort vorlegen !

An das
Reichssicherheitshauptamt, Referat IV B 4.
z.Hd. SS-Obersturmbannführer EICHMANN o.V.i.A.

B e r l i n

An den
Inspekteur der Konzentrationslager

in Oranienburg

An das
Konzentrationslager

A u s c h w i t z

          Am 11.9.1942, 8, 55 Uhr hat Transportzug D 901/25
den Abgangsbahnhof Le Bourget-Drancy in Richtung Auschwitz
mit insgesamt 1000 Juden verlassen.
          Der erfaßte Personenkreis entspricht den gegebenen
Richtlinien.
          Transportführer ist Feldwebel HAVENSTEIN, dem die
namentliche Transportliste in zweifacher Ausfertigung
mitgegeben wurde.
          Mitgegebene Verpflegung wie üblich pro Jude für
14 Tage.

                              I.A. I.V.

                              SS-Untersturmführer

A Nazi letter about transporting Jews—as cold as transporting goods

Among the documents that my brother received from one of the
organizations he contacted is a copy of a page, reproduced above, from

an SS officer to the overseer of the "Final Solution," Adolf Eichmann. In this letter the officer tells Eichmann that one thousand Jews will be transported in Convoy No. 31, on September 11, 1942. Israeli agents abducted Eichmann from Argentina, where he was hiding after the war. The trial in Jerusalem, which inspired the play *The Man in the Glass Booth*, was covered by Hannah Arendt who interviewed Eichmann and wrote the book *Eichmann in Jerusalem: A Report on the Banality of Evil*. This book generated a lot of controversy. Briefly, in it she made a distinction between an individual *doing* evil and *being* evil; that Eichmann was just a functionary doing his job, with no personal animus against Jews. In the case of Eichmann himself, that was hotly contested by critics of the book. But I do believe that in many cases "the banality of evil," is an apt descriptor of those who were cogs in the murderous enterprise who went about their "work" as a nine-to-five job with no more thought about their activities than workers in an abattoir.

I try not to, but every so often I cannot help thinking about my parents' last days; I see them mounting the steps to an overcrowded and stifling railroad car meant for cattle. I see them selected by the SS guards and marched to the gas chamber, and when I try to feel their pain all I feel is rage. When we hear about the murder of a single individual, we are full of condemnation for the perpetrator and sympathy for the victim, but when the murders are in the thousands, or millions, our brains freeze. The human mind cannot absorb a tragedy of such magnitude, and only the numbers register, not the pain and suffering of each individual. I can't put these thoughts more eloquently than Susan Zuccotti, whom I quote below.

Between August 17 and 31, seven trains left Drancy for Auschwitz carrying about one thousand people each. Between one-third and one-half of the passengers in each train were unaccompanied children—the children from the Vél d'Hiv'. We do not know how many of them died alone in the boxcars during the journey. Nor do we know how they were unloaded at Auschwitz. Did they panic at the incomprehensible barking of orders in German? Did they weep when they lost their bundles, their last memories from home, or when they were separated from siblings, friends, or attendants? Did they obey orders to disrobe and wait patiently in front of showers that were the gas chambers? Did they scream when the lights went out, when they died in total darkness? Were they actually asphyxiated, or were they trampled to death in the mad struggle within the chamber to reach the last bit of oxygen near the ceiling? How many survived the gas chamber, trapped in a tiny pocket of oxygen beneath a pile of dead bodies, only to be thrust alive into the crematorium? We do not know. Even asking such questions is unbearable. We do know, however, that none of the deported children from the Vel' d'Hiv' returned to the France that had betrayed them.

My parents' convoy, number 31, had one thousand "passengers"—not one survived.

In June 2001, on the thirteenth, specifically, I happened to notice a short article in *The New York Times*, entitled "U.S. Suit Says French Trains Took Victims to the Nazis." This article made my blood boil. The French trains in question were operated by the French national railroad, SNCF (the abbreviation in French). To quote several parts of the article: "It (the death of the Jews) could not have happened without the S.N.C.F."; "The railroad was paid per head, per kilometer..."; "... the French often outdid the Germans at their own anti-Semitic game."

This article shattered my naïve view of France, which portrays itself as upholding *liberté, égalité, fraternité*. I joined the lawsuit. Ultimately, the lawsuit failed for complicated legal reasons. The SNCF got away with murder, but at least I had fought back. It wasn't until 2011 that the SNCF formally apologized to the Holocaust victims.

In 2012, Joan and I took another vacation to France, this time starting in Strasbourg, then to Nancy and finally to Paris, three or four days in each city. We were walking in the street in Paris when we saw one of those cylindrical billboards common in Paris, but this one announced an exhibition at the *Hôtel de Ville* (City Hall) intriguingly entitled *"C'était des Enfants,"* "They Were Children." The city was observing the seventieth anniversary of the July 1942 rafle and paying homage to the children that had been swept up and murdered.[74] There were photographs and poignant letters, and in the corner of one room there was a monitor (screen) rolling pictures every few seconds. From a distance they looked very familiar. As I approached, lo and behold I recognized these were my brother's wartime drawings when he was hidden in Normandy, and on the wall was a very short biography about my brother. I was stunned. I have no idea how this landed in the Paris City Hall. Somehow the past and the present had melded. I took out my camera and started to take a photograph, whereupon a guard approached and said, "No pictures!" in French, of course. I explained to him that I was not a random tourist, but what we were looking at was my brother's work. He remained unmoved, but our conversation (I was a little loud due to my frustration) started to attract a crowd who had heard much of what I was saying, and surrounded the guard in an unfriendly manner. He then shrugged his shoulders in the typical French way and departed.

That exhibit reminded me again that, if not for my mother, I would have been one of those children on the same convoy as my parents. I repeat: That convoy, number 31, had one thousand "passengers"— not one survived.

XIII

GROWING NEW BRANCHES OF THE FAMILY TREE

IN AMERICA

As I write this, I can't put out of my mind that I should have been dead eighty years ago. What comes to mind is a jumble of thoughts: missing my parents, love-hate for the French, marriage to Joan, and the birth of our sons and grandchildren.

Psychologists tell us that the effects of childhood trauma last a lifetime, and I suppose I can attest to that verity. There are different kinds of trauma: chronic hunger, neglect, beatings, none of which happened to me. But the overnight loss of parents for a five-year-old boy is surely devastating. I venture to say that, unconsciously, I yearned to recreate a family like the one I had originally.

Nevertheless, I must attribute the strength to persevere as one of my parents' genetic gifts. My coping mechanism was to suppress the sense of loss and try to adapt to whatever situation I was in. In this matter, I was fortunate to find emotional support in several ways prior to meeting Joan. There was the Leclère family, who gave me a home and wanted to adopt me. Then, after the war I lived in the *maison d'enfants*, which was in effect an extended family. In the States, I developed a family-like connection with the Schwartz family and then the Goldbergs. And most of all, of course, my brother and my sister were always steady anchors, and in *loco parentis*.

Until my brother's discovery of our parents' fate and the role played by the French police, we had been firm Francophiles. After all, it is the country of my birth, my first language, the forming of my palate. Somehow, I absorbed the lofty principle of *liberté, égalité, fraternité*, even though it was practiced selectively, which I didn't actually understand till much later. But when I learned that French police had arrested my parents, interned them, and sent them to their deaths, my affection for France turned to anger. It did not have the intensity of that against the Nazis, for whom rage simmers in my heart. But perhaps an even stronger feeling was the image-shattering disappointment and sense of betrayal, because it so violated that high-minded triplet. And the reluctance of France to acknowledge and apologize for its responsibility in the Holocaust was another blow to my idea of France, at least until President Jacques Chirac did make a poignant official proclamation, decrying France's role.

But, by and by, my stance against the French role in the war softened, primarily because of the simple fact that there were "good" French people, ethical individuals with a strong sense of rightness, without whom I would not be alive, nor my siblings, nor thousands of other children who were hidden. I don't know if one can say that the good deeds of the few, much too few, absolve the guilt or inaction of the many, but however that may be, I owe my life to the few.

I have said that religion does not speak to me, but there are strong ethical strains in Jewish texts. There is a saying in the Talmud, freely translated, *"He who saves one life saves the world."*[75] For a time I pondered its meaning, and my interpretation is that one moral act can have a lasting ripple effect, that a life saved leads to another life, which leads to still another life, and so on, until a family tree is rebuilt far into the future, with as many branches as there would have been a century, or seventy-five years ago, had they not been chopped off in the war.

My life with Joan allowed my two boys, now young men, to come into being.

Contrary to my own childhood, I wanted theirs to be "uneventful" other than in a rewarding way. Our boys had a more or less typical suburban upbringing: neighborhood elementary school and high school, boy scouts, little league baseball, summer camp, birthday parties, and eventually college. For Claude it was Skidmore from where he graduated with a degree in computer science, which he puts to use in his profession; and for Kenny, Wesleyan and then Georgetown Law, graduating with a JD and an LLM in taxation. Kenny and his wife, Kayla, have three girls and one boy, and Claude and his wife, Olga, have two boys and one girl. I know that my sons' grandparents on my side would have been proud of them and loved them very much (as was the case for Joan's parents) and would have been delighted to be great-grandparents. Some people say they "know" their dear departed ones are "looking down" on them. Skeptic that I am, this time I wish it were true

Kenny, Michel, Claude

And our boys' lives allowed further lives to come into being. With my survival and my siblings' as well, the branch started by our parents can carry on to the future. The family tree in the opening pages shows the branches emanating from my brother, my sister, and me. Not one of the names there would exist if the three of us had not survived.

People are fond of saying that children are the future. Of course, it's true. But the future must be informed by the past, unless they fall into the seemingly eternal trap implied by the saying "Those who cannot remember the past are condemned to repeat it," attributed to the writer/philosopher George Santayana. I hope that this memoir will give these children, my grandchildren, a sense of their past and learn something from it.

The newest leaves on our family tree...

Gloria, Serah, Joseph, Hope

Alina (front), Alan and Eric (back)

NOTES

NAMES AND HISTORY

1. NAMING CONVENTIONS

Earlier, I mentioned that my father-in-law's grandfather had been ordered by the German authorities to take on a family name (surname), which until that time had not been mandated in Germany. His grandfather wanted *Wolf*, but the powers that be told him there were already too many of that name, and so he settled for *Wolfgang*. This renewed my interest in searching for the origin of my last name. My brother and I had an interest in this many years ago, but we did not extend much effort in the research. Now, as I write this memoir, I find this goal more compelling.

One obstacle in such a search is the fact that Jews in their ancient homeland, present-day Israel, did not have surnames. The standard practice was to give a first name to a boy, appended with "son of father's name" (e.g., Saul ben Joseph, "ben" means "son of" in Hebrew); a similar practice held for girls but as "daughter of mother's name" (e.g., Rebecca bat Sarah, "bat" means "daughter of" in Hebrew). In the Bible, one does not find a surname given to the prophets! As a result of wars with powerful kingdoms over several centuries, Jews began to disperse from their land into other places and continents, the Jews in foreign lands being collectively referred to as the *Diaspora*. There, to integrate into the new society, they began to acquire surnames, but the timing of this practice varied greatly with the particular country they settled in. In some places this process started as early as the tenth century, but in others, particularly in the Austrian Empire, Germany, and eastern Europe, this process did not begin until the nineteenth century. Since Jews had settled all over the world, the acquisition of surnames followed different practices and often reflected occupations, the local culture, or variations on the names of current or previous family locations.[76]

In western Europe in general, given names are easy to interpret and read (for English-speaking people) because they are written in the Latin alphabet. Many Jewish families would give sons transliterated biblical names, like those of patriarchs, such as Abraham or Isaac, or prophets, such as Joshua; daughters' names would replicate those of matriarchs, like Rebecca or Rachel, or heroines like Esther. Of course, these were originally created with Hebrew characters. In more secular societies, given names were often commonly used by the population at large: Witness my first name.

In eastern Europe, Jewish given names are a bit more difficult to interpret. Even though the practice of given names was also generally based on those of biblical personages, the transliteration would have been into the predominant language of eastern European Jews, which was Yiddish, but written with the Hebrew alphabet. In Poland, a Jewish person interacting with the population might have his name transliterated into the Polish alphabet (a variation of the Latin alphabet), or possibly use a typically Polish name. For example, my father's given name was Wolf Shmuel; Wolf is a Germanic name, which reflects the German influence on Yiddish, but Shmuel is a transliteration of Samuel, as it would be pronounced in Yiddish. My father's younger brother, one of the few who survived, Uncle Chil, simply adopted the name David when he lived in France. So, this system applies to all the names of relatives from Poland whom I mention in Chapter III.

As for our last name, my son Kenny advances the following explanation of its origin. Here I am reproducing an edited version of the letter he sent to me.

The Jeruchim name seems to go back at least to the early 1830s in Poland. It was likely the first name of the father of the first person in our family who used it as a last name. He would have been "*Ploni ben Yerucham*" (so-and-so son of Yerucham), as was the custom. But when Jews in Poland began acquiring surnames, in many cases the "son of" was dropped and the first name of the father became the surname of the son and those that followed.

The name Yerucham was not uncommon as a first name in European (Ashkenazi) Jewry. The name Jeruchim derives from the Hebrew יְרֻ חָם – Yerucham. This name has been pronounced in different ways in different countries, likely pronounced with a Yiddish accent by our grandparents, with a French lilt in France, and here in the States still differently. It should also be pointed out that in Polish the letter "j" is pronounced as "y." Because Yerucham is itself a transliteration, that is, written in Latin letters to replicate the way it sounds, our name could just as well have been written Jerucham, and from there it's a short hop to Jeruchim. The name actually has a beautiful meaning. The root from which it is derived means "compassion" as often used in the word *rachamim*, a word I mentioned in Chapter II as part of the prayer *El Maleh Rachamim*.

The word Yerucham itself means something like "he who receives compassion"—or another way to translate it would be "en-wombed"—colloquially it means something like "he who is loved." A slightly different version, Yerocham, is used as a first name several times in the Torah. Back to Yerucham, a verse from the Torah in Hoshea[77] 14:4 refers to "the orphan who is granted mercy" which literally reads in the Hebrew "the orphan Jeruchim" which is a striking expression given our family history.

2. BACKGROUND HISTORY

World War II in the European theater is a subject of such enormous scope that it defies a meaningful summary. The military operations, the behavior of each country under occupation, direct or by puppet governments, and the causes leading up to it all require unending scholarship and no easy explanations. In the Prologue, I said that it was not my intention to write history, which is the case, as I am not a historian. In any event, my interest here is much more limited, which is what happened in France, and in particular to the Jews of France, and here I mean both French citizens and those living in France from other countries.

There is a voluminous literature on the subject, written by historians and scholars of the period. However, after many discussions with friends, acquaintances, and colleagues, all well-educated individuals, it became clear that my story would not be comprehensible without setting some context, which inevitably includes "history." History, after all, is the story of what happened before. What happened yesterday may well affect you, or what you do, today. So, wherever I have touched upon history, it came to me instinctively, as a natural setting to the topic at hand, not an attempt to "teach" history. Nevertheless, history is the backdrop of my story, and it feels like a stab in the heart to say that the history of Europe, the events that led to WWII, and the Holocaust are slowly disappearing from the collective consciousness, as reported in recent polls. We humans seem to have a short memory. Already I can see Santayana's warning becoming true. A full understanding of the history and causes of the Holocaust era, and the war itself, would make for endless reading, much of which is fascinating, if not chilling. There is a voluminous bibliography on the subject, online and in books.

With that in mind, I feel compelled to give a thimbleful of background about the defeat of the French forces in 1940 in almost unbelievable rapidity, an event I take personally because for me it is not simply history, and also about the role of the Vichy government in facilitating the Nazis' murderous pursuit.

The defeat of the French forces was not preordained, which is particularly galling. In a sense, the defeat follows my theme of randomness because the perception of German forces as an unstoppable juggernaut did not exist in 1938–1939. But, the seeds of Germany's rise had been planted and had yielded the rotten fruit of Nazi Germany leading to the invasion of Poland on September 1, 1939.

Dozens and dozens of decisions, independently made by both the Allies and the Germans bumped into one another, like particles in a gas. At the beginning of the war, according to one account, the Germans could well have been defeated, but indecision, reticence, lack of imagination or daring, and perhaps even hubris on the part of the Allies—the French military in particular—among other failures, all conspired to bring defeat.[78]

One of the articles below gives perhaps too facile a reason for the French defeat—leadership on one side and the lack of it on the other—but makes a good case for it. After that, the Germans essentially controlled Europe. It took five long years to uproot the bad seed.

About the conditions in France that led to the murder of about

75,000 Jews, two books already mentioned were of great value: *The Holocaust, the French, and the Jews* by Susan Zuccotti, University of Nebraska Press, 1993; and *Vichy France and the Jews: Second Edition* by Michael R. Marrus and Richard O. Paxton, Stanford University Press, 2019.

A mind-numbing number of laws, statutes, ordinances, and orders—several hundred—removed Jews from public life, dismissing them from professions or imposing drastic quotas, particularly those in teaching, law, public administration, and virtually any profession. Vichy also participated in restricting Jews to a minuscule fraction of artisans in various occupations, supporting demands from French professional organizations who wanted to eliminate competition. The list is unending. These restrictions were followed by the "Aryanization" law in 1941. Basically, this program confiscated and pilfered Jewish property, which was nothing other than systematic plundering, described by some as legalized theft. Rabid anti-Semites in the Vichy government apparatus, as well as somewhat neutral bureaucrats who were simply "doing their jobs" were cogs in a repressive regime that interned Jews, mostly "foreign" ones, in camps in the unoccupied zone, whose prisoners were eventually sent north and then to Auschwitz. In all these oppressive activities, contrary to a perhaps generally held assumption, Vichy did not act under pressure from the Nazis, but acted on its own.

Although the Vichy regime did not have mass murder as an objective, they were accomplices of the Nazis in doing so. Vichy provided the services of the French police to round up Jews, to put them on trains, and to guard them in the detention camps, in which several thousand prisoners died from the abject conditions, malnutrition, disease, and starvation, before they could be murdered in the death camps.

Here, I would like to quote Marrus and Paxton in part: "In the final analysis, the Vichy government made the outcome worse. Instead of asking why so many Jews survived in France, we should ask why so many perished..." Approximately 75,000 died after (and sometimes during) deportations and several thousand more in the internment camps, as just mentioned.

In Chapter XIII I mentioned my disappointment in the actions of the French government during the war, to which I can add anger. After the war, some have wanted to blunt the stain on France by claiming that Vichy was not a legitimate government. But however that is, there is no doubt that survival of many Jews in France was due to heroic and selfless actions by the ordinary people of France.

3. A FEW WORDS ABOUT THE RÉSISTANCE

In Chapter V, I mention that Gaston had said to me, when we reconnected, that Marcel (his father) had been in the Résistance.[79] At that time I think I had a romanticized view of the Résistance as swashbuckling guerilla men and women who performed daring acts of sabotage and kidnapping of German officers, but it did not occur to me then to ask for details. The truth is more complicated and nuanced. Below, I muse about what kind of activities Marcel might have engaged in.

In Chapter IV, I mentioned that Professor Baldenweck had compiled list of Résistance members in the lower Seine, in which Marcel Leclere's name did not appear. Assuming that Gaston's assertion that Marcel was in the Résistance, in what capacity might that have been? Professor Baldenweck opines that Marcel could have acted alone, independently, but doing what?

Professor Baldenweck, in his voluminous history of the lower Seine region[80] (where I was hidden) offers a categorization of Résistance activities, one of which he calls Résistance civile. He defines it thusly:

Civil resistance is all forms of refusal of the occupier and of collaborationist policy. These actions, harshly punished, mobilized several hundred or even several thousand people, beyond the Résistance movements. For example, one act of civil resistance was to hoist the French flag on a chimney during the night. Conceivably, Marcel could have been in this category, but he would have had to be very, very, circumspect.

Another category was called "passive defense," which referred primarily to the following: ensure the food supply of the inhabitants, create an underground hospital, help the wounded, fight fires, and maintain good morale among our fellow citizens. This, perhaps, might have been a more apt description for Marcel's activities, but we'll never know.

The other activities described by Professor Baldenweck are more or less daring, or destructive, and dangerous, both in terms of the actual acts and punishment from the Nazis, if caught:

- Destroy construction
- Destroy or cut electric or telephone wires
- Sabotage boats
- Sabotage railroads
- Arson
- Deliberate slowing down of the building of military infrastructure, especially ships
- Theft of ration tickets and of weapons
- Making false papers
- Infiltrate administrative offices
- Attack individual German soldiers

However, not all of these activities occurred during the same time period. The more overt physical attacks increased as the war progressed, but killing or wounding German soldiers were met with asymmetric reprisals (e.g., executing twenty innocent villagers for one German casualty).

It is unlikely that Marcel participated in these latter activities.

<<<<<<<<<<<<<<<<<<<<<<<<<<<<<<<<<<<<<<<<<<<<<<<<<<<

THE VÉL D'HIV RAID: THE FRENCH POLICE AT THE SERVICE OF THE GESTAPO

The title of this section says it all: the corruption and descent, not only of the French Police, but of the French sate.

In Chapter 4, I speak about the raid on July 16-17, 1942, which arrested men, women, and children, who were murdered in Auschwitz soon thereafter. But my description there does not tell the whole story. This raid and its deadly consequences could not have occurred without the willing cooperation of the French police and many of the Vichy ministers. Although other arrests had previously occurred, and more to come, this raid played a central psychological role in the trauma of the Jewish population of Paris and *environs*. For the first time, women and children were arrested, irrespective of their age or condition. France, the land of Liberté, Egalité, Fraternité, could no longer be trusted.

This raid is often described as the "Vél d'Hiv" roundup because those initially arrested were confined to the Vélodrome d'Hiver, a sport stadium in Paris, before being dispersed to various concentration camps in France, including Drancy, the point of departure for Auschwitz. Here, the term "concentration" camp does not quite correspond to the same term for those that existed in Germany or Poland. Nevertheless, the conditions there were atrocious and are a blot on the history of France. Many people did die there simply of disease, malnutrition and despair, before they reached Auschwitz.

There is a book, entitled *The Vél d'Hiv Raid: The French Police at the*

Service of the Gestapo, by Maurice Rajsfus, translated from the French, which describes in detail the close cooperation between the Nazis and the French state at the time (Vichy). The French Police and high-level functionaries in the Vichy regime were more than cooperative – they were enthusiastic participants and were fully involved in the planning. Reading this book is like watching a crime unfold slowly in a silent film. One wants to turn away, but cannot. I hung my head in shame and anger. Here is a related extract from the Internet:

> *Though many Jews had been forewarned of the danger, they had assumed the deportation would only target men, as they had in the past; consequently, women and children did not go into hiding. In the week following the arrests, the Jews were taken from the Vél d'Hiv to the concentration camps of Pithiviers and Beaune-la-Rolande in the Loiret region south of Paris, and to Drancy, near Paris. At the end of July and the beginning of August, the Jews who were being detained in these camps were separated from their children and deported. Before deportation, each prisoner's head was shaved, and his or her body was subjected to a violent search. Most of the deportees were sent to Auschwitz and murdered. More than 3,000 babies and children were left alone in Pithiviers and Beaune-la-Rolande. At the end of August and during the month of September these children were deported alone, among adult strangers, in sealed railway wagons, to Auschwitz, where they were murdered*

APPENDIX 1

MY TEACHING RECORD WITH CEI-EUROPE

In recognition of your outstanding merit as lecturer in our international advanced technology programs, and in conjunction with two decades of continuing education CEI-Europe gratefully awards this anniversary certificate to

Dr Michel C. Jeruchim

Record of Lecturing Service

Wireless Communications Systems: Modeling and Simulation, Wireless, Mobile, Optical, and Radio Links
September 24-28, 2001, Dublin, Ireland

Modeling and Simulation of Wireless Communication Systems
February 19-23, 2001, Nice, France

Modeling and Simulation of Wireless Communication Systems
October 16-20, 2000, Barcelona, Spain

Modeling and Simulation of Wireless Communication Systems
April 3-7, 2000, Davos, Switzerland

Modeling and Simulation of Wireless Communication Systems
October 25-28, 1999, Barcelona, Spain

Modeling and Simulation of Wireless Communication Systems
June 14-17, 1999, Helsinki, Finland

Modelling and Simulation of Communication Systems - The Physical Level: Wireless, Mobile, Satellite, Optical and Radio Links
February 9-12, 1999, Nice, France

Modeling and Simulation of Communication Systems - The Physical Level: Wireless, Mobile, Satellite, Optical and Radio Links
March 23-26, 1998, Davos, Switzerland

CEI-Europe | Advanced Technology Education
CONTINUING EDUCATION INSTITUTE - EUROPE

CEI-EUROPE • PO BOX 910 • S-612 25 FINSPONG • SWEDEN • PHONE +46 122 175 70 • FAX +46 122 143 47 • cei.europe@cei.se • www.cei.se

Modeling and Simulation of Communication Systems - The Physical Level: Wireless, Mobile, Satellite, Optical and Radio Links
November 3-6, 1997, Barcelona, Spain

Modeling and Simulation of Communication Systems - The Physical Level: Wireless, Mobile, Satellite, Optical and Radio Links
October 15-18, 1996, Baveno, Italy

Modeling and Simulation of Communication Systems - The Physical Level: Wireless, Mobile, Satellite, Optical and Radio Links
March 19-22, 1996, Davos, Switzerland

Modeling and Simulation of Communication Systems - The Physical Level: Wireless, Mobile, Satellite, Optical and Radio Links
October 16-19, 1995, Barcelona, Spain

Modeling and Simulation of Communication Systems - The Physical Level: Wireless, Mobile, Satellite, Optical and Radio Links
March 27-30, 1995, Cambridge, UK

Modeling and Simulation of Communication Systems - The Physical Level: Wireless, Mobile, Satellite, Optical and Radio Links
November 14-17, 1994, Cambridge, UK

Modeling and Simulation of Communication Systems: Wireless, Mobile, Satellite, Optical and Radio
May 2-5, 1994, Stockholm, Sweden

Simulation of Communication Systems: Computer-Aided Modelling, Analysis, and Design
October 18-21, 1993, Madrid, Spain

Simulation of Communication Systems: Computer-Aided Modelling, Analysis, and Design
March 8-11, 1993, Davos, Switzerland

Simulation of Commuication Systems: Computer-Aided Modelling, Analysis and Design
September 21-24, 1992, Cambridge, UK

CEI-EUROPE • PO BOX 910 • S-612 25 FINSPONG • SWEDEN • PHONE +46 122 175 70 • FAX +46 122 143 47 • cei.europe@cei.se • www.cei.se

Simulation of Communication Systems: Computer-Aided Modelling, Analysis and Design
March 16-19, 1992, Garmisch-Partenkirchen, Germany

Simulation of Communication Systems: Computer-Aided Modelling, Analysis, and Design
October 14-17, 1991, Madrid, Spain

Simulation of Communication Systems: Computer-Aided Modelling, Analysis, and Design
March 18-21, 1991, London, UK.

Number of courses: 21   Friday, September 07, 2001

Dr. Birgit E. Jacobson
Executive Director

CEI-Europe — Advanced Technology Education
CONTINUING EDUCATION INSTITUTE - EUROPE

CEI-EUROPE • PO BOX 910 • S-612 25 FINSPONG • SWEDEN • PHONE +46 122 175 70 • FAX +46 122 143 47 • cei.europe@cei.se • www.cei.se

APPENDIX 2

LIST OF PUBLICATIONS AND MEMORANDA IN THE OPEN LITERATURE

When my grandchildren become old enough to be interested, they may ask, "*Grandpa, what did you do when you were working?*" And I will reply, "*Here's a reading list!*"

1. *A Note on Limiter Outputs*, Proceedings IEEE, Vol. 56, No.6, June 1968.

2. *A Technical Basis for Communication Satellites to Share the Geostationary Orbit*, Paper 70-441, AIAA Third Communication Satellite Systems Conference, Los Angeles, CA, April 1970 (with Don Jansky).

3. *Orbit Utilization*, EASCON '71 Record, Electronics and Aerospace Systems Convention, Washington, D.C. October 1971.

4. *Interference in Angle Modulated Systems with Predetection Filtering*, IEEE Transactions on Communication Technology, Vol. COM-19, No. 5, October 1971.

5. *Orbital and Frequency Sharing between the Broadcasting-Satellite Service and the Fixed-Satellite Service*, ICC '72 Conference Record, Philadelphia, PA June 1972 (with D. Kane).

6. *Controlled-Carrier Transmission of AM/VSB Television from Space*, IEEE Transactions on Broadcasting, September 1972 (with A. Geia).

7. *Spacing Limitations of Geostationary Satellites Using Multilevel Coherent PSK Signals*, IEEE Transactions on Communications, Vol. COM-20, No. 5, October 1972 (with F. Lilley).

8. *Digital Computer Simulation of Satellite Quadrature Data Communication Systems*, Conference record, Vol. 2, National Telecommunications Conference, New Orleans, LA, December 1975.

9. *On the Estimation of Error Probability Using Generalized Extreme-Value Theory*, IEEE Transactions on Information Theory, Vol. IT-22, No. 1, January 1976.

10. *A Survey of Interference Problems and Applications to Geostationary Satellite Networks*, Proceedings IEEE, Vol. 65, No.3, March 1977.

11. *A Statistical Approach to Satellite Interference Levels*, Conference Record, International Conference on Communications (ICC '78), Toronto, Canada, June 1978.

12. *Some Modeling Aspects in the Simulation of Digital Links*, Proceedings of the International Telemetering Conference, Los Angeles, CA, Nov. 14-16, 1978.

13. *Regulatory and Technical Factors in Orbit Utilization*, IEEE Transactions on Communications, Vol. COM-27, No. 10, October 1979 (with H. Ng and D. Jansky).

14. *Implications of Power Flux Density Constraints on Satellite Systems*, Conference record, Vol. 3, National Telecommunications Conference (NTC '79), Washington, D.C., November 1979.

15. *On the Characterization of Noise in the Simulation of Nonlinear Wideband Satellite Digital Links*, Proceedings of the International Telemetering Conference, San Diego, CA, October 14-16, 1980.

16. *Empirical Study on the Variability of Monte Carlo Simulation*, Proceedings of the International Telemetering Conference, San Diego, CA, October 14-16, 1980 (with J. Moore).

17. *Performance of CPFSK over Nonlinear Satellite Channels*, Conference Record, Vol. I, International Conference on Communications (ICC '81), Denver, CO, June 1981 (with J. Moore).

18. *The effect of Station-Keeping Error on the Distribution of Carrier-to-Interference Ratio*, IEEE Transactions on Communications, Vol. COM-30, No. 7, July 1982 (with J. Moore).

19. *The Effect of Companding on Orbit Utilization of FDM/FM Carriers*, Symposium Record, IEEE 1983 International Symposium on Electromagnetic Compatibility, Washington, D.C., August 23-25, 1983 (with A. Shadman).

20. *Techniques for Estimating the Bit-Error-Rate in the Simulation of Digital Communications Systems*, IEEE Journal on Selected Areas in Communications (Special issue on computer-aided design of communication systems), Vol. SAC-2, No.1, January 1984.

21. *On the Relationship between Geostationary Orbit capacity and the Interference Allowance*, IEEE Transactions on Communications, Vol. COM-32, No. 5, May 1984 (with R. Hedinger).

22. *On the Application of Importance Sampling to the Simulation of Digital Satellite and Multi-Hop Links*, IEEE Transactions on Communications, Vol. COM-32, No. 10, October 1984.

23. *BER Estimation in Digital Link Simulation*, Conference Record, Vol. 2, Globecom Conference, Atlanta, GA, November 26-29, 1984.

24. *On the Steady-State Simulation of Equalized Digital Communications Links,* Conference record, Vol. 1, Globecom Conference, New Orleans, LA, December 1985 (with T. Klandrud).

25. *On the Coding Gain for Degraded Channels,* IEEE Transactions on Communications, Vol. COM-34, No. 5, May 1986.

26. *Developments in the Theory and Application of Importance Sampling,* Presentation at the IEEE Workshop on Computer-Aided Modeling, Analysis, and Design of Communication Links and Networks, University of Kansas, Lawrence, KS, May 6-8, 1986 (with P.M. Hahn).

27. *Implementation of Importance Sampling in Multi-Hop Communication Simulation,* in Proc. Globecom '86, Vol. 1, Houston, TX, December 1896 (with P.M. Hahn and T.J. Klandrud).

28. *Systems Modeling and Simulation techniques,* Invited Presentation at Workshop on Advanced Communication Systems, organized by University of Southern California Communication Sciences Institute and Army Research Office, Sedona, AZ, May 1987.

29. *Developments in the Theory and Application of Importance Sampling,* IEEE Transactions on Communications, Vol. COM-35, No. 7, July 1987 (with P.M. Hahn).

30. *Computer-Aided Modeling, Analysis, and Design of Communication Links: Introduction and Overview,* Guest Editorial, IEEE J. Select. Areas in Communications, Vol. 6, No. 1, January 1988 (with K.S. Shanmugan, E. Biglieri, and P. Balaban).

31. *On Efficient Implementations of Importance Sampling,* Proc. 1988 Conference on Information Sciences and Systems, Princeton, NJ, March 16-18, 1988 (with R.J. Wolfe and P.M. Hahn).

32. *An Experimental Investigation of Conventional and Efficient Importance Sampling*, IEEE Transactions on Communications, Vol. COM-37, No. 6, June 1989 (with P.M. Hahn, K.P. Smyntek, and R.T. Ray).

33. *Modeling Nonlinear Amplifiers for Communication Simulation*, International Conference on Communications (ICC) Record, Vol. 3, Boston, MA, June 1989 (with R. Blum).

34. *Estimation of the Signal-to-Noise Ratio (SNR) in Communication Simulation*, Proceedings, Globecom Conference, Vol. 2, Dallas, TX, November 27-30, 1989 (with R.J. Wolfe).

35. *On Optimum and Suboptimum Biasing Procedures for Importance Sampling in Communication Simulation*, IEEE Transactions on Communications, Vol. COM-38, No. 5, May 1990 (with R.J. Wolfe and P.M. Hahn).

36. *The Analysis of Phase Noise Degradation in a Coded Communication Link*, IEEE Military Communications Conference (Milcon 1990), Conference Record, Vol. 2, Monterey, CA, September 30 – October 3, 1990 (with R. Ray and D. Hatzipapafotiou).

37. *A Computer-Aided Analysis of the Effect of Phase Noise in Interleaved Block-Coded Communication Links*, IEEE Journal on Selected Areas in Communications, Vol. 16, No. 3, April 1993 (with R.J. Wolfe, C.D. Garthwaite, and S. McGlynn).

38. *Improved Methods for Using FIR Filters in Simulating Discrete-Time Systems*, Presentation at 5th International Workshop on Computer-Aided Modeling, Analysis, and Design of Communication Links and Networks, Princeton, NJ, April 24-27, 1994 (with J.A. Adkins and R. Blum).

39. *Modeling and Simulation of Wireless Channels*, Half-Day Tutorial

ENDNOTES

1. An excellent and poignant description of the multitude of psychological and physical needs of hidden children is given by Anne-Karine Jovelin, in *Sur la trace des enfants cachés – histoire d'une reconstruction* (*On the Trail of Hidden Children – Reconstructing History*); extract of a thesis at the University of Rouen.

2. In France there are many places named after the same saint, distinguished one from another by some sort of suffix, typically a local reference. You may be accustomed to the French word *"les"* as the plural form of the. However, lès with the accent is an archaic term meaning next to. Thus, "my" St. Aubin was affixed with the nearest large town, Elbeuf, St. Aubin lés Elbeuf. For brevity, I will refer to my town simply as St. Aubin.

3. The connection to the Résistance is more nuanced than I realized originally. Thanks to Professor Baldenweck, I learned that there were different types of Résistance. I address this briefly in the endnotes.

4. It may strike the reader that Monsieur Ledauphin is absent in this telling. When Alice arrived at the farm, he was a prisoner of war, one among approximately 1.8 million. This placed a great burden on families, especially farmers. So, refugees from the city who were old enough to work were especially welcome. Some of these were Jews, and the fact that they may have helped with chores does not diminish the risk the farmers took. (Later, I clarify this notion of risk.) My sister was now an almost young woman, old enough to help, and she did all kinds of chores at the farm. My brother, although younger, had a similar experience, as he describes in his own memoir cited earlier.

5. *Neighbors: The Destruction of the Jewish Community in Jedwabne, Poland,* Princeton University Press, 2000.

6. This honor is called "Righteous Among the Nations." I will return to this briefly in Chapter IV.

7. Joan has written an extensive recollection of this trip.

8. Actually, if I read it the prayer right, what it does is praise God's name, but I don't make that distinction.

9. I had wondered how this photo could have survived since we did not have the luxury of collecting our possessions after the July 16, 1942 rafle. Alice gave the obvious answer that David, who survived, was in possession of it.

10. Hasidic Jews basically follow a very Orthodox practice of Judaism. There are a number of variants of Orthodox practice that evolved over time in eastern Europe.

11. Given names are Hebrew/Yiddish, written in Polish characters. The original tree did not have Feiga. In France, my father used Samuel, the equivalent of Shmuel. Information about our Polish ancestors appears in Polish archives, part of which was sent to me by my son Kenny, our last name appearing there at least as far back as 1834. In the endnotes there is a little longer discussion about names.

12. This updated information is a result of an unexpected coincidence that I'm about to share.

13. A great deal more about Jewish life in eastern Europe can be found at this website: https://www.jewishgen.org/yizkor/ostrow/ost017.html.

14. In the endnotes, I give a little more background to this demoralizing episode.

15. The entire article can be found at the following website: https://iht-retrospective.blogs.nytimes.com/2015/06/11/1940-parisians-flee-the-city-as-german-troops-advance/. Many more can be found by googling "Paris France exodus in 1940."

16. Courtesy of the German archives.

17. These conditions were harsh in both zones, but the unoccupied zone was somewhat safer, at least until the Germans occupied it later on. A bit more about this appears in Chapter IX and the endnotes.

18. The intertwining roles of the French (Vichy) government and the Germans in pursuing Jews are much more complicated than this simple statement. A bit more on this is given in the endnotes.

19. University of Nebraska Press, 1993.

20. The specific circumstances for each of these raids is discussed in varying degrees of detail in the following references: http://www.genami.org/culture/rafle-paris-20-aout-1941.php; https://blogs.mediapart.fr/albert-herszkowicz/blog/230811/memoire-la-rafle-meconnue-du-20-aout-1941- paris; http://www.aloumim.org.il/histoire/grandes-rafles.html. See also the books by Zuccotti and Marrus and Paxton cited elsewhere.

21. As indicated, this was not the first rafle, just the largest one. The roundup continued until the next day.

22. Marrus and Paxton have a slightly different number, but still close to thirteen thousand.

23. Here "camps" means detention or internment camps.

24. Here I point out the bitter irony that this celebration of freedom for the French people was almost immediately followed by the exact opposite for the Jews of France.

25. Many Jewish rescue networks had by then been established, and it is possible that this dentist was part of one. These networks played an important role in saving many lives. For a detailed review of these networks, see "Unarmed Combat: Jewish Humanitarian Resistance in France during the Shoah" by Nancy Lefenfeld, Chapter 5 in *Jewish Resistance Against the Nazis*, Patrick Henry, Ed., The Catholic University of America Press, 2014. However, Marrus and Paxton point out that ordinary French people saved more than these organizations, either by hiding Jews or simply "ignoring" their presence in their towns.

26. My brother was a witness to this scene, but much remains cloudy. I am extrapolating his description a bit.

27. However, the largest rescue networks had already been established by Jewish organizations, who often worked hand-in-hand with Catholic and Protestant churches and their leaders. An accounting of the Jewish organizations can be found in the essay by Nancy Lefenfeld cited earlier. Even though the Bonneaus were Protestant, subsequent events indicate they may have worked through the Jewish organization OSE.

28. It's appropriate to note in passing that a ceremony awarding the title of Righteous Among the Nations has taken place in Marseille on September 10, 2017, in the presence of the Bonneaus' grandson. My brother and his wife attended as well as my sister's daughter and granddaughter.

29. Later on I will say more about the Résistance, which is more multi-faceted than the popular impression of physical resistance like blowing up railroad tracks.

30. For brevity, I shall sometimes abbreviate the name of this town to St. Aubin.

31. The Seine has an almost mythical aura in France. Many songs have been written about it, even giving it human character. In one of the songs, the Seine and Paris are portrayed as lovers! Only the French! I remember this song from long ago.

32. https://www.wikimanche.fr/Savigny-le-Vieux.

33. Le Chambon-sur-Lignon is a commune in southeast France, where over three thousand Jews were protected from the Nazis for the duration of the war, in essentially a communal pact. The people were primarily Huguenot or Protestant and their own history of persecution in France had made them feel a kindred spirit of association with Jews. I mentioned earlier that the Bonneaus were Protestant.

34. In 2021, Professor Baldenweck very generously offered to travel to St. Aubin, from his home (more than once), to see if there were any trace of my wartime identity in the town archives; there were not. On a later trip he made an appointment with school authorities in St. Aubin. Unfortunately, the school archives did not go back far enough. So, the answer to this question will unfortunately remain a mystery.

35. This deception campaign was an extremely complex operation. See, for example, https://en.wikipedia.org/wiki/Operation_Fortitude.

36. See, https://www.unicaen.fr/mrsh/vc1944/haute-normandie.html (in French); Haute-Normandie (Upper Normandy) is where I was.

37. See, for example, https://en.wikipedia.org/wiki/Normandy_landings#Allied_order_of_battle

38. My brother became a professional artist, but discovered his talent while hidden during the war. He made a number of water colors which were subsequently donated to the Holocaust Museum in Washington, D.C. His memoir, mentioned in the Prologue, contains all the details.

39. That there were few German soldiers in St. Aubin prior to D-Day comes from Professor Michel Baldenweck. Here I must digress a bit because almost all of the updated information about the war years has been given to me by Professor Baldenweck, about whom I will say more in the Acknowledgments.

40. Most of what follows was sent to me by Professor Baldenweck, including a priceless fifty-year commemorative copy of the *Bulletin of the Historical Society of Elbeuf* which contains recollections of French participants in the liberation. This material would have been nearly impossible to find otherwise.

41. Later you will see that the Lecleres' house was on the rue de Tourville. Many

of the geographical references appear on the map below, hand-drawn by Monsieur Brisson.

42. Initially the Résistance were more or less individual groups operating on their own. At this time, they became a cohesive organization: FFI stands for Forces Française de l'Intérieur, "French Forces of the Interior," which later became incorporated into the French army.

43. This information comes from the website of St. Aubin, http://www.ville-saint-aubin-les- elbeuf.fr/Histoire5.html, but it does not specify the actual days of this battle.

44. This information appears in the *ARCHIVES DEPARTEMENTALES DE LA SEINE-MARITIME*, the archives of this region (in French) for the years 1940–1946. I am indebted to Danièle Easton-Thomas, the former French consul in Philadelphia, for bringing this publication to my attention. However, at that time I did not have access to the detailed information later provided to me by Professor Baldenweck.

45. I thank Maj. (ret.) Harold Skaarup of the Canadian armed forces who gave permission to reproduce this photo and provided its source, the Library and Archives Canada, which I gratefully acknowledge.

46. Wikipédia: Saint-Aubin-lès-Elbeuf; Démographie.

47. https://fcit.usf.edu/holocaust/people/rescuer.htm. There are many other resources online that attempt to explain the mystery of ordinary people responding to a moral imperative, even with potentially terrible consequences.

48. Here is a translation of an email from Professor Baldenweck concerning this question: "I have built up over time for my thesis and for my book, and using all sources that could be identified (including direct testimonies of resistance fighters and deportees) a file of members of the Résistance, and Résistance fighters in Lower Seine (now Seine maritime), namely, eleven thousand names. I found neither Leclere nor Ernst...but it is possible that they did individual acts of resistance: the best thing was to welcome you!!!" Alas, my friends who are members of the historical society did not know the Lecleres who must have been very discreet.

49. Our friend in Philadelphia, Bill Untereker, lent me a copy of a new biography of Blum, *Léon Blum* by Pierre Birnbaum, Yale University Press, 2015.

50. But here I must interject that Simon did not escape military service altogether. After our arrival in the US he served in the army in the Korean War, an experience that he relates in his second book, Frenchy.

51. Here, Simon says another glitch happened.

52. There are a number of Holocaust museums in the States. The one I'm referring to is the United States Holocaust Memorial Museum located in Washington, DC. For brevity I refer to it simply as the Holocaust Museum.

53. Simon Jeruchim, *Frenchy*, Fithian Press, 2005.

54. So soon after escaping the Nazis, my brother put his life in jeopardy again near the front lines. His book Frenchy details many of his harrowing experiences there.

55. I say "at the time" because political pressure later instituted an open admission policy which plunged the system into disrepute. I believe it has recovered somewhat since.

56. Literally, this expression means "more royalist than the king" but has now taken on the larger meaning of a person who has an exaggerated loyalty toward a group, person, etc. In Berthe's case, she extolled everything French, to a degree she probably would not have done were she living in France.

57. Bob did eventually graduate with a bachelor's degree in civil engineering and immigrated to the west coast. But his real love was cooking, likely transmitted from his mother in the womb, and he started a restaurant some years later.

58. Thomas H. Cook, Mysterious Press, 2012.

59. IEEE stands for Institute of Electrical and Electronics Engineers. I am not a self-promoter, but I want my grandchildren to know what I had done during my work life.

60. The names of groups and organizations were forever changing in response to whatever trends were current, but the word "Communication" was always in it. So, for the rest of this story I'll just call it that.

61. OTP was then one of the offices in the Executive Office of the President (of the US). It was reorganized and renamed under Nixon, and shifted to the Department of Commerce.

62. The notion itself was not new, but its application to problems requiring intensive computation was, and this became possible because of the advances in computing.

63. When I say "my" company, it's whatever it was at the time. Although I started with GE, in February 1961 the Space Division was sold to the Martin Marietta Company in April 1993. Then, in March 1995, Martin Marietta merged with the Lockheed Company to become Lockheed Martin Corporation (LMC). In November 2010, LMC divested itself of the division I worked for. At that time, I was working part-time and already retired.

64. There is a fascinating history on Jewish family names and how they were

acquired in different countries, in https://www.onjewishmatters.com/ archives/7426, article by Gideon, "The history and evolution of Jewish surnames," June 27, 2015.

65. It's worth noting that at the time we were completely ignorant of the eastern European (Ashkenazi) Jewish tradition of naming a child after a departed relative.

66. This was my attempt at humor. Were I writing this today, I would have found a different metaphor.

67. The book alluded to is the first volume of Kenneth's chronicle that Joan faithfully kept up.

68. Bar mitzvah is a coming-of-age ritual. It is not literal manhood, but in the sense that he becomes responsible for his own actions relative to Jewish observance and ethics.

69. I do not remember the name of that restaurant, but there is in fact a restaurant in Milan that's been in operation since 1696. It's called Boeucc; it may well be the one we went to.

70. More about this cemetery can be found at https://www.jta.org/2004/05/03/ lifestyle/polish-stone-for- cubas-shoah-memorial.

71. Polish names are transliterated, but not always the same way. My mother's name was also written as Syme, and she was known in France as Sonia.

72. Almost all of the convoys operated by the SNCF were destined for Auschwitz, only a few were not.

73. The description of Vichy France here gives only the most basic sense of it to set the stage for my parents' arrest. There is much literature on the subject, in articles, online, and in books. Here I must mention one such book by my friend Dr. Henri Parens, who, as a boy, escaped the Rivesaltes internment camp in southern France. His book, *Renewal of Life – Healing from the Holocaust* (Schreiber Publishing, 2004) gives a description of the abject conditions there. Henri made it to America where he became a well-known psychiatrist and professor.

74. We actually had been alerted to this exhibition by our friend Danièle Thomas-Easton who had been the head of the French Consulate in Philadelphia for many years and now splits her time between Philadelphia and Nice. But I had forgotten her information until we stumbled on the billboard.

75. This quote, or a version of it, appears in the following text: Mishnah Sanhedrin 4:9; Yerushalmi Talmud, Tractate Sanhedrin 37a, written approximately two thousand years ago.

76. There is a fascinating description of this process in different online resources. One such is https://en.wikipedia.org/wiki/Jewish_surname and another is www.onjewishmatters.com.

77. Hoshea was an early prophet who lived approximately 2,750 years ago.

78. There are many analyses of the cause and conduct of the war; however, the online references below give a fairly succinct description of the Battle of France. https://en.wikipedia.org/wiki/Battle_of_France; http://www.bbc.co.uk/history/worldwars/wwtwo/fall_france_01.shtml; https://nationalinterest.org/blog/the-skeptics/the-super-simple-reason-nazi-germany-crushed-france-during-1940; *The Survival of the Jews in France; 1940–44*; Jacques Sémelin; Translated by Cynthia Schoch and Natasha Lehrer; Hurst and Company, London; 2018.

79. I capitalize this word to distinguish it from the common use of it.

80. Michel Baldenweck, *Histoire de la Seine Inférieure 1939–1945 (The War, the Occupation, the Résistance, the Liberation)*, 586 pages, Wooz Publishing, 2022.

at etaCOM Conference, Oregon Convention Center, Portland, OR, May 7-10, 1996.

40. *Modeling and Simulation of Communication Systems: an Overview*, Journal of the Franklin Institute, Vol. 332, No. 5, pp. 521-533, September 1995.

BOOKS AND BOOK CHAPTERS

1. "Technical Factors and Criteria Affecting Orbit Utilization", (with D. Jansky), chapter in *Communications Satellite Systems for 70s: Systems*, Vol. 26 in AIAA progress Series in Aeronautics and Astronautics, N.E. Feldman and C.M. Kelly, Editors, MIT Press, 1971.

2. "Modeling and Simulation of Communication Systems," Chapter in *Encyclopedia of Telecommunications*, F.E. Froelich, Editor, Volume 11, 1995.

3. Papers 7, 8, and 10 above have been reprinted in the IEEE Press book, *Interference Analysis of Communication Systems*, P. Stavroulakis, Editor, 1980.

4. *Communication Satellites in the Geostationary Orbit*, Artech House, Needham, MA, 1983; Second edition published in 1987 (with D. Jansky).

5. *Simulation of Communication Systems*, Plenum Press, 1992 (with P. Balaban and K.S. Shanmugan).

6. *Simulation of Communication Systems: Modeling, Methodology and Techniques*, (2nd Ed.): Kluwer-Academic Plenum Publishers, 2000 (with P. Balaban and K.S. Shanmugan).

ACKNOWLEDGMENTS

This memoir would not have been written without the indispensable contributions to memory by my brother, Simon, and my sister, Alice. My brother's memoir, mentioned earlier, filled in much of my early history, and his later book Frenchy gave me more details about our American beginnings. My sister's long letters brought my mother's history to life, as well as other details. They both graciously accepted my many phone calls to clarify one question or another. My brother also generously contributed his illustrations, which appear on pages 36, 85, and 204.

My wife, Joan, gave me unflagging encouragement. She also read and reread different versions of the manuscript as they emerged, and made many good suggestions, most of which I followed.

My son Kenny reviewed the part of Chapter III dealing with the history of my father's family and also made excellent suggestions, in addition to which he researched genealogical data, found the key to the meaning of our last name, and provided other biblical information.

Our friend Danièle Thomas-Easton, former French consul in Philadelphia, has been generous in providing me various links to French things, even contacting colleagues in France for specialized topics like citizenship laws in France, and led me to the wartime archives from the Normandy region. And for connecting me to an indespensible resource who became a friend and profound source of information, Professor Michel Baldenweck.

My friend Vince Rotondi used his PowerPoint skills to edit several of the graphics that appear in Chapters IV and X.

James Frazier very kindly used his technical skills to prepare all photos and illustrations in the manuscript for the required resolution.

Dr. Jean-Marc Dreyfus clarified a number of questions about events and conditions during the Nazi occupation.

Stefanie Seltzer explained the history of the hidden children and the formation of Holocaust support groups. Stefanie also deserves credit as one of the original forces behind the recognition of hidden children as a distinct category of survivors. This was a key to my own "coming out."

I learned a lot from the very well-written books, *The Holocaust, the French, and the Jews* by Susan Zuccotti, University of Nebraska Press, 1993, about what happened in France during the Holocaust and conditions leading up to it; and from the meticulously detailed *Vichy France and the Jews: Second Edition* by Michael R. Marrus and Robert O. Paxton Stanford University Press, 2019.

A very different and interesting view of wartime France is given by Jacques Sémelin, *The Survival of the Jews in France, 1940–44*, Hurst and Company, London, 2018.

As I mentioned in the introduction to the second edition, the feeling of amnesia about the circumstances surrounding the liberation of St. Aubin was totally relieved by the information supplied to me by Professor Michel Baldenweck, for which I am profoundly grateful. I am also indebted to Professor Baldenweck for many other pieces of information that would have been very difficult to unearth otherwise, and that fleshed out the narrative.

And finally, as the saying goes, last but not least, I want to thank my stellar editor, Joy Stocke, for her unerring guidance and literary and emotional sensitivity. She kept me on the straight path.

ABOUT THE AUTHOR

Michel Jeruchim was born in Paris, France and was a hidden child during the Nazi Occupation of France. He immigrated to the United States when he was 12. He received his Ph.D. from the University of Pennsylvania and went on to work in the telecommunications industry. An expert in satellite telecommunications systems, he was selected by the State Department to participate in the first Space World Radio Administrative Conference (WARC) where he helped develop the first set of technical rules for geostationary satellites. Dr. Jeruchim has authored or co-authored forty journal and conference papers on various topics in communications, and is co-author of two books, *Communication Satellites in the Geostationary Orbit* (Artech House, 1983, 2nd Ed., 1987), and *Simulation of Communication Systems* (Plenum Press, 1992, 2nd Ed., Kluwer Academic/Plenum Publishers, 2000). Michel lives with his wife Joan in Center City, Philadelphia, has two sons, and seven grandchildren.